A STRATF

A Stratford Story

Angela Hewins

Oxford   New York

OXFORD UNIVERSITY PRESS

1994

Oxford University Press, Walton Street, Oxford OX2 6DP

Oxford New York
Athens Auckland Bangkok Bombay
Calcutta Cape Town Dar es Salaam Delhi
Florence Hong Kong Istanbul Karachi
Kuala Lumpur Madras Madrid Melbourne
Mixico City Nairobi Paris Singapore
Taipei Tokyo Toronto

and associated companies in
Berlin Ibadan

Oxford is a trade mark of Oxford University Press

The Dillen first published 1981 by Elm Tree Books/Hamish Hamilton Ltd.
Mary, After the Queen first published 1985
First issued as an Oxford University Press paperback in a single volume 1994

British Library Cataloguing in Publication Data
Data available

Library of Congress Cataloging in Publication Data
Data available
ISBN 0–19–283182–8

1 3 5 7 9 10 8 6 4 2

Typeset by Pure Tech Corporation, Pondicherry, India
Printed in Great Britain
by Clays Ltd., Bungay, Suffolk

for Brian

CONTENTS

List of Illustrations and Acknowledgements   viii

The Dillen   I
Foreword to *The Dillen* by Ronald Blythe   3
Preface   5

Mary, After the Queen   235
Foreword to *Mary, After the Queen* by Paul Thompson   237
Preface   241

Glossary   383

LIST OF ILLUSTRATIONS

Unless credited otherwise, photographs are from the author's private collection.

The Dillen

1. George Henry Hewins on his ninety-eighth birthday (by permission of Herald Photographic Services)
2. The view from the Shakespeare Memorial Theatre
3. Inside Warwick Gaol
4. The Shakespeare Memorial Theatre under construction (by permission of the Shakespeare Birthplace Trust)
5. Cal Cook's cottage (by permission of the Shakespeare Birthplace Trust)
6. Dancing bear (by permission of the Shakespeare Birthplace Trust)
7. Sheep Street, Stratford-upon-Avon, 1870s (by permission of the Shakespeare Birthplace Trust)
8. The new Shakespeare Memorial Theatre
9. Cal Cook's daughter, Nance, with baby (by permission of Mrs E. Cordwell)
10. Barford Street, Birmingham (by permission of Birmingham Public Libraries, Local Studies Department)
11. Errand boy on the Parade, Leamington Spa, 1880s
12. Waterside in summer (by permission of the Shakespeare Birthplace Trust)
13. Roasting a bullock outside the 'Prince of Wales', Stratford-upon-Avon Mop (by permission of the Shakespeare Birthplace Trust)
14. Building workers posing in their Sunday best
15. Shottery football team, 1901–2
16. Harry Bayliss
17. Garrick Court (by permission of the Shakespeare Birthplace Trust)
18. Old Court, off Sheep Street

19. George at twenty-two
20. Lucy's mill (by permission of the Shakespeare Birthplace Trust)
21. Waterside in the floods, 1901 (by permission of the Shakespeare Birthplace Trust)
22. Waterside after the floods (by permission of the Shakespeare Birthplace Trust)
23. At work on the river Avon (by permission of the Shakespeare Birthplace Trust)
24. Building workers, old Almshouses, Stratford-upon-Avon (by permission of the Shakespeare Birthplace Trust)
25. Cyclist, Bordon Hill
26. Peapicking (by permission of the University of Reading, Institute of Agricultural History and Museum of English Rural Life)
27. Blackberrying lane, Luddington
28. High Street, Stratford-upon-Avon *c.* 1906
29. Mop Fair, Stratford-upon-Avon, 1912 (by permission of the Shakespeare Birthplace Trust)
30. The River Restaurant, *c.* 1912 (by permission of the Shakespeare Birthplace Trust)
31. The officers of the 2/7 Battalion, Royal Warwickshire Regiment, 1916
32. The Hewins family, 1915
33. Wounded soldiers queuing at the Town Hall, Stratford-upon-Avon (by permission of the Shakespeare Birthplace Trust)
34. Waterside, 1932: the second official visit of the Prince of Wales to Stratford-upon-Avon

Mary, After the Queen

35. Mary aged fourteen
36. The boy with red hair, aged fourteen
37. Emma, outside 20 Park Road, Stratford-upon-Avon, *c.* 1919
38. Else and Jess with friend in Red Horse yard, Stratford-upon-Avon *c.* 1920
39. Emma, early 1920s

40. Hockey team, Church of England School, Stratford-upon-Avon, late 1920s (by permission of Mrs V. Cooke)
41. Sis, Mary, and Doll on a brewery trip to Weston-super-Mare, 1930s
42. King Edward VII Memorial Chest Hospital, Hertford Hill, near Warwick (by permission of Mrs M. Halladay)
43. The School House, Alcester Road, Stratford-upon-Avon, 1983
44. 'The bottling end', Flowers Brewery, Stratford-upon-Avon, late 1930s
45. 'The Golden City', Flowers Brewery, Stratford-upon-Avon (by permission of the Shakespeare Birthplace Trust)
46. Lunch break at the 'Canning' during the Second World War
47. Brian
48. Stratford-upon-Avon Produce Canners Ltd., Second World War
49. Cyril in Italy
50. Street party to celebrate victory, 1945
51. Mary's young man, 1940s
52. Stall at Stratford-upon-Avon Mop, 1940s (by permission of the Shakespeare Birthplace Trust)
53. Post-war Mop Fair, Stratford-upon-Avon (by permission of the Shakespeare Birthplace Trust)
54. Porch, Church of England School, 1983
55. Mary in 1985

The extract from 'The Song of Wandering Aengus' on page 247 is taken from *The Poems of W. B. Yeats*, edited by Richard J. Finneran (New York: Macmillan, 1983), and is reproduced by kind permission of Michael B. Yeats, Macmillan London Ltd, and Macmillan New York.

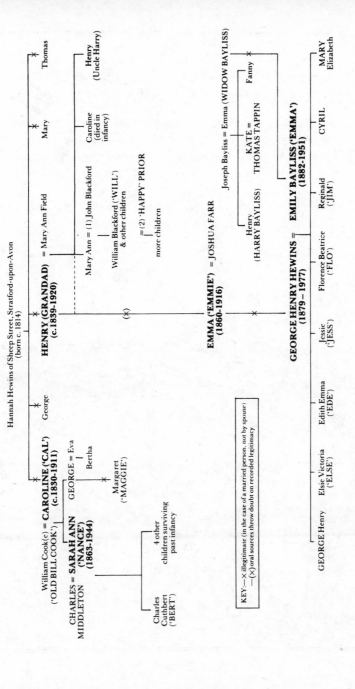

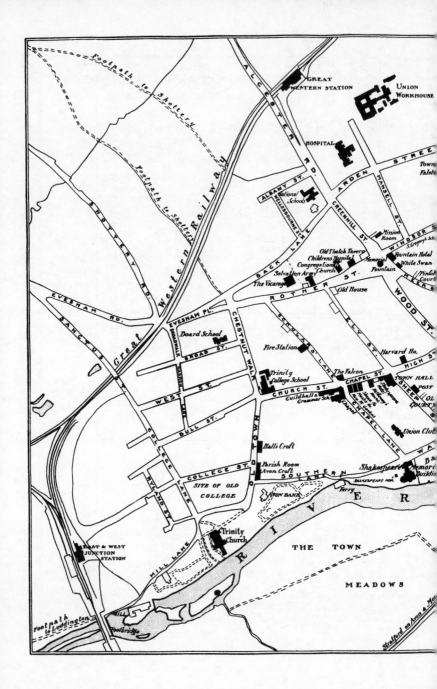

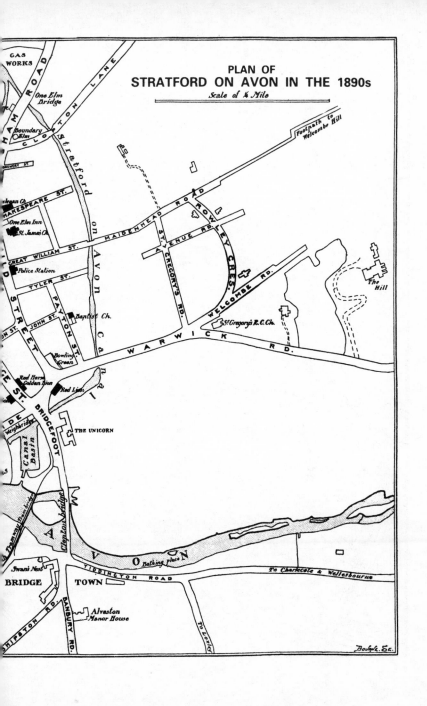

PLAN OF
STRATFORD ON AVON IN THE 1890s
Scale of ¼ Mile

The Dillen

Memories of a Man of
Stratford-upon-Avon

FOREWORD

by Ronald Blythe

The Dillen is an astonishing achievement. It is as if one of those rough little figures glimpsed in picturesque Victorian photographs had darted from his mute sepia world and, in a torrent of disturbing language, had changed the vague notions we may have held of that world once and for all.

Before the Great War, and indeed up until 1940, there were the 'poor' and the *poor*. The latter were an immense army of bread-liners, not just confined to industrial and metropolitan rookeries, or agricultural hovels; they could be seen clinging to existence as best they could in the cathedral city, the select resort or, in George Hewins' case, Stratford-upon-Avon. Such people have always beguiled poets, novelists and historians, and literature is full of attempts to interpret them. Theirs was the socially powerless group which sprawled below the respectable working class. For all our sociological insights we can scarcely comprehend their helplessness or their tenacity to survive. Dickens dramatized their world and did more than any other writer to reveal its teeming strangeness and sickly vitality. And we find unforgettable glimpses of it in the stories of A. E. Coppard and Mary Mann. There are, too, many vivid recollections of it on the tapes of today's oral historians.

But there is nothing quite so total as this description of his first forty years which George Hewins gave to his family just before his death in 1977. Avoiding easy classification (it falls somewhere between autobiography, novel—or tale—and social history), it takes the reader by the scruff of the neck and forces him to taste the food, smell the smells, agree to the tricks and breathe the air of a cheerful, dreadful England which would do for you if it could. George is articulate above all things and able to say what he thought and did without stricture or self-consciousness. The book is kept in good shape by the chronological pattern imposed upon it by Angela Hewins, the wife of George's grandson, and this probably is the reason for its excellence. A continuity prevails which some outsider's scientific or literary ear might have fractured. The confession ends, not in agedness, as might be expected, but when this little (five foot-three) Warwickshire cock-sparrow returns, not quite dead, from the Great War. By which time an entire experience trailed behind him, passionate, hopeless, merry, scrambling and sane.

PREFACE

This is the story of a man who grew up, lived and loved in Victorian England. With a few 'h's added and some repetitions omitted for the sake of readability, the words are his, recorded by his grandson Brian (my husband) and myself over a period of three years, 1975–77. When we began it had been with the idea only of taping one or two songs from his large repertoire, for our collective amusement. What I discovered between the songs was the start of a story. In mounting excitement I realized that here was something extraordinary and possibly unique, not only in the telling (George was a born story teller in the old oral tradition, with a truthfulness, humour and innocence all of his own, that illumined even the most chilling event) but in the historical evidence that he was unwittingly laying before us. For George's world was the world of the submerged tenth: the world of the very poor who were dependent on casual labour, charity and their own wits, where '*crafty*' was a word of highest praise. They lived, as George himself puts it, 'from meal to meal . . . from one week to the next' not in the metropolis or some bleak industrial city, but in one of the most picturesque market towns in England, and certainly the most famous—Stratford-upon-Avon.

His story provides a rare, personal insight into the emotions and attitudes of people caught in the poverty cycle of ill-fed, deprived childhood, early marriage, a big family, irregular work and ill-fed old age, and into the intimacies of family life in a largely matriarchal society—from a man's point of view. Agencies for social welfare had not yet reached the very poor, or had only managed to brush the surface of their problems. Against these there were only two bastions: the family was one, the other was the community.

Between 1878 (when George's story begins) and the 1920s, the wider world beyond Stratford started to impinge, albeit slowly, upon this close-knit community which Shakespeare would have had no difficulty in recognizing. Indeed, the language of the town labourers, though by no means as rich as that of their country cousins, had not yet been fatally diluted by mass education and the

1. George Henry Hewins. This photograph was taken on his ninety-eighth birthday, during a 'behind scenes' visit to the Royal Shakespeare Theatre.

mass media. Witches, ghosts and devils held more powerful sway than later, Christian myths. 'I seed a ghost once,' says George, 'at Pebworth.' If his reader—or listener—occasionally finds himself or herself projected into medieval faery tale (beholding a bear that 'ate a little girl called Laura Eddens, once upon a time' or a table miraculously piled high with food that 'looked as if we'd all had three wishes') the images more often seem to come from darker and more distant ages still. There are the half-spoken ancient legends of the eels, the parsley that goes 'seven times down to Hell afore it chits', the mysterious stone. One of the last images is of the leader of the elite of predominantly Anglican Stratford—the Vicar—silhouetted against the flames of a Monday morning fire and bearing a remarkable resemblance to a more satanic personage.

In this community strangers were ever the source of greatest excitement. Flitting in and out of the lives of the very poor and giving George a semblance of mobility he never really had (until he was thirty-five he had never been further than Weston-super-Mare) were travelling men—and women. In his story we meet vagrants and roadsters on their way to the workhouse or the peafields, tarts on their way to 'Brummagem', or temporarily fleeing it, like red-haired Annie Salmon, discharged soldiers on their way to nowhere, gaolbirds seeking sanctuary, craftsmen seeking work, like stonemason Joshua Farr who 'wore a top hat on the job' but whose greatest misfortune may have been possessing (for Emmie) a 'magical name'. The first of these travelling men, of whom the listener only catches a tantalizingly brief glimpse is the anonymous street musician, who sang with the band and for Emmie in particular on a sunny Whit Monday in 1878. He was a candidate—certainly a more attractive one than the mealy-mouthed Tom Farr—for George's paternity.

It comes as no real surprise that the very poor in Stratford were as maligned as they were everywhere else by their middle-class documentalists—as feckless, undeserving, drink sodden or down-right criminal. Accounts of meetings of the Guardians, the editorial columns of the local press, the pages of the Parish Magazine, all bear witness to this. Even well-meaning charity workers shrank back. Before they moved to the other side of the street did they see the clear hard looks of the poor, who knew their townsmen's sexual proclivities intimately (Cal's mother, for example, had been a most prolific whore), their treatment of aged parents of whom they had become ashamed, their tendency to light fires and leave others to take the blame? Did the lady who came to sketch Pimms Court—'It's just like Italy!'—hear their laughter?

The ignorance of ladies in big white hats was not always their fault. The listener to George's story has only to speculate on how Cal Cook, his redoubtable mentor and guardian, would have dealt with such a visitor, let alone a census investigator. George's and Emma's impulsive forgery of the marriage register is one tiny proof that traditional, hitherto trusted primary sources can be unreliable when researching the lives of the very poor. There are many more.

Can oral evidence do any better? The answer must be 'yes' and 'no'. No, in so far as the written word must always be necessary, for those matters which lie beyond memory, for simply verifying names or dates or events. Here George's schooldays, spent drilling or learning by rote, paid dividends. He had a trained memory, and could quote at will from the yellow cuttings, fragile as dead leaves, bequeathed to him by his mother, poor foolish Emmie. They were his only birthright. The written word may also fill gaps. All memories have their own silences and selectivity, just as the local press, the Poor Law books, the police records, have their political or bureaucratic biases, their own exasperating omissions. Every community has its taboos and George's was no exception. It was not sex or death or defecation which caused him to hesitate; it was pauperism.

'Shut up, George,' says Emma, when he starts to question one of the cherished tenets of the Guardians. Why were people punished for being poor?

'Shut up!' shout the customers at the 'Oddfellows' when he strikes up with a song about the workhouse. 'We don't want to 'ear *that*!'

And George himself confesses: 'I'll tell you what I never told nobody else till this minute—she [Cal] had a pauper's funeral.'

No other sort of evidence can identify these attitudes so directly—this is how they saw it, this is how they felt—or condemn so positively the system of 'less eligibility' by which all help was refused until every resource of the family, including self-respect, had been exhausted.

Money, or lack of it, seems at times to dominate George's story. He counts from the start with a precision and an abiding interest that befitted a pupil of Cal's—'she could neither read nor write but she could add up'—in pennies and silver threepenny pieces, in George shillings and spade guineas. Even the cost of a broken chamber pot is noted. Clearly for George nothing, except women, offered the same sensual satisfaction of touch and promise as a gold sovereign. The power of money over the minds of the poor was paramount: it was necessary for survival. Lack of it brought debts and thievery, sickness and death, the dreaded pauperism; the acquisition of it (not the earning, at fourpence an hour) might bring a sudden fortune or be the means of deflecting authority's savage retribution.

'Money,' comments George of a lucky escape, 'won that.'

Notwithstanding, he was never a mean or a greedy man; he was rather inordinately generous, a fact noted sadly by Cal. Her own son George, who returned to the town of his birth as a successful war profiteer, clad from head to toe in fur, had learnt his lessons well. The other George, the 'dillen' on whom she lavished a late flowering of tenderness and who had loved her in return, dissipated all—in an astonishing zest for life. This stayed with him for nearly a century.

A. H.

CHAPTER ONE

'This is how it happened,' said George.
He chuckled. It was a late winter's afternoon; we were huddled round the
fire in his near derelict cottage, more self-conscious than he of the intrusion
of the tape recorder. Above the perpetual walloping of the black kettle on
the hob and the wind outside and in—at ninety-six he seemed to have
been cured, like leather, against all discomfort—he chuckled again, spat
into the flames and began:

An old chap on the canalside told me. Years and years ago, he said,
afore you was born, they used to get six or seven canal boats down
those locks in one week. You could a-gone down the tow-path
and not picked a weed off the banks. They kept them clean, like
emerald green lawns. A boat would come out that last lock, go
through the basin to the mill with wheat and take a load o' flour
back. Some opened the river lock and went on down to Tewkes-
bury. Two or three came loaded with coal, or picked up skins and
left another load o' carcasses. Cox's timber yard stacked up; the
Bancroft was all wharfs and small factories. Early morning you'd
a-thought you was on the docks instead o' Stratford, all the bustle
and smells and folks a-shouting and heaving stuff about. The boat
builders did well then, the old chap said.

Whiles he was stoking his pipe he gave me a funny look, as if
he knowed me from somewhere: 'You've heard tell of Tommy
Womack?'

'Loggin the chemist were supposed to owe im for 'is recipe for
cough mixture?' That tale had been about town for donkey's years.

'Well,' he said, 'Tommy Womack nearly had 'is knuckles rapped
once.'

I laughed. 'More'n once, I'd say.' Womack was a rogue, everybody said so.

'E sold your mother some medicine to get rid o' you!'

It was a nasty shock.

'It's true,' the old chap said, 'and this is how it happened.'

*

The railways came to Stratford, and the trippers; shops opened, hotels. The boat builders, those who was crafty and saw the way the wind was a-blowing, turned to pleasure boats, quick. The river trade died; canal boats was fewer and farther between. During the spring gales of '78 an elm tree fell across the Avon; nobody shifted it. Locks rotted and gave way and the water ran free. Only the rushes flourished, and the eels. Not that Emmie Hewins gave much thought to all this. She was eighteen years old, a silly young wench but pretty! Oh, she was pretty—eyes as blue as forget-me-nots, dark hair that curled on its own. For her, the world was full o' promise. She was in service at Leamington Spa, and she'd come home for the Whitsuntide holiday. The sun shone and a band was playing in the street when she stepped out in her best dress with the flounces, and her dainty little shoes. One of the musicians—they were travelling men—he sang for her, called after her along Waterside: 'I'll

2. The view from the Shakespeare Memorial Theatre, the foundations of which were laid in 1877. Lucy's Mill can just be seen, on the far bend of the river, beyond the Parish Church.

treat you, Princess!' But today she didn't speak to him. She tossed her head, looked neither to the right nor the left; she was on her way to meet Tom Farr! In fact, she had an appointment. Tom knowed how to *do* things, and he was most pernickety about appointments: 'Meet me by the Sale Yard,' he'd say, or 'back o' the "Unicorn".'

Folks outside their cottages listening to the band tut-tutted as she went by. The Farrs was a class above *that*, they said. For a start, they was well off. Old man Farr owned houses in West Street, ran a boat building business at Emscote Dock, Warwick, and another on the canal at Stratford. Emmie Hewins might have high hopes of the son—over two year now it was—but a fat lot o' good it would do her, walking out with the likes o' him, and lately they'd been doing more'n walking! Ask Humpy Heywood at the mill, they'd given him a terrible fright. Then there was her *aunt*, if aunt was what she was . . . So they went on goggity-goggiting till Emmie passed out o' sight, head high, in a blaze of glory.

Little did those folks know just how soon she'd meet her come-uppance. Whitsuntide came and went, and she started to worry about her condition. Tom Farr was worried and all: 'I'll keep in touch,' he said. She weren't happy with that. 'I'll'ave to think what to *do*,' he said; he was stuck for once. 'And I'll let you know. If you gets a postcard askin you to meet somebody, it'll be from me.'

'Alright,' she said.

She had a postcard stating: 'I WILL BE ON LEAMINGTON STA-TION TONIGHT SEVEN O'CLOCK'. Seven o'clock went by, she paced up and down the platform; eight o'clock, she kept looking at the postcard, she didn't know his hand; nine o'clock, she was starting to get anxious—anxious, not desperate, cos although Emmie had been well and truly babbed (there was no doubt about it now) she really did believe Tom Farr would wed her.

Just as she thought: 'This is it, e bain't a-comin!' a train pulls in and out jumps Tom. He'd been at camp at Stoneleigh, with the Volunteers. There he was in his uniform: scarlet tunic, helmet with a spike on top, smart as a new carrot. 'I got a name,' says Tom. He said nothing about wedding. 'You'd best meet im, your next day off'.

So Emmie got Womack's name and bought the medicine. Womack was an ordinary working chap who made up pills and medicines for folks as couldn't afford the doctor or the chemist. He'd got the *gift*, they said. Well, soon as she'd took a couple o' swigs of Womack's medicine Emmie stopped fretting. She knowed it would work, like a spell, make the babby vanish; that's what Tom said and he was always right. She never gave it another thought. Come July she was back in Stratford for the Riverside Gala, carefree as a butterfly and twice as pretty. 'See you eight o'clock for the dancin,' Tom Farr said, 'be'ind the Big Tent.'

It was what you'd call a *perfect* day. Emmie and her friend Kate went early; they strolled about together, arm in arm, kept themselves to themselves even though they did get a lot o' looks and whistles from the young chaps. The Militia band was there, playing selections, the meadow was hung about with flags and coloured streamers. There was a half-mile flat race, and little tents for the older uns as wanted shelter from the sun, and all sorts of amusements—skittles, Aunt Sally, walking the greasy pole, kiss i' the ring. Eight o'clock—more prompt'n at the station!—Tom Farr turns up. He'd brought a pal for Kate. They danced and they danced. They was still dancing when dusk starts to fall and, lo and behold! A balloon goes up, with magnesium lights, hovers for a minute and sails over the town.

'Ohhh!' went the crowds.

Fireworks started to bust in the sky.

'Ohhh!' they went.

And little coloured flares lit up the trees by the river.

Oh, they was happy.

And after the fireworks Emmie and Tom Farr made love again.

*

She didn't know 'A' from a bull's foot. The baby was *still there*! It had been there all the time. Womack's medicine weren't strong enough; it hadn't worked. She growed bigger and bigger. She had to leave her job in Leamington and come back to Stratford, for good. Still she hoped Tom Farr would wed her, but he made no sign. Her aunt, Cal Cook, took her in. Cal lived in a cottage on the corner of Waterside and Sheep Street; Emmie did the cooking for her, waited on Cal's lodgers, slaveyed. It was a come-down from Leamington, harder work, but beggars can't be choosers as they say. It was better'n the workhouse, by God.

Tom Farr took to crossing the street when he seen her a-coming.

'Tom!' she cried, but he looked the other way and his pals started laughing: 'I seen you drinkin at the "Garrick",' calls Tim Baker, he was a mouthy one, 'and the "Cross Keys", Whitsun, wi that singer!' And whiles she was feeling her face catch fire and everybody gawping and wished she could die, Tim Baker shouts across Sheep Street: 'Humpy Heywood told us a thing or two 'bout *you*, Emmie Hewins!'

Tom Farr, he said nothing.

As for the neighbours, they had a field day. Emmie was in tears most o' the time, but her aunt Cal weren't: she was no more frit of words than she was of folks. She didn't care what she said, who she offended. She told them all to go to hell, and old mother Freeman in particular. That's how Cal came to be summonsed—'for usin profane and obscene language'. The copper told the Magistrates she'd been in a very drunk state: 'This bain't the first time neither. Three weeks previous, sir, she was 'elplessly drunk, lyin on the pavement. Shall I summons er for that an all?'

Cal pleaded guilty to 'sayin a little wrong'. 'But I never used them words *er* said, your Worship—what was they?'

They was so bad the Magistrates had to whisper them!

'Caroline Cook, you are guilty by your own confession of usin this language. We think it is the most 'orrible, beastly an brutal language as can be used by one human bein to another—'specially too for one woman to use to another un. This is not the first time you 'ave been 'ere, and the language used on this occasion is, to our minds, the most 'orrible that can be conceived, to say nothin of Christianity . . .'

How long in gaol if she didn't pay?

'Fourteen days.'

Says Cal: 'What's the money, sir?'

'One pound an eight shillin.'

'I will go to gaol, sir.'

This throwed them all in a flummox. 'If you don't 'ave the money to pay after what you've said, the commital will 'ave to be filled up an that'll raise the price and there'll be the run over to Warwick Gaol. Are you sure you ain't got the means to pay?'

'No, my Lord.'

So Cal went picking oakum, left Emmie on her own. It couldn't be helped. One week later at 22 Waterside, ninth o' March 1879, ten-past-twelve in the morning, she was 'delivered of a male child'—that's how the law put it. She had a hard time; they said afterwards she'd never have another un. She called me George Henry Hewins, after her Dad. What about *my* Dad? 'E's Lord Mayor o' Brummagem!' she'd say, and a faraway look would come into her eyes. But that was years later. *Then*, she laid me at Tom Farr's door.

3. Inside Warwick Gaol

16

Cal was back from Warwick 'We'll take im to court for the money,' she said, and she egged my mother on. Old man Farr egged on Tom. At the Police Court the Farrs' lawyer said: 'My client often seen er walkin the streets, your Honour. She's been heard to say, "If Tom Farr ain't the father of my child, e's the most respectable young man I been with, and I means to put it on im!"'

My mother was a-sobbing. 'I never! And I never 'ad money off im neither, sir!'

'This gal can't be *believed*,' said the lawyer. 'Whiles in Stratford she 'as spent a great deal of 'er time in public houses!'

There was a murmering in the court then, you can bet your life! It was lucky my mother was pretty and she knowed how to behave. Service at Leamington had taught her that. 'My father lives on Ely Street,' she said, 'but I 'ave my home wi my aunt. I ain't been to public houses no more'n once or twice in my life, and then only to fetch beer, sir.' She made a good respectful impression on the Magistrates.

Womack, he'd been called as a witness, wobbled up to give his evidence; pale and sweaty he was like a big lump o' dough. He used to wobble when he walked.

'You say this gal come to you. Did she ask for anythin?'

'Er asked for some medicine—a tonic.'

'The same you give in a case at Shipston some time ago?'

'Ah.'

'And that was a "tonic" sold to some young gentleman for the purpose of givin it to a gal, weren't it?'

Womack played dumb, so Alderman Kendall, he was a Magistrate, he had a go. He made chemicals for the brewery, ran a factory on the canal; likely he knowed a lot about tonics. 'What was the mixture?'

'Quinine and iron.'

'Folks in er condition don't usually require medicine.'

'Er said er wanted summat,' said Womack, 'but er didn't specify any partick'ler purpose.'

'Hmm,' said the Mayor.

Yes! It seems this paternity case was so extraordinary the Mayor himself had turned up! Charles Edward Flower—folks reckoned he'd soon, be *Sir* Charles!—he was Mayor of Stratford that year, and owner of the brewery. He'd made a fortune out o' selling beer! The Mayor asks Womack: 'Are you in the habit o' sellin young gals medicine wi'out knowin whether they wants it or not?'

'Well—er says, "I ain't very well, Mister Womack", and I prescribed for er.'

They had him on that! Says Alderman Kendall: 'You ain't told us what she said was the matter wi er. Did she not state it was to "correct irregularities"?'

'Just so,' says Womack.

And they all bust out laughing. For them it was a big joke.

Things was starting to look bad for my mother. To top it all, Tom Farr was denying everything. No, he said, the postcard weren't in his hand; no, he said, improper intimacy never took place between them. The first time he'd set eyes on her was at the Riverside Gala. 'I was about to dance wi her—well er's a good lookin piece.' That was the only thing he never did deny. 'But my companion conveyed er *character* to me. I left er immediately, o' course.' He couldn't a-kept her company at Whitsuntide, nor the night o' the fireworks, could he? He had a witness would vouch for it—here, in the Police Court! Everybody looked round—Womack!

'Hmm' said the Mayor. Nobody cared for Womack, with his lying ways and his pale pikelet face, for all he'd got the gift. Folks used him, but nobody cared for him. 'Hmm' said the Mayor. He was busy laying plans for the opening of the new Theatre, just a few days hence, on Shakespeare's birthday. He'd given the land for it, and a lot o'money asides, and it was going to be a really posh occasion. All the toffs would be there—nobility! Stratford was going to get *tone*; it was the start of a new chapter. 'The defendant can pay three bob a week for the babby', he said, 'and all the costs!'

*

Tom Farr was arrested for not paying. When Bobby Harris brought him in he found a knife and a bunch of keys on him, a gold watch—and *fifteen shilling and elevenpence*! They let him off, soon as he'd settled the arrears. The coppers said his character was 'previously good'. That weren't enough for his Dad, though. Old man Farr was furious. He weren't going to let some little hussy get the better of his only son: 'I'll take this to Warwick, to the County Court! We'll appeal!' he said. He'd reckoned without Cal. She knowed the breed and seed of *him*, she said. He'd got too big for his bloody shoes. The boat trade wouldn't last much longer, even canal boats; any fool could see that! The Farrs'd end up begging *her* for a bob. 'Mark my words,' said Cal. 'Boats will fly and carriages will go wi' out horses, tomorrow day.'

She was in fighting mood; she bought a lawyer for my mother, and folks as would go over to Warwick to give evidence. And so it was that Tom Farr got cold feet and talked his Dad into withdrawing from the 'Extraordinary Affiliation Case'—that's what the *Herald* called it. He did, at the last minute. But the damage was done.

✍ CHAPTER TWO ✍

My mother was branded. She changed her name to Cook—that weren't much good in a place like Stratford. She got a job at a house on Henley Street, offal work, but it was a job. Then what should she go and do but get caught with a couple o' books she'd borrowed from the bookcase—she'd meant to put them back, afterwards—and a piece o' ribbon to do up her hat.

'We's disposed to deal leniently wi you,' they said, 'on account of your recent trouble'—that was me!—'So we's only givin you fourteen days.'

They gave her a character and all: 'Suspicious,' they said, 'she can read an write.'

*

Then she had a bit o' luck. One of Cal's lodgers took a fancy to her. Well, as I said she was nice-looking and neat. His name was Joshua. He was a stranger and he wore a top hat—on the job! He'd come to Stratford to do the carving on the Theatre, and for a time on that tower he was the highest bloke in town. The neighbours on Waterside gawped and tattled: 'What's e want wi that giddlin gal?' they said. 'A man like that!'

He got good money for that time o' day: *eightpence an hour*! It provoked the local brickies and masoners into asking for more and when they didn't get it they went on strike—a strike in Stratford! You can bet their gaffers was glad when the Theatre was done and all the strangers packing their traps and ready to go, and things could settle back to normal.

Sat'day night my mother's young man cleaned and polished his tools and spread them out on the table for her to see: tiny tools they was, like knitting pins.

'Oh!' she said, and he look pleased.

But it weren't his tools, no more his money set her heart a-beating

4. The Shakespeare Memorial Theatre under construction. Work began in 1877. Although opened for productions on April 23, 1879 (the first play performed being *Much Ado About Nothing*) the Memorial buildings were not completed until 1881.

fast as his. My mother was a dreamer and it happened this bloke had a magical name for her just then: *Farr*. He weren't no relation to Tom, but his name was Joshua Farr.

The two of them goes to see Cal. My mother says: 'It's like this—'is people's against it.'

Cal said nothing.

'Won't you understand?' he says. 'I'll take er, but I can't take *im*.'

Still Cal said nothing. But she understood alright, and she gave him a look as made folks say she rode up the fields a-nights, on a besom.

And so my mother went off with Joshua Farr.

I never missed her because I was never with her. I looked on Cal as my real mother. I called her 'Gran' and she called me her lad—'My Lad'. It was a marvel, folks said, how she loved me.

Caroline had never been soft with her own, and didn't she choose hard labour sooner'n pay the fine and help poor Emmie when she was in the fashion?

'Ah,' said Cal, 'er's "Poor Emmie" now.'

As for me, I was such a little minute a puff o' wind would a-blowed me away. When I was five I was the size of a kiddie of three. And I was spoiled. 'You can see e's Granny-reared,' they said.

Each year, ninth of March regular, I got twenty-four penny stamps from Brummagem. Cal sold them to the man at the liquor vaults; when I was older she bought them off me. Once, I thought about writing, but I never did.

Cal brought me up. She was a good soul but she'd had a hard life, learnt to stick up for herself early. No one could make a fool out of Cal. When my mother left she took a young girl in to do the chores—wash the crocks, make the beds—and Hetty *tried*. This is how it came about.

As long as I can mind, Cal slept downstairs in the front room, which was by way of being a greengrocery shop and a second-hand clothes shop. That way she stopped folks as was *in* getting out without paying, and folks as weren't, getting in. There was a big chain on the door to Waterside; every night she saw as that was in place. Not that nobody ever robbed us—there weren't nothing to rob. So they thought! She always pleaded poverty. If anyone went there with half a sovereign she said: 'Guvner, you got me beat! You'll 'ave to go over to the public and get it changed—I ain't got that much money in the house!' If anyone came with a sovereign her eyes gleamed. She shook her head and she said: 'I never seen that much money in Stratford!' And they'd believe that tale!

A lodger might say: ' 'Ave you got a bob, Cal? Just till Sat'day?'

'When did I ever 'ave any money?' she said.

Hetty had to sleep with Cal, so's she knowed what she was up to. Cal didn't trust nobody, and Hetty had been in the knife box, for all she looked no more'n thirteen. She weren't pretty, not like my mother. She had a funny face, longish and white, and she scrobbled about the place all on a-side, like a bird with one wing. I reckon she'd got rickets. She was always fussing and cuthering

22

me, and she soon found out I had a bed to myself, over the passage. When Cal was snoring away, when she'd had a skinful, Hetty snook up the stairs in her shift and got into bed with *me*. That shift had took on the stink of everything in the house; I can smell it now, all stale piss and gin and smoky fires and the new plums she'd been helping Cal to sort that afternoon. Well, Hetty wraps herself round me—her hands was like dabs of ice but she soon warmed up—and there she'd stay till five o'clock in the morning when she snook back down the stairs. I figured she didn't like sleeping with Cal when she was drunk.

One night she brings someone up with her. 'S'alright, George, it's only ole Mister Anderson—e's come to tuck me in.'

It was hard to tell if she liked Mr Anderson tucking her in or no. *I* didn't, that's for sure, and maybe Hetty wouldn't a-done neither but for the three-penny pieces he left by the candle. What with his wheezing and farting and trying to get her shift off—he never did get it off, it was part of Hetty, that frowsty old shift, like a skin—it was an irritation and a puzzle to me, that nightly perform-ance. He never did give up, old Mr Anderson, but he never did manage it neither. The most amazing thing was him paying for all his bother.

When he'd gone Hetty lit the candle and went to the loose floorboard under the mat where the others was hid. I was making out to be asleep. And I can tell you, it was a picture to see Hetty counting her money. Her face went all holy, transmogrified. I wondered what she was planning to do with it. She'd got five shillings and ninepence already!

This went on for two year, off and on, maybe three, whenever Cal had had too much. Then up she comes one night, not half as drunk as Hetty reckoned, looking for the warming pan. 'You slivin slummocky bitch!'

What she didn't call her! She pushed her down the stairs—I heard the chain a-clanking—and straight out into the night. *Bang* went the door. And up the stairs comes Cal and chucks Hetty's clothes out after her, and her shoes. Like a toad out a tree—*thump!*—you could hear them hit the road.

You'd a-thought old Mr Anderson's wits had sailed out after

them. He stood there start-naked, dithering with cold, looking like death on a mop-stick. I crept to the casement and peeked out. Hetty's face was white and ugly—I'd never seen a face so ugly. When she sees me she starts making signs but I made out I didn't understand. Well, I weren't supposed to, was I?

That very night Cal moved her bed right to the door, where the wind from the river blowed through the cracks and made the old clothes at the back of the shop shiver and flicket in a most fearful way. She'd told Hetty not to show her face again, and no more she did. Nobody ever asked after her, not even Mr Anderson. There's no accounting for folks. I thought he might a-done, 'specially as Cal let *him* stop. She weren't going to lose a shilling a day. He had his breakfast, a plate o' stew a-nights and a clean shirt when he wanted it, and Cal made sure that was all he had. She watched him like a hawk, after that.

One day she said, out the blue: 'You never seen er with money, did you?'

I knowed she meant Hetty. 'No!'

I was frit, but I lied, thinking of all those threepenny pieces and the dust settling nicely on them. Four pounds, one shilling and ninepence, in silver threepenny pieces.

She must a-seen my face change. 'Now don't you go thinkin about it no more, My Lad—bury it!' She ruffled my hair and I thought: 'I done it!'

I'd done what nobody else in Stratford could do—got the better o' Cal.

*

A few doors away on Waterside lived Police Sergeant Cross. Red faced and pudgy, he had a big tub and a big family, even for that time o' day: a dozen lads, and right little Rodneys they was, too! They'd tie up one of the neighbour's window frames, kick it and shake it and then run away—or terrify an old chap's cabbages. Half an hour later there'd be their Dad, struggling with his notebook and pencil at old mother Freeman's door, not knowing it was his kiddies all the time—*she'd* soon point the finger!—and looking as if he'd boil over with the effort of writing.

'What's a penny made of?' we yelled. 'COPPER!'

Bobby Cross was supposed to check up on Cal: see as she kept the earth closet from stinking—some hopes o' that!—and didn't cram too many folks in a bed and aired the rooms. We did that each spring: March-open-the-winders-and-let-the-fleas-out. It was all laid down, he told her, in the book o' rules, what he was supposed to do:

'Keep movin along the edge o' the pavement an be carefully observant of all that is passin, partickerly any strangers of suspicious appearance . . . ' That was the bit I liked best. 'Cautiously observe their movements and take care to visit the common lodgin houses on your beat frequently, and observe the characters as is locatin there!'

There was one by Market Cross, another on Windsor Street . . . If he bumped into a superior sort o' travelling man looking for a bed he might direct them to 'Caroline Cook's on Waterside'. On the other hand, he said, if he looked rough he'd point him over the bridge, towards the 'Shoulder o' Mutton'.

Cal and Bobby Cross got on well. I reckon he looked up to her—she kept better order'n his missus—and many an early morning on his way home she slipped him a few taters, a peck o' peas or a colly.

He said: 'Cal! If there's any trouble just pop out—or send the lad down.'

But we never had no fights. When the men got rough she dealt with them herself. She weren't a big woman but she looked big, stout and stern, more like the widowed Queen than anyone I knowed. She always wore black: old-fashioned long skirts as dragged the floor, a black bonnet. She dressed poor, out the shop. 'I don't mind the *company*,' she said, meaning the fleas, 'but the buggers do 'alf bite.'

Mostly they was arguments over the frying pan. Maybe one bloke had snared a rabbit on his way home from work and another one had got a couple o' rashers o' bacon. If things looked nasty she'd give them a bit out our pot and send me to the public for some beer. She'd please them—quick! When they got drunk she took no notice: 'They'll get sober again!' was her motto. When they got sick—well, that were a different matter. She couldn't afford to have them sick. She sent for Doctor Lupton and he ordered them to the workhouse.

Cal started off renting one cottage. It weren't much to look at: a plain brick building on the corner of Sheep Street and Waterside, with a lamp outside where folks gathered of an evening to pass the time o' day, and the young chaps met their wenches. It was a situation you couldn't ignore if you'd got brains and Cal weren't behind the door when those was handed out. She served in the shop; even when business looked to be blooming she wouldn't let nobody else do that! She'd sell folks a pennoth o' mixed veget-ables—a couple o' taters, a little turnip and a carrot and a parsnip.

'I'm losin' money on this!' she'd say. 'But bein as you's so poor I'll 'elp you out a bit!'

But you could take your oath those taters was good. She went to the Sale Yard early, pinched a tater out each pot, marked them and cooked them to see which was the best cooker. She always bought taters as cooked nice. She didn't buy *all* her vegetables— don't worry! The roadsters called at Cal's, peapicking time, and they always came loaded up.

All year round I looked forward to the roadsters a-coming. And suddenly one day in June they'd be there, filling up the doorway; with long black coats and black beards and black tea cans a-dangling in my face and shoes that looked as if they'd tramped to the ends of the earth and back. Cal knowed their names and strange names they was and all, like feet hitting gravel: Dag and Lop and Clommer and Grauncher and Dink.

'Evenin, little fella!'

Their tales came straight from faery-land: strawberries big as taters, cider-apple country, fields upon fields o' lilies, all colours of the rainbow, as far as the eye could see, an army of wapses, each one fierce as a ferret, man traps, wading through peppermint 'till you stank o' nothin else!'

'You'll dub the point o' that knife against the bricks!' said Cal, smiling. 'Come in!'

5. Cal Cook's cottage on the corner of Sheep Street and Waterside

Our teacher called them the *Peapicking Menace*. Mothers on Waterside shouted their kiddies indoors and such a clucking started up you'd a-thought the old fox was in the hen coop. Bobby Cross laid low. Cal's lodgers chuntered and grumbled but it didn't do no good: she liked the roadsters too. 'You'll 'ave to shove up round this fire,' she said. There was always a fire going, even in June. Her look said: 'If you don't like it, you can lump it and that's all as is!'

Soon you could hardly see for the pipe smoke. Old Mr Anderson sounded to be choking to death, but she took no notice.

'Us shan't be pickin for a week, Cal. It's a back'ard season, back'ardest ever I knowed. Us'll stop 'ere if that suits you.'

She always had a room upstairs put by for them. They got a slice o' bread and a jar o' cocoa for fourpence—they golloped that down!—and the use of the fire. More often'n not they'd be wanting new strides and a pair o' shoes. You see, they came to Cal's to get fitted up for the year ahead. They'd show her the size.

'Gimme a day—I'll see what I can do.'

27

Where Cal found her shoes I never did know, but they always fitted a treat.

'I can't pay you till the peas is ready.'

'Move those taters and carrots for me in the shop,'—she was planning to make room for the peas, her mind was ticking over— 'sweep it up for me and I'll say that's square.'

Or he'd pinch a fowl off the farmer.

One of these blokes was Ram, he was a favourite of hers. I reckoned he was called Ram on account of his curly hair, part black, part silver. I asked him about his name once and he laughed and said: 'Hiram O'Sullivan at your service, sir, a Popish Protestant bastard!'

He always called me 'sir' and Cal 'ma'am'. This year he turns up smart as a carrot in a *new suit*! It was splattered with muck but you could see it was a good un.

'Shittin luck is good luck,' he said, and grinned. He'd got it off his last landlady, Pershore way; she was a widow woman, well off, and she'd fell in love with him. She had a packman come and he said: 'Get me a suit will you, Nancy darlin?' She gave him the suit and he was off, with no rent for her, no more the pack money and two gold sovereigns! Everybody laughed. He let me hold one for a while and Cal's eyes gleamed.

'Got a shift, ma'am? A pretty shift wi ribbons on it?'

She showed him one. It weren't all that pretty: whitey-brown calico. You could see Ram thinking the same. 'Oh, that ain't long enough.'

Cal was snappy: 'There's four and twenty men where she is, Sullivan, and they've all 'ad a look while you've been away. It's long enough for *er*!'

A couple of roadsters always brought their women with them, and kiddies—more hands for picking, see. They slept on the floor of the shop with their kiddies in their arms and whilst they was there they got a new set o' clothes. They was old-fashioned tats! They changed in the shop and left their old uns with Cal. Peapicking time she sent me running to Tinker Freeman's with sacks o' rags.

'Does e 'ave to watch? E's a growin lad!' the women said, laughing like, cos I was only as big as a bee's knee, and pulling off their old petticoats, layers and layers of them. I dodged out the road—you could see the fleas flying. They'd had them on for a *whole year*! And I'll tell you summat else—they had no knickers! The gyppos came to Stratford too, at peapicking time. They mostly slept in the 'Unicorn' yard, at the back o' the cattle pens, but they called at Cal's for clothes and some of them was fine-looking women, with black hair greased down with hedgehog oil into little curls round their faces, gold earrings. They'd be puffing away at their clay pipes and making lace as they stood in the shop—lovely lace.

'Look at them,' said Cal, 'they don't waste a minute!'

But when the peas was ready! Dink and Ram, Lop and Dag, gyppos and tramps, they all lived in their tents on the land, slept in a barn or up the Tram, and they picked all night or very near, as long as they could possibly see. Many a sack o' peas they dumped in Cal's front room, late o' night. Cal knowed who it was a-knocking!

'I bet it's them peapickers!' she'd say, looking pleased, and it was. 'Go and fetch em some beer, My Lad.'

I was off like one o'clock. The pub was only just over the road. Cal sorted out the loot.

'*Sixpence a peck!*' The shopkeepers came round town hawking the peas on trucks. 'Sixpence a peck brought to your door!'

But sixpence was sixpence then. Our peas was the cheapest in Stratford.

*

I told you Cal was a marvel with money. This is what she used to do. When an old chap went round who looked a bit better off'n most she said: 'Are you insured? Cos I can't 'ave no-one lodgin 'ere oo ain't insured! Yes? Gimme your book. You can't afford to pay *that*! I'll pay it for you!'

Later she got me to read it out for her: the details—it might be a penny a week—what Society it was and that. Cal could neither read nor write but she could add up! She had the old chap's book and if he died she'd got the policy. She made a lot o' money out of all those deaths; a lot died there—oh yes they did!

I was six when I saw my first corpse laid out at Cal's. I didn't know but what he was asleep; I didn't have the sense to be frit. She never was. She always said: 'Never be afeared o' the dead, My Lad! They can't hurt you. It's the livin as does that!'

I helped to carry them downstairs. One day I was away from school and Cal says to me: 'I got Doctor Lupton a-comin. Get a bucket o' water an go an wipe that room up.' There was two up there dead—they was lying there dead! It was a shock. I went through the pockets. Sometimes I found old-fashioned knives with horn handles, proper beautiful ones. These two had nothing, not even a cotton handkerchief. That was peculiar: one of them always weared a cotton 'kerchief round his neck, a red un with stars busting all over it. It had *distinguished* him. But the most mysterious thing was—somebody had cut his beard off!

If he was an old chap who had sons and daughters in Stratford Cal said: 'Do you want 'is clothes?'

'No,' they said, they didn't want to take them. So she hanged them on the line at the back of the shop. If he was a stranger, if he had no relations—well she had them just the same. I didn't like the way those old coats and flannel shirts flapped about, I can tell you, it was enough to scare the crows. All over the place they fluttered, above the tater baskets, at the top o' the stairs, like ghosts when the souls have gone, and that's what most of them was.

CHAPTER THREE

The first school I went to was the National School, Alcester Road, cos Cal believed in keeping in with the Vicar. 'There's no pickins from Chapel,' she said.

It was in the days of the Reverend George Arbuthnot—Black George, we called him. Many a time he punched my ear-hole. 'Wipe that grin off your face, boy! Now,' he said to the class, 'can anyone tell me why *our* Sunday School is so popular?'

My hand shot up. 'Please, sir, cos of the Clothin Club!'

You had a card marked twopence, every time you went—twopence a week for clothing. Some of us snook out the back, once we'd got our cards marked, and at the end of the year you got the money. Who would have gone, else?

I got another clout for that.

It was drill, drill, drill. We was paraded in four companies on the Vicar's cricket field, down Back Lane, even the tiny tots, with staves for guns. The best boy had sixpence. Timmy Large, the teacher, rushes over to me. 'You'll never get the sixpence, Hewins!'

I didn't care about his old sixpence and I reckon he knowed it. That was what got his back up. Plenty of them *did* care—I was lucky, I was better off'n most. Cal gave me as much as I wanted. She'd say: 'Don't go to school wi'out some coppers in your pocket.'

They was always bribing us. There was the School Attendance Prize. The first Monday morning of the new year we was all stood up for the Vicar as usual—in dead silence, you could hear a collar creaking or the softest fart. He stood in front o' the fire and he bellows: 'The reward which we offer for regular and punctual attendance 'as produced good results, and we are goin this year to try an extend its usefulness by making CLEANLINESS a further condition for winnin it. The untidyness an dirtiness of some boys, mentionin' no names, is a disgrace to the community. SOAP is cheap,' he says, 'and the new supply of WATER to Stratford will

31

doubtless soon make this commodity plentiful, so I 'ope for good results from this NEW RULE.'

He stared long and hard at one of two of us, and the Evesham Road boys started sniggering. I thought: 'I'll get you later, Fatty Taylor.' Our teacher looked upset. We knowed why. The lad who'd stood to win the prize lived on Meer Street: there was no hope of Danny Andrews getting cleaned up. I didn't like teachers' pets but I didn't like the Evesham Road lot neither. Danny was *poor*, that's all he done wrong.

Soon as the Vicar had gone, Timmy Large our teacher started shouting; he didn't talk to us, he shouted—well, he had to, to make himself heard. Some days if another teacher was took bad there was as many as a hundred of us, in one class. 'THE OLDER THE BOY THE GREATER THE ASS!' Then it was a different sort of education: threepence a week to go to school and once you'd paid they didn't care if you didn't go again till next Monday. If it was raining, or the steeplechases, or peapicking, a lot of us *didn't*. The School Attendance Officer, he never troubled once your money was paid in. And plenty o' kiddies spent a penny or a ha'penny of it on jibber-and-jumbles afore they got to school. They had a good swipe o' the cane: the teacher told them to bring another ha'penny— quick! 'The older the boy the greater the ass!' he shouted. Timmy Large was always in a lather about one thing or another: he reckoned the School Attendance Officer weren't doing his job, or Lieutenant Hutchings of the Volunteers was drilling us that hard we couldn't learn when we got back to school, or the Vicar was coming, or we was laughing at him behind his back. It was true!

*

We got off school as much as we dared. We ran wild in those days—those of us as weren't earning and didn't want no prize neither—down by the river, up the Tram. We ran up the fields by the tramway to meet the old grey horse as pulled the trucks; we jumped on the buffers, had a ride to Cox's timber yard. As soon as it saw the crowd waiting on the wharf it sat down, that old grey horse: it wouldn't budge till it had had some buns! It was crafty!

We helped unload the timber, for the ride. Then they'd take a load o' coal back to Shipston or Moreton-in-the-Marsh.

You can see from this that I done what I liked. Once I got up a steeplechase with some sheep, on the sheeps' backs. We was in those fields behind the 'Shoulder o' Mutton'. Someone must a-seen us. Next day Bobby Cross was waiting round the corner, catched us coming home from school. *That* time it was just two or three stripes with the ash plant—mind you, you knowed you'd had it!—and 'I'll tell your father!'. I laughed—it was handy not to have one. And I weren't worried about Cal neither. She'd say to Bobby Cross: 'If you think I'm goin to hit My Lad—I ain't. The world'll knock im about enough!'

I don't remember ever having a tap off her in my life.

The 'Shoulder o' Mutton' public house stood on the river bank, opposite Waterside. They had pleasure boats moored at the front and a doss house at the back. Well you see from the Banbury Road, Shipston Road, Warwick Road they got all the really rough uns as had fourpence to spend: beggars and tramps. Cal had her regulars, like Ram. She wouldn't take *any*body; no more would the other lodging houses. Those as couldn't pay went on to the workhouse. The tramps used to go to Warwick workhouse and Shipston workhouse, then work their way to Stratford workhouse, then Alcester workhouse.

'Spring is 'ere,' folks said. They hadn't seen the first crocus, they'd seen the first tramp!

We had some fun by the 'Shoulder o' Mutton'. There was Sam the Pig Poker:

> 'Sam Sam dirty ole man,' we hollered after him,
> 'Washed 'is face
> In the fryin pan,
> Combed 'is hair
> Wi' the leg of a chair—'

He used to chase us with his frying pan! He was a beggar, peapicker, scrap iron, rags, bones, *any*thing. Tramps in those days had to earn a living. One of them had a Russian bear, twice as tall

6. Dancing bear

as me, a great fat thing. We kept well back when we saw that bear! He came every year to Stratford—they knowed the places where they'd done well—and slept at the 'Shoulder o' Mutton', in the stable. He was a regular Russian tramp, with baggy trousers and ribbons hanging down. He'd got no musical instrument, just talked to the bear in his way and it danced! Then he went round with his hat for the money. The bear grunted and pulled on its chain and *we* ran off! We'd heard tell that bear ate a little gal called Laura Eddens, once upon a time.

*

I was coming home from school one day when what should I see but the Town Crier a-ringing his bell and crying out: 'Anybody oo wants firewood come down to the Parish Church and 'ave some!' They was taking the gallery down: it was getting rotten.

I thought to myself: I'll fetch some for that ole lady down the road there, she'll give me a few coppers.

34

So I takes Cal's coal truck. The first person I sees in the church is Bobby Cross.

He says to me: 'I'm glad *you've* come!' They'd got the ground out by Shakespeare's tomb, to test the columns, see if they was safe. 'You see that hole,' he says. He could hardly see it himself. As I said, he was a big fat fella, with a tub. 'Next time I 'ave any trouble wi you—you'll be put inside that hole and left in all night.' I reckoned he should a-started with his own lads, but I kept my mouth shut.

Well, I was getting some firewood together when I noticed an old tin box—and just aside it a *spade guinea*! I slips the guinea in my shoe and I shoves the box on the truck, under the firewood. It was a fancy box, but I never thought anything of that. In those days they used to stick coloured transfers over things. When I got home I opened it up. I fetched some old pressed flowers out, and a stone.

Cal says, quick as lightning: 'You go round to Mr Pearce, Bridge Street, ask im what it makes.'

I took twenty-one shillings for my spade guinea and Mr Pearce says: 'I don't think much o' that stone you got. I'll give you a nice red un for it.'

I hadn't been brought up by Cal for nothing!

'Alright,' he says, 'I'd better come back wi you.'

He walked into Cal's shop and I went into the next room. There was a glass panel so's she could see if anyone had come in. I saw him look at the stone again. He chatted with Cal. Then he gave her *five guineas* for that one stone. *Five guineas!*

I kept my marbles in the tin box. I was playing in the street one day when a group of Americans happened to come by, in top hats and greatcoats. They wanted to know where the Theatre and the Church was, but they kept looking at my box. One of them says: 'Where d'you live, child? I'd like a word wi your parents.' He follows me down Sheep Street. 'What's your age?'

'Eight,' I says, 'comin up for nine.'

He looked surprised: I reckon he thought I was younger'n that. Cal was in the shop. The American comes straight out with it: 'D' you know this young man's playin wi a *fortune*?' You should a-seen

Cal's face change! 'This is a most valuable casket!' he said. They must a-been precious stones on that old tin box!

In a trice Cal locked up and we all went round to Mr Pearce the jeweller's. 'Now,' says Cal to Mr Pearce, 'what ud *you* give for this box?'

He ran his hands over it; he did half caddle it. 'Eighty pounds,' he said. *Eighty pounds!* 'But it ud be a shame to break it up to make small articles. Where d'you say you got it, Cal?'

'I didn't.'

The American says to her: 'I'll 'ave it if you'll sell it.' He paid for it in gold sovereigns. One-two-three . . . Cal counted them again, one by one, just to make sure.

Now Cal had a grown son and daughter, a 'pigeon pair' as they say, George and Nance. George had just finished his apprenticeship at a barber's on Henley Street and he was out o' work: the shop had closed.

'Mam, there's a barber's shop goin at Leamington—I could do wi that eighty pound.'

Says Cal: 'It's My Lad's nest-egg, y'know.' She was a hard dealer. 'I'll want interest.'

George took the money quick, afore she changed her mind—and left her with Maggie. It didn't seem a very good exchange. Maggie was his daughter by a Stratford wench: she was younger'n me, no more'n five or six year old, and she was—well, poor Maggie had come out the oven half-baked. Maggie's mother didn't want her, left her on the doorstep when she heard George was planning to leave town. So I didn't have a penny of all that money. And I lost my bed. 'You'll 'ave to shove up,' said Cal, but she gave poor Maggie one of her looks as made me think it wouldn't be for long.

Then I got into terrible trouble. The canal boats used to anchor in the basin next to the Theatre—there was two basins then. They got ashore by planks: they couldn't get the boats close to the bank cos of the mud, you see. And while the canal boat folks was out boozing a-nights, at the 'Wheatsheaf' opposite Cal's or a few yards higher up Sheep Street at the 'Dog' where beer was eight pints a bob, we snook up the plank and had a good feed. We was all right till past midnight. They'd get well-oiled, start arguing about their boats, telling the others what their parents was—not fit to black *their* boots! There was many an argument over whose boat was best. Sometimes the pleasure boatmen joined in and all. They'd fight and then they'd make up. You could hear the canal boat folks dancing down Sheep Street at midnight and along Waterside, wives and wenches too.

Well, they got wind of us in the end. The copper—Bobby Harris—he comes up the plank. Like fools we didn't know we was trapped. We laid low and when he got half way up this plank we tipped him in. He was up to here in mud and a-hollering to folks on Waterside to get him out. They had us this time! I was booked for the birch, and naturally I was took bad at the thought of it.

Doctor Lupton—he was a nice chap—comes to see Cal. 'Where's the lad, Cal?'

'E's bad in bed.'

7. Sheep Street, Stratford-upon-Avon, 1870s, the 'Dog' public house on the right. The state of the road was typical.

'E weren't bad t'other night when e nearly got that fella drownded.'

'D'you think e's fit to 'ave the birch?'

'The birch rod?' says Doctor Lupton.

She put two sovereigns in his hand and he passed her a note to take to the police.

He told me afterwards: 'Behave yourself, lad, cos I can't get you off again, you know.'

Money won that. But my five pals went to Weston Reformatory, for five years. Some of them came back to Stratford. They'd learnt to play instruments while they was away—they was in the Weston Reformatory Band!

When Cal's daughter, Nance, who'd been away in service, came home to get married and said: 'I'd like to take im back to Leamington wi me for company, Mam,' I reckon Cal was quite relieved. *I* couldn't believe my ears!

'Just till this trouble's blowed over,' Cal said, and a look passed across her face. 'If you takes the dillen you can take er too,' meaning Maggie.

Nance's husband-to-be Charlie Middleton weren't keen, I could

8. The new Shakespeare Memorial Theatre

see that—'Er's cakey!' he kept whispering—but Nance didn't care. It was her wedding day.

She had me and Maggie put up on the box. All the neighbours had turned out and did they gawp!

'Up you go, Little Jack.'

And I rode with the coachman to the Parish Church. The new Theatre trotted past—the Grand Tower and the turrets striped like sticks o' mop rock—and the Flowers' big house and the elm trees and the rooks a-cawing. It was April. Nance had a bonnet with primroses on and I thought she was the most beautiful young lady I had ever seen.

When her brother George heard about it he said: 'E can come an be lather boy for *me*!'

✥ CHAPTER FOUR ✥

I started shaving when I was nine! I'd got a white apron and a white smock. I had threepence a week for being lather boy and if George got any rough uns off the road come he'd say: 'Would you let the boy practise on you?'

'I dunno,' they said. There was no safety razors, blades, nothing o' that then, just a open razor.

'E's alright!' George said. And they'd get a shave for nothing.

Hair cutting was three ha'pence, penny a shave. It was pretty good practice with the rough uns cos they'd got goodish beards, I can tell you. I had to dip the lather brush in the boiling water, then the soap. 'Ow! Oi'll be buggered!' they cried out. 'That's 'ot!'

After that, George told me how to put my finger in, to see how hot it was. Some of the beards was very hard. I cut them right down first, rubbed them with a sort of paste we made, lathered them well and shaved them. 'Ow!' they shouted.

But mostly our customers was ordinary working folk. In those days blokes didn't reckon to shave themselves; they went to a barber's twice a week. When it was quiet I learnt how to do ladies' combings. They brought them in, I labelled the packets and drew the combings into strands. Then we worked them into plaits, fringes—that sort o' thing was in fashion. My teacher came into the shop to have his hair cut and his beard trimmed, he'd got a beard. I remember his name—Lamsdale. He was headmaster of Trinity Street School, opened in 1868, the notice outside said: 'To give the children of the poor residing in the upper part of Leamington an education suitable to their rank in life,' whatever that was.

I listened by the door whiles George was trimming his beard and I heard George say: 'Ow's e getting on?'

'Not as good as needs be,' says Lamsdale. 'I clouted im today.'

He used to make me take a class. I was well advanced, see, quick on the uptake; when I was ten I was specially commended by the Inspector. This day it was reading. The kiddies gave me rock, not to let them read, and when Lamsdale comes back I was about four pages behind. He gave me such a sock o' the ear-hole! There was nothing to what he did to two lads. They had cheeked him, I expect. He tanned them and whaled their backs—we thought he were never going to stop. *Whack! Whack! Whack!* You could see the marks where he'd hit them! The skin was broke! We stared in silence, never said a word—we daresn't.

Next morning we heard a cuffufle in the entrance. The two mothers had arrived! Oo, there weren't half a performance! In they barged. They rolled their sleeves up and one of them shouts, 'Come on!' They said they'd smash him up, give it *him*! All the kids stamped with excitement, desks was knocked over, and these two mothers was a-trying to get Lamsdale. The school was one long darkish room—it stopped all the lessons. Lamsdale jumped over the desk and we followed suit, jumping from desk to desk. They'd have given him summat if they could have copped him, but he escaped out the back door and it was our turn to laugh. The two mothers joined in.

But most of the time we was bored. We used to get locust pips and spit them on to the neck of the lad in front—it made a change from learning by heart. If you was caught you had to empty your pockets. Everybody craned their necks to see what you'd got. Singing was the only thing you might say I *enjoyed* at school. Lamsdale was a musical bloke and we had concerts, school concerts. They invited the parents, so Nance went with Maggie when she could. I was picked to sing solo. I stood there and sang like a robin. Nance beamed with pride, and Maggie—well, she smiled all the time anyways. I didn't like any of the rest of school.

*

The organ grinders came to our shop on Oxford Street. They was Italians, all of them. They said: 'Where's our boy?' Yes, they was my friends. I used to lather them.

George said: 'Now stop talkin to the lad, else you'll get a mouthful.'

41

As they was going out they'd give me a penny or twopence. They was very kind. Late o' night, after the shop—I was in the shop from four till eight, and Sat'days—I went down Satchwell Street where the organ grinders lived. Summer nights, the barrel organs would be outside the pub and they let me turn the handle so's they could have a dance themselves. There'd be a sort o' hiccup and a gasp, then up it would start in the middle of a tune and they'd be a-dancing! Many an hour I've played the barrel organ while they danced up Satchwell Street.

> Oh Oh, Antonio,
> E's gone away.
> Left me all alone-io
> All on me own-io.
> Oh I'd like to meet im
> With 'is new sweet'eart,
> Then *up*! would go Antonio
> And his ice-cream cart!

I seen many a scrap. Summat would upset them. Well, they always had an idea that if there was two folks talking and looking their way they was talking about them. Or p'raps one's wife had been boozing. He'd start on her, then if she had a brother or father they'd have a go at *him*. Soon there'd be a big excited crowd and they was fighting on the ground and the blood flowing. There was a lot of Antonios in Leamington at that time o' day, and there was one they reckoned was the boss—he sold more ice-cream than the rest of them put together. They called him 'The King of the Italians'. His real name was Al Farini.

Sometimes they went down the back streets, but most of them worked on the Parade. They had six barrel organs there. They weren't their own: they hired them from Brummagem, so much a month. They put a card on one of them: 'ALL THIS GOES TO OUR BOY!' That was me! There was an art in turning the handle: just one pace, depending on what song it was. *Mother Macree* was the favourite in Leamington. The organ grinders was all for gay stuff themselves, they didn't like solemn songs. Those who'd made a bit, like 'The King', they had a monkey, a little un, on a chain—sad looking little fellas. Folks fed them as they passed by, with a biscuit or a bun. Well, in a few weeks I'd collected pounds! Asides pennies for a grind some folks paid you to move on! Shop-keepers did and the Regent Hotel sent a footman out with a tanner. Those organ grinders made some money! Sometimes they skipped up the Parade aside a likely customer, grinning and jabbering away in a sing-song voice till he paid up just to get rid of them. They made some money, and they helped one another, if one didn't do well: they was a clique together. But they lived *any*how—ate macaroni, slept on straw!

Nance said low: 'Don't you go down that street no more, Jack. It's rough.'

She didn't really mind, it was Charlie. He was a fussy sort o' chap, Charlie Middleton, a painter by trade. If he was working where a lot o' folks went, like the Pump Rooms or the Post Office, he reckoned to pick up a *Courier* somebody had forgot, or finished with. Maggie ironed it out for him, sheet by sheet. She'd really took to him, I couldn't see why. He made you feel uncomfortable. He didn't go to the public a-nights—he sat there reading! Some-times there was a page missing and he chuntered under his breath. Maggie smiled and smiled and went on smiling, cos she didn't understand. You could hear the clock ticking. Nance and me whispered and giggled; we couldn't stand the quiet. Sometimes he read aloud if a bit took his fancy.

'Listen to this—a bloke's summonsed 'The King!' I was horrified. He *was* a king, to me.

'Didn't I say so, Annie?'

''E ain't like Grogan! Now e *wants* lockin up!' Grogan was a hawker, the terror of Satchwell Street. His stock in trade was six packets o' needles. He stopped folks and forced them to buy a packet for twopence or it would be the worse for them. He was a bully.

'Or Gallagher,' said Nance. ''E's lived off poor Fanny Tew for years, they say, and all e gives er is a black eye an a beatin' of a Sat'day. "*Please, sir e'd 'ad a drop o' beer and e slapped me on the face, that's all, only once!*" At least the Antonios earn a livin an give Fanny a bit. Folks is jealous.'

'Well, listen to this,' said Charlie Middleton, getting a bit ratty:

'Applicant stated as e was sent down from London by a friend of Farini's to assist im in the ice-cream trade in Leamington. Farini met im at the railway station and engaged im at 'alf a crown a week, and 'is board an lodgin. E sometimes went out wi an organ but 'is usual work was sellin ice-cream. E handed 'is Master on some days . . .'

He paused and peered. If they'd had the money he'd a-weared spectacles; he had to get to an inch of the paper.

. . . 'As much as *fourteen shillin*!'

Even Maggie was impressed by that. She stopped smiling. Fourteen shilling a day!

'An two-thirds was *profit*!'

'What ud our Mam say to that?' said Nance.

Charlie Middleton read on:

' 'Is Master did not pay im regular, but let im 'ave 'is money when e wanted.' And 'ere's a letter from one of the shopkeepers!' Nance snorted.

'The sons o' Joobal, an their ice-cream compatriots seem to be drivin a flourishin trade in the Royal Spa . . . When *fourteen shillings* in one day can be made in Leamington out o' ice-creams it is no wonder there is such a rush to this El Dorado. There is many an many a hard-working tradesman on The Parade oo don't make fourteen shillings profit in a day. But all the luck is on the side of the ice-cream sellin Italian. E'as no rents, rates an taxes to pay, and e takes 'is shop with im.
I cannot understand why Leamington juveniles 'ave such a stomach for ill-made ices!'

'It's a wonder,' Charlie Middleton said, looking straight at me, 'they ain't poisoned nobody.'

'They're goin to buy im a suit!' said Nance. 'A new suit an a shirt, ain't they, Jack? That's more'n the old shopkeepers would a-done!'

You could see Charlie Middleton didn't believe a word of it.

But they *did*! I got rigged out well at the market. Was they pleased to see me with my new clothes on! They laughed and jabbered away in their own language and 'The King' sat me on his shoulder and ran up to the public with me and bought me a beer. 'This is Our Boy!' he said. Folks stared! I'd sooner have had an ice-cream.

Nance gave me a kiss when I got back and said: 'My, you look smart! Mind they don't kidnap you!' She was scared the Italians might kidnap me, or adopt me.

Charlie Middleton kept hoping. He was painting a big house at the bottom o' Leamington, on Leam Terrace, about a mile off. Every morning Nance sent me down with his breakfast, and every morning he gave me a couple o' pears he'd pinched from the garden. ''Ere! Take these!' he said. 'Quick!'

They was hard as hell, but I ate them. Then he comes home one night—I shall never forget it!

9. Cal Cook's daughter, Nance, with baby

'I bet those pears is a-gettin' ripe, Annie.'

'*Pears?*' said Nance.

'Those pears I gave Jack to put i' the cupboard.'

I helped Nance all I could. By now she'd started to have babbies—one, two, three—one after another I pushed them up the
Kenilworth Road in an old pram. And I done the washing, I helped
with the mangling. Just over the road from us was a place where I
took our things. There was a notice in the window: 'MANGLING
DONE HERE!' Folks waited while he mangled them. He'd got a
long mangle, six foot or so, with a box filled with stones on top
o' the rollers, to weight it. When he'd done I'd take them home
and help Maggie to iron them. I'd a-done *any*thing for Nance.

Me and my pals used to meet the trains and carry the visitors'
bags, and I always gave Nance what I made. 'Carry yer bags, sir?
Carry yer bags, sir?' Retired folk, old maids, vicars, they flocked
like crows to Leamington to take the waters. But when the actors
arrived to play at the Theatre Royal in Holly Walk we carried *their*
bags for nothing. It was a sprat to catch a mackerel. We got in with
them, and if it was a poor play and didn't go well, they'd pay six
of us to go up in the gallery. When they came on the stage we
clapped and cheered! We got about a tanner for that, and we
watched all the plays. There was robberies and convict mutinies
and railway collisions and chases after escaped gaolbirds and shooting and that sort o' thing. The best one was *The Strangler of Paris*.
He was disguised as a whitewasher—just like Charlie Middleton!
Well, he strangles this bloke and takes the money:

'The law give im me daughter's money, but the law didn't say
ow long e could keep it!'

We learnt them off by heart. When a nigger minstrel show came
to the Theatre Royal we copied it. We picked it up and we started
on our own.

We called ourselves The Bakehouse Minstrel Troupe. We put a
notice on a pole 'ADMITTANCE ½d' and blacked our faces with
burnt cork. We was in Teddy Ivins' bakehouse, in Oxford Street.
He had a big loft. There was stairs up but you had to sit on the
boarded floor. Folks knowed where their kiddies had been! 'You've

been to that damned minstrel loft again!' They was smothered in flour!

Word spread. Every night it was packed—kiddies, chaps and their wenches. When he saw it was a paying concern, George took over. There was nine of us altogether. I was Bones on one side with the clappers—I got them out the Sunday meat—and there was a Tambourine t'other. The one in the middle told jokes and you had to answer them:

'Now if I've four oranges—an I give *im* one—ow many oranges should I 'ave left?'

'Three!' I'd say.

'Wrong! I shouldn't 'ave give im one!'

It was all songs and jokes. That's where I first sang that parody of *Queen of my Heart*. I was dressed up as an old woman.

> E turned up 'is nose at 'is vittals,
> And the pickles e then at me threw.
> E swore as the taters was skittles,
> And the steak it was like chewin glue.
> E struck me three times wi the fender,
> And e made this poor eye such a fright,
> But I bet there's a part of im tender—
> And I'll give im *beans* tonight!

And I pulled a brick from under my shawl! Laugh? I'd say they did!

''Ave you writ that essay I wanted you to?'

'Please, sir, I kept fallin off.'

'Fallin off? What d'ye mean, "fallin off"?'

'Well, you told me you wanted me to write an essay on the bicycle.'

I liked it, I liked everything about it: dressing-up, singing, folks clapping and cheering. I could have gone on, if I'd had someone behind me. But there was nobody really *owned* me.

*

I was still getting twenty-four penny stamps from Brummagem—Nance bought them off me now. Cal kept in touch through the carrier. One night there was a message to go and fetch a dillen pig she'd found at the Sale Yard. The carrier had left it at Warwick. It was pitch black and everybody was in their beds when I got there. I tucked the pig under my arm—it was a-squealing! I was frit to death the coppers would be after me for making a commotion at that time o' night. Folks kept coming to their windows and peeping out. 'Oo's that?' I reckon they thought there was a murderer about, the noise that tiny pig was making. In the end, it got stuck up my sleeve; Nance had to cut it out when I got home!

We kept it in the backyard, fed it on scraps. It growed bigger and bigger. When it was ready we couldn't a-bear to kill it. We sold it. Me and Nance couldn't touch bacon for months afterwards. Then she started rearing some ducklings Cal sent. You wouldn't a-thought you could get fond o' *ducks*, but Nance did! She found an old bath for them and set it in the yard full o' water so's they could have a swim and a paddle. They followed her everywhere, into the house, down the passage, pulling at her skirts.

One day Nance said: 'Mam's sent a message, Little Jack. You's to go with er to Brummagem.'

'*Brummagem?*'

Nance said: 'Mind you don't let *er*' (meaning my mother) 'make you stop, or kidnap you. She's in trouble, I'll be bound.'

And so we went to Brummagem: me and Cal and Cal's husband, old Bill Cook, carrying a big carpet bag. I forgot to say Cal had a husband. You always forgot about old Bill Cook, he was that sort o' chap. He worked on Hutching's coal wharf. He was a clerk—he couldn't read, but he chalked on the trucks who the coal was for. It was the first time I'd been on a train. One and sixpence return from Stratford the fare was then. They came round and gave us an iron hot water bottle, two foot long, filled with boiling water, to keep us warm. Some lads met us at the station: 'Carry yer bags, sir?' They took the carpet bag—and they flied like hell! They was terrors. Old Bill Cook couldn't keep up with them; they'd gone down the streets and he saw no more of his bag. Cal cussed. It didn't do no good. I was scared. There was buildings everywhere made of stone, and the smoke from the trains and the smoke from the steam trams—they had steam trams in Brummagem at that time o' day—had turned them all *black*!

48

10. Barford Street, Birmingham. When this photograph was taken, in 1905, the street was about to be demolished. The posters advertise a soup-kitchen.

My mother kept a sweet shop in Barford Street. We walked. It weren't far from the station when you found your way. Rough? Was it! The shop was in the front room, the window faced the street.

My mother said: ''Elp yourself!' She sighed. 'It's all of a mullock in 'ere! I can't manage on me own. You don't know what it's like on your own.'

I didn't know her—well, I'd never had a day with her afore. But I could read the signs and I minded what Nance had said. I played dumb. I sat in the shop eating, eating my way through the profit. There weren't much o' that: you could get a *farthingsworth* of sweets then.

'E's gone to India, to the temples—e's carvin inside,' she said. 'Three months.'

The young devils was a-standing outside the window in the rain. They kept licking it—*Aagh*! They was some rough uns!

49

'Last time e'd gone as thin as a lath. I didn't know im I didn't.'

I was thinking: I daresn't go out! I'm better off in 'ere!

I had plenty o' rock while I was there, you can bet your life I did. But even in the house you weren't safe!

She said: 'Go an 'ang this bath in the kitchen will you?' I thought she meant the passage.

Later she said: 'Funny, I can't see that bath.'

I said: 'I put it in the passage.'

She said: 'It's gone!' She starts wringing her hands.

Cal snapped: 'Pull yourself together, Emmie—it's only a bloody bath.'

Yes. They'd pinched it, one of the neighbours had pinched it! It weren't like home. They didn't stop and gossip at back doors in Barford Street—they'd got other things to do. You could see Cal didn't like the look of it neither. When it came to parting she said: 'I bain't a-goin to leave My Lad 'ere, Emmie—' My mother was sobbing. 'E'll kill im and you knows it.'

Cal was still frowning in the train. '*Brummagem!*' she said, '——!'

Other folks in the carriage gawped. 'Well, er's made er bed, er's got to lie on it and that's all as is. I can't do no more.'

What she meant I didn't rightly know, but I was glad to get home, I can tell you.

*

All this time I was getting to be a handy little chap at cutting and shaving. I could see myself as a master barber one day. Lamsdale the teacher came in for his hair cut.

'Any improvement?' George asked him.

'E's got the gift o' the gab, I'll say that.'

I had! I never could stop talking and that's how I came to leave Leamington. It happened like this.

A butcher's widow from Warwick Street started bringing her combings in. George picked up with her, he never missed his main chance. Soon it was '*Eva.*' She'd got more curls and rolls and puffs'n a fancy bantam.

One day George says: 'We's a-goin to emigrate, Jack!'

My heart leapt. There was two boys at school had emigrated.

They'd had to stand up and the teacher said, 'Tommy and Albie Cox is goin to New Zealand. It's the other side o' the world and the rivers is that 'ot you can boil your dinner in em.' Now it was my turn!

'New Zealand?'

'Canada! It's the Land of Opportunity, Jack!'

Suddenly I guessed from his face he weren't planning on *my* company. 'Take me with you, George! I'll be handy for you!'
But he weren't so struck on me as Nance. 'Wish I could, Jack lad, wish I could. It's out o' my control. I'll send you a postcard though, keep in touch.'

He started off well on the boat:

DEAR NANCE AND ALL, NOT FORGETTING LITTLE JACK AND MAGS—HERE'S A TURN UP FOR THE BOOKS! I MET A WEALTHY GENTLEMAN WHO NEEDED A VALET. I'M LOOKING FOR A CHAP WHO CAN SHAVE AND CUT HAIR, IS THERE ANYONE ON BOARD? HE SAYS. YOURS TRULY!
P.S. YOU CAN KEEP THE SHOP.

Nance tried to keep the barber's shop on. But she had to find a bloke to run it for her, and she had to give him too much: she couldn't make it pay. So I left school—I'd practically left afore, with all the lathering I'd been a-doing lately—and looked round for work. I was eleven. They generally posted it on a window pane: 'BOY WANTED' or 'GIRL WANTED'. Education? It was a waste o' the teacher's time. He taught you all he knowed, but you'd got no interest cos *you* knowed what was going to come, all the while. Life was what learnt you.

*

And I was soon learning! I got a job at Chilcott's the draper's, on the Parade. 'High Class Tailors, Hosiers, Hatters and Shirtmakers.' Was I pleased with myself! I had my clothes—a uniform, a peaked cap—and I had all the old pattern books as they sent to the gentlemen and ladies, to pick their suits, what colour and stuff they wanted.

'We'll 'ave the poshest rugs in Leamington, eh Maggie?' said

11. Errand boy on the Parade, Leamington Spa, 1880s. The Regent Hotel is on the right.

Nance. ' 'Ere's a funeral wi four black horses, and 'ere's the Lord Mayor's trousers and 'ere's more stripes'n the poor old butcher!' We called Eva's late husband the poor old butcher.

The samples made good rugs—they was new, they'd only been opened for customers to see. 'Look at this Bobby Dazzler!' Nance waved a piece o' tweed.

'The King!' I cried.

'Off to mass at St Peter's!'

We laughed.

Mostly I was taking parcels round, but sometimes I was a tailor's dummy. I went to the dressing-room and had a sailor suit fitted on me. The tailor as made it was there. He looked at Mr Chilcott: 'Ain't e a bit old for this un?'

'Same size as Master Smart! E's small for 'is age!'

'What ud they say . . .' He meant what would the Smarts say if they'd a-knowed *I'd* been in it! His mouth twisted about a bit. 'Supposin . . . well, they's . . . if . . .'

'E ain't crummy,' said Mr Chilcott. He was a business man, he got on with it. 'Asides, what the eye don't see, *I* allus say.'

He showed the tailor the faults—it weren't high enough there, it weren't level enough on the coat. He was brisk.

When I'd done at the shop I went and washed up and scrubbed for his old lady. They'd got a lovely house at Milverton, between Leamington and Warwick, it was very fashionable then—'Cleeve Lodge'—but she couldn't keep servants. She used to get drunk, you see, knock them about. Mr Chilcott put a tanner in my hand and said low, so's the staff couldn't hear—they all knowed about it, don't worry!—'Now don't you drink none o' that lemonade when you gets there—tip it away when she ain't lookin.'

I did. Lemonade! She made me have *gin*—half a pint glass of it! But I didn't mind doing the washing up. I'd a-done anything for her—I washed her feet, cut her nails, combed her hair—cos there was all her second-hand clothes. I used to bring them home for Nance—a bundle! Sometimes there was summat new in, by mistake. You should a-seen Nance's face!

'I'll get a hat next week,' I said. 'A hat wi green feathers on!'

Nance clapped her hands! She danced me round the table. 'Mind you take care!' But Mrs Chilcott was a good old soul, she never carried on at me at all. She was always too drunk.

I did well at Christmas time, with parcels. I said to Bert, that was Nance's little lad: 'Come round wi me, Bert, we'll see what the pickins is!'

I had as many tram tickets as I liked—I pinched them off the roll at Chilcott's—and we went about Leamington for nothing, Bert and me, on the top of the two-horse tram. They all gave us summat when we called, cos it was Christmas. We was full up with pop and food—*and* we took some money home! Afore the week was out I'd got too cheeky. One woman didn't give us nothing and I told her off. 'You'll fetch your own parcels in the future!'

She reported me.

I was fed up with Chilcott's anyway.

So Charlie Middleton got me a job at Teddy Ivins' bakery. He was a relation of his. I think I got five bob a week; I know it was more money'n Chilcott's—and it was harder work! The night afore, we had to grease the tins for the tinned loaves, set the sponge—it was all like a foam—then five o'clock the next morning if I weren't up they'd come over, knock the door till they *beat* me up, kept knocking till I answered. It was all ready for us—there was another lad there asides me. The flour came down the chute in the early morning from up above. It landed in the trofe and then we had to punch the dough and twist it and turn it about.

'Punch it, Jack! It's got no friends!'

The flour came from Stratford—Lucy's Mill—from that old mill by the river. A relation of Nance's brought it with a horse and a big van, delivered flour there. We helped make the bread, and the buns, nick the loaves—you know, the nicks in the cottage. Come Sunday he heated the oven and cooked folks' dinners, those as hadn't the facility to do it, charged them twopence.

When the bread was made I went all round Leamington with it, pushing a cart with two shafts. Every day right down to Shrubland Street, under the railway bridge, Leam Terrace East I went, delivering it. I was home more in the evenings—well, I was beat! Now this evening Charlie Middleton was sat reading a book—as I said he was a fussy, quietish sort o' chap—and I would keep chattering to Nance.

'Your Mam must 'ave fed im wi a shovel!' he said. We giggled. Then suddenly he shouts: 'Get out! I wants to read! I wants to be quiet and read this book!'

I'd just got to the middle door to get out of the room. It had a half glass panel. He'd set it in himself. It had flowers and birds engraved on it; he'd got it from a house they'd been altering. And I made a face. He chucked the book at me—I ducked—and he smashed the panel.

'That's the last bloomin straw!' he said.

So next day I put my top coat on—Nance was a-crying—and I set off on the road for Stratford.

It's a long career!

I reached Stratford by dusk. It was late summer and judging by the smell the river was low. I couldn't see it, but I could picture it, slow and sluggish and brown. To me it seemed like the smell of the River Avon was the sweetest smell on earth. A few trippers was still larking about in punts. You could hear them shouting to one another and laughing. I started to hurry. Nothing had changed, not as I could tell. There was the cottages on Waterside and the pop factory opposite and a kiddie running with a jug to the

12. Waterside in summer

'Wheatsheaf', as I'd used to run, for Cal. Her chimney was smoking. Once I seen her chimney smoking I knowed everything was alright.

I walked straight in. She was just locking up. 'I was expectin you! You've been a little devil, I've no doubt! *Look!*' she cried. ''Ere's My Lad, back from Leamington!'

The old chaps turned their faces from the fire and stared. I got my first shock. I didn't know none of them, only old Mr Anderson.

''Is pension's still comin in,' said Cal. Then I knowed it weren't the vinegar had been preserving him all those years. 'Let's 'ave a look at you!' She couldn't hide her pleasure.

But next morning when she woke me she was black as thunder. 'It's bad news, My Lad. Your Grandad's been round wi some runner beans.'

Runner beans? I thought.

'Wait till I catch the blabbermouth as told im!' I wouldn't a-liked to be in *their* shoes, the way she looked. 'E says "Send im down, e can do a bit o' labourin, e can 'elp *me*."' She gave the old bloke laying next to me a nasty poke. 'It's 'is right.'

'Me *Grandad*?' It took me a minute to think who he was.

'Ah,' said Cal, ''e's remembered you, thirteen year after.'

She didn't get on with her brother. There was something bitter there—I never could get to the bottom of it. Cal was deep as the cut, when it suited her. All I knowed was, I was on her side.

'The best thing about im's 'is bloody veg,' she said. She gave the old bloke another poke. He whistled and wheezed but he stayed put. 'Well, that's saved me makin *this* bed—e'll be in for the day now.'

I was wide awake and I could see she was upset. 'I'll soon be back—don't worry Gran—and I'll stop for good!'

'Huh!' she said.

But I meant it.

*

So I had to go and live with my Grandad. As soon as you get out of Rother Street, round the corner into Ely Street, he lived there, in the first cottage. When I went for a crap I couldn't believe my eyes—the earth closet was fifty feet up the longest garden I had ever seen, and the miskin. A lot of the cottages in Stratford had miskins then; folks chucked their ashes from the grate in them, along with their refuse and tack and shit. You could see what my Grandad did with his: it was dug in when he dug his garden for his vegetables. And you never seen such monsters! Rhubarb thick as your arm, a forest o' sparra grass, rows of onions popping up like Chinamen's heads. Woe betide the kid who tried to terrify *them*! He'd get a belting off my Grandad he'd not be likely to forget. And if anybody pinched so much as a parsnip he'd know. He'd call the copper and he'd take them to court.

There was a cousin living there already, a-learning the trade, about the same age as me—Will Blackford. Will was the favourite there alright! Every time we had rabbit for Sunday dinner—my Grandad and his mates went poaching at night with nets and ferrets—Will had a back leg, *I* had the shoulder.

'You got a *leg*!' my Grandad shouted, thumping on the table, and he'd cuss. He'd got a bad temper—he could cuss too! That didn't stop me answering back: 'Yes, but it's a front un!'

They sold most of the rabbits Sat'day night, in the 'Oddfellow's Arms'. That was the builders' public, where the bricklayers and the painters met and had a drink together and a bit of a sing-song. The carpenters went to the 'Bull's Head'—they liked to keep themselves separate. They reckoned there was more skill in chippying, and maybe there was. But in the 'Oddfellows' I could see my Grandad was somebody. For a start, he'd never been caught. Night poaching was a serious offence in those days. There was no knowing how long you'd get for taking one stringy old rabbit. Might as well be hanged for a sack-full of plump uns was *his* motto. He was crafty as the old fox.

He tipped them on to the floor: 'With the compliments of Sir Arthur—fresh Clopton bunnies!' They all laughed. They was from the wood behind Clopton House. 'Four good onions an a nice turnip an a couple o' sticks o' celery and you've got a Sunday dinner fit for the Queen—and er family! *Fourpence* an *sixpence* apiece! What about this un then?'

He'd got the gift o' the gab, my Grandad. The trouble was, he was unpredictable. Next minute he'd be telling a young chap to watch where he spat his baccy in future, or it would be the worse for him. It was the same in the house. He'd be nice as pie one minute—

'Now there's a copper,' he told us Sunday dinner time, between mouthfuls o' rabbit, done just as he liked it. 'There's a copper covers Snitterfield to the Alcester Road, we won't mention 'is name—' He winked. We all knowed it, o' course.

'Now this copper says to me "Get us a copple, Judy!" So—I gives im the nod, says they'll be there, two ditches away. Course, e's got a good excuse, 'asn't e? If anybody sees im e can say e's disturbed the poachers an they runned away and left the rabbits. "This 'ere's the evidence, your Honour!" Ah. E'd easily get out of it!'

We was all agreed on the treachery of coppers. You just had to put it to best advantage.

'One night,' my Grandad went on, he was really warmed up, 'I 'ears the sound of horses' hooves a-comin down Snitterfield Lane. *Clipotty-clop, clipotty-clop*. I hides in the ditch. Oo should it be in the brougham—so near I could almost a-touched it—but the *Prince o' Wales*! There was no mistakin im. Two coachmen in the front and two in the back—stood up i' the back, in uniform!' His wife nodded. She must have heard the tale no end o' times, but she was as round-eyed as me and Will. How many folks in Stratford had seen royalty?

'E'd give Lady Mordaunt up at Walton Hall four white ponies, an bugger me if 'er husband don't catch em together, Lady Mordaunt an the Prince o' Wales, and shoots em dead—'soon as e's sent the Prince packin. Four white ponies! It might a-been that very night I seen im.' You could have heard a spider spinning.

'Let's see what you made today then. Empty your pockets!'

He sent me and Will nutting. We took them to the 'Oddfellows' just afore Sunday dinner time, while he was digging his garden, and sold them to the customers, as many woodnuts as they could shovel up in their hands for a penny. One was burning a hole in my shoe. Well, I knowed he'd take the rest—all of it.

When he'd done counting and put the money in his pocket he said: 'Send some round to Russell Court, May, there's plenty left in the pot.'

That was our second helping down the spout!

He scowled at me. 'You'd eat enough for three bears!' No danger! I thought. 'Old is poor an poor is starvin. Not 'ungry, *starvin*! We'll all be old one day and don't you forget it.'

He seemed old to me already—he had grey hair and a humpy back—but I never said nothing. My Grandad was a man you learnt not to argufy with.

I ran down Ely Street—the smell from that basin was tormenting me—nipped up Russell Court. Then I drawed up sharpish. Always it minded me of under the canal arches, that room; I didn't want to go in. It was clammy and pitch black. When your eyes got accustomed you could pick out the old chap and his wife sat one on either side o' the fire—what fire there was, it was always warmer outside than it was in, that place—and an old kettle walloping away on the hob, making a bubbling sound that gave you the creeps even after you'd found out what it was. The old chap couldn't see much, but he could hear alright and shift about a bit, holding on to the chair and the table and the bed. There he stood, giving me a funny wall-eyed stare. I never seen her stir, not once, all the times I went. You'd a-thought she was dead 'cept for her head nodding up and down. Me and Will reckoned she *was*. Some of the neighbours reckoned she was dead idle, more like, and said, 'It's a shame! Poor ole chap!'

'It's Judy,' he croaked, 'come wi some dinner!'

'Judy's lad,' I said. I plonked the basin down and I was off. If I'd a-felled down I wouldn't a-stopped to get up. The truth was, me and Will had talked ourselves into being afeared of that room up Russell Court. I reckon we *enjoyed* it.

When I got back and my Grandad saw my face and said: 'It's better'n the workhus, lad,' I didn't believe him.

One day we called at Harris the builder's yard. He was one of the old folk's sons, Lieutenant of the Fire Brigade, *got on*. Could we borrow a ladder, cos ours was at Shottery?

'I dunno,' he says. 'I 'as to buy *my* ladders.'

'Alright,' says my Grandad, flaring up, 'never mind. You couldn't a-bought all this stuff while I was giving your father an mother many a meal, could you?'

John Harris turned pale. 'Judy!' he said, they called him Judy. 'Judy
'ave anything you like out the yard—and keep your mouth shut!'

I almost forgot to say my Grandad was a bricklayer. I had the
shoulder every Sunday but I learnt a lot. One thing I learnt was
how to set grates and lay floors and backyards and walls—general
knocking about. Our work lay mostly on pub yards and farms,
farmhouse repairs. He didn't do no new building: he weren't well
enough off to build houses. We did all the old thatched cottages at
Welford: 'Rough cast between the old timbers, paint the timbers
black, paint the rough-cast white' the order said. We was handy
for him like that, cos we could read. He found the work, then he
served me and Will, passed us the bricks and the mortar. He was
learning us, you see. He was doing well out of us and all, charging
fourpence an hour for labourers. It was fourpence then, sixpence
for brickies. He gave us so much a week—it weren't much, I can
tell you, when he'd took our board and lodgings out of it.

He worked us hard, but we played hard too. We found an old
boneshaker bike and repaired it! It looked like a cartwheel with
pedals, iron rims. We used to start it just past the top o' Sheep
Street, run with it, jump on, rattle right down Sheep Street, bump
into the gates and through into the Bancroft Gardens. *Wheee!*

Then, come the end o' blackberrying time, there was the Mop
Fair. My Grandad and Will and me built a fireplace the length of
a beast, outside the 'Prince o' Wales' on Rother Street, all amongst
the fair organs and sideshows and painted horses. The publican
bought the beast—eighteen pounds was the highest price beef out
that Sale Yard—had the butcher kill it, take all the insides out.
Then a pole was set up across our fireplace, with two hooks with
screws on as went round the pole and through the beast's back.

Now my mother's sister had married a man named Blackford.
He'd gone and died, leaving her with a load o' kiddies—Will was
one of them, folks said Doctor Barnardo had took the rest—and
she married a chap called Prior and had another load. Happy Prior
they called him, a joking sort o' chap, though Lord knows, folks
said, what he'd got to laugh about. He always helped my Grandad
turn the wheel with the beast at the Mop.

My Grandad would go along and say: 'Now, Happy, it's only ten o'clock, keep them halves down!'

'Gramp,' he said, 'don't you worry! I'll get *inside* the beast an backen im!' Happy got well-oiled whiles he was roasting.

As soon as those lids started to crackle, to turn, and the smell of roast beef was in the air I thought: 'Oh I should love a piece o' that curlin!'

Happy said: ''Ere you are! That ole bugger,' meaning my Grandad, 'when e starts e'll eat the lot!'

He let me inside the rails and, as the heat began to cook the beast, I had to get the spanner and keep tightening the screws or it wobbled about.

'Keep it tight!' my Grandad called out.

Always when we fired it we fired the back part o' the neck: we didn't fire the middle cos that was the thinnest part, it would have scorched up. My Grandad did the carving. He started at the neck, in case there was any left. If there *was*, then he'd got the best part o' the beast left, the nicest joint. He'd be on the right side—he could sell that. I'd got my pockets stuffed with stale crusts and I catched the dripping and ate it while he was a-carving there. It was lovely, that beef dripping.

Happy let me hold the wheel a bit. He was kind. He minded me of Nance—I was missing her at that time o' day—laughing and kind. He broke up the crowd about dinner time and my Grandad said: 'We got a lot o' beef left, Happy. Watch out for the next trip.'

''Ere they come!' I shouted, above the din of the organs. And they filled the road up—all Greenhill Street—a mass o' folks coming from the station, and not one without a hat on. They bobbed about like apples in a tub.

'We shall be alright now,' said my Grandad. 'What we makes now is profit.'

Those as couldn't get in the 'Prince o' Wales' sat down under a big tarpaulin done up on hurdles. The waiters brought the dinners out: ninepence and a shilling. I helped if they was rushed.

'I'm sorry! There's no ninepenny dinners left, they're all a shillin!' I said.

They paid their shilling and they had a glass o' beer with it, two

13 Roasting a bullock outside the 'Prince of Wales', Stratford-upon-Avon Mop. 'Judy' Hewins, George's grandad (third from right) roasted here for over fifty years. His assistant (far right) also appears in the photograph on p. 71, and is probably a relative. The large gentleman in the hat is Sir Arthur Hodgson.

slices o' beef as long as your hand, sprouts and taters. Oh, it was a good dinner!

There was a lot o' folks came and took it away—bought a joint to take away. Even the Vicar turned up. All of a sudden there he was, out of nowhere, glaring at my Grandad and Happy and me. 'There is nothin more *repulsive* than an 'alf consumed carcase in the roadway!'

The folks around looked astonished. He told them: 'I shall be speakin about this Annual Saturnalia on Sunday at the Parish Church.'

It didn't have much effect. Most of them was Brummies and Happy was up the pole. My Grandad cussed, under his breath, but I could hear it and I reckon the Reverend Arbuthnot did and all.

My Grandad weren't frit of no black mark. He could see no usefulness in the church, he said, not like Cal, ''cept for talkin and berrin'.

We even sold the bones! Brummagem trippers, they'd give us a penny or a ha'penny for rib bones—and they'd got nothing on them! At night about seven we got the saw and cut the backbone off, a piece like that. My Grandad wrapped it in a towel. 'That's for the missus—take that home wi you—*nammus!*'

He'd got the horns to send to my mother. He said they was for her friends, the Lord Mayor and so on, they liked to cure them and hang them over the doorway he said, decorate their halls with them. Well, I'd seen no halls in Barford Street, but I didn't say nothing.

And next morning! Next morning folks went round to the public houses to get a quart basinfull o' dripping—twopence! They knowed it was pure beef or pork dripping. We sold it all next morning at the 'Prince o' Wales'—a good basinfull for twopence. I loved bread and dripping and beef dripping from the beast was best. I was at that awk'ard age when food was on my mind almost all the time. When I didn't get enough I slipped down to Cal's: she'd feed me up. 'The skinny ole toad!' she said. ''Ere, 'ave a bit more, My Lad. Don't spare!'

And I pumped the water for the fire engine. Here's how it came about that pumping water got us a good feed.

My Grandad was contracted to ring the bell at the Guild Chapel, for twelve month. He sent anybody to ring it as would go—you can guess who that was. We got nothing for it neither. We rang the curfew six in the morning, that was to get you up for work, and eight o'clock at night. In the old-fashioned days you was supposed to be indoors then, everybody; you'd got to be in the house when the curfew rang. Me and Will, we'd got my Grandad's pocket watch between us, we studied it and soon as it was eight . . .! My first toll, I shan't forget it! There was a trap door where the rope comes through, and I'd never rung a bell afore. Instead o' letting the rope slip through my hands, I kept hold of it—it took me up! We tolled the minute bell for funerals, the muffled bell, me and Will, every minute at the Guild Chapel when a funeral went by. *Dong*! Muffle it, they did, with a flannel, tie a flannel round it and it went *Boom*! An awful sound it was. And we rang for the Fire Brigade.

The Guild Chapel was for the Fire Brigade too. There was two bells rung for a fire and my Grandad relied on us to do it. When the alarm had been raised we rung the bells and we waited. The fire station was in Scholars' Lane, opposite the Guild Chapel. We watched them scrambling on the engine in their helmets and uniforms: Captain Campbell—Harris the builder was his Lieutenant—my Grandad. Yes, he was a fireman and all! We waited at the top o' Scholars' Lane and when the horses slowed down to take the corner we jumped on, me and Will. They always took us, cos it was a hand pump, a big engine and they had to pump the water by hand. Asides, my Grandad always arranged for us to get paid the week after.

If the fire was no more'n five mile it was only two horses, if it was further, it was three. One fireman rode the third horse, the one in front, postillion. We all clung on for grim death. The horses belonged to a man in Wood Street, Bill Smith. He let out carriages and pairs, went to funerals with them, stood two of his men outside Shakespeare's house with a landau to pick up Americans and take them to Shottery. Those black horses got around. Today they'd got a change of pace alright! We went hell for leather over Clopton Bridge and up the Banbury Road. It was a rick fire—mostly it was hayricks caught fire, straw, beanricks—and it was spreading towards the buildings.

When we got there the fire had been going for over two hours and the ricks was blazing away. They weren't insured neither. The flames had spread to the barns and farm buildings and was making for the house. We started to pump by hand from a shallow farm pond. Rumours flowed backwards and forwards. Somebody had seen a tramp on the Banbury Road, early morning—there was gyppos in the neighbourhood—moppers. It was hard work, hot thundery weather with storms all around. The sweat was pouring off us. We knowed the pond would dry up soon. The firemen was six-a-side and we helped till the villagers started arriving, and folks from Stratford. Then we let them take over. The hayricks was lost, and most of his barns but the house was safe. We'd stopped the flames spreading to the house.

As soon as we'd got the fire under control the farmer's man said: 'Into the home barn, lads!'

There was liver and fry sizzling away and casks o' cider— *scrumpy!*—sent our heads a-reeling. 'You'll be fallin off the engine again, Judy!' They all laughed. Many a fireman slipped off the engine going home, but it didn't matter cos the horses knowed there weren't no rush. They went funeral pace, going back to Stratford.

Now while we was in this barn having a good feed I was listening to the old uns laughing and joking and watching the fowl pattering around the bean rick. They put beans in a rick then, let them ripen and shoved them in a rick. The fowl pattered around, picking as much as they could get out the side. Ah—they was crafty, weren't they? Sometimes I thought creatures had more brains'n human beings. Only thing was, they weren't free, really free. I was starting to use *my* brains at long last. I said to myself: 'I'm near fourteen-year-old and earnin and nobody owns me. If I stays with *im* I'll be a labourer for the rest of my life and no better off'n one o' Smith's old horses—or this little fella, a-pokin and a-scrattin.'

So that night I went up the garden for a crap. *So they thought!* I took a run up the bury where all his taters and turnips was hid and I vaulted over the wall. I felt like I'd escaped from gaol. Why didn't I walk out the door? Maybe I weren't as grown as I reckoned to be.

✥ CHAPTER SIX ✥

'You returned?' said Cal.

I said: 'Aye, I thought it was about time I came now.'

'I didn't think you'd stick im long. You'd better 'ave a trade, then. I'll get you apprenticed.'

And so she got me apprenticed to Teddy Kennard the builder. He was doing a job nearby for the Corporation—alterations to the Art School on Sheep Street—hoping to be a Councillor soon, folks said. A lot of contracts came your way, then. Cal called him in and she said: 'What about this lad learnin the trade?'

'I dunno,' said Teddy Kennard. You could see he was playing for time. He had a sneaky look round. Cal had expanded. She was renting the two cottages next door now; the second-hand clothes shop was separate from the veg. He took in every detail.

'Shockin business, that neighbour of your'n going like that.'

Cal said nothing.

'Buyin an eel!'

''E knows a lot already,' said Cal. She hadn't fetched him in for coffin talk.

'Eels is funny creatures to deal with. They say,' said Teddy Kennard, 'the Devil took er off.'

Cal looked at him. I seen nobody so discomfort folks as Cal, when she wanted.

'Course, I don't hold wi superstitions like that myself, I'm a *God*-fearin man.'

'Will you start im or won't you?'

'Ah, e can start,' he said.

'What's the money?'

'I'll give im five shillin a week for seven year. Fifty-six hours and a half.'

Cal nodded.

When he'd gone she said 'I don't want nothin off you.' So five bob was my pocket money! I was never so well off in my life!

I made it up to her. She was doing well, business was getting better all the time, and I was handy for her. Asides the roadsters—they was seasonal o' course—she had as many permanents as she could cram in: four to a room and the rest over the passage.

'Now I'm back I'll make the beds for you,' I said. 'Just learn me ow to do it.'

She bought old bedding at the Sale, as much as she could get hold of, made you wonder who'd died on them and *how*, but Cal never worried. Stained and frowsty they might be, crummy they was; she put them in a new tick and that was that.

'Ere!' she said, 'gimme a hand to get this stuff off!—Ey! What's this?' Her eyes gleamed. Hullo! I thought. And sure enough, in a corner of that old mattress there was *sixteen gold sovereigns*, sewed in the corner.

She laughed and laughed and laughed. I thought she would never stop. 'Eh!' she said. 'Eels!' I never seen her in such a merry mood.

'Take this bottle,' she said. She'd got a blue bottle, like a medicine bottle, with 'NOT TO BE TAKEN' on it, in big letters. 'Fetch us two pennoth from the liquor vaults.'

I learnt to cook too. I used to get their dinners, the lodgers' dinners—mostly mutton stew cos she'd taken to having all old chaps as had finished work and hadn't got no teeth. They liked my cooking. I took more trouble'n Cal: I skimmed the fat off, popped some nice veg in from the shop when she weren't looking. We had a big pot as went from hub to hub, stirred it occasionally. Meal-times I sat at the end of the table, like the son.

'My, George, that smells a treat!'

Cal got nettled. 'I'll be raisin my price if you don't shut up!' she said. She turned to me: 'What you put in it?'

They used their fingers and a hunk o' bread for eating: Cal didn't have no knives and forks, stuff as could be pawned for beer money. No fear! Now and then they brought out a shut knife, or had a cough and a spit. The only sound else was champing.

Then there was the crocks to be washed. And afterwards the old chaps sat round the table with their clay pipes, they'd talk about their experiences and that, about their children, droning away like humblebees in a churn. Me and Cal sat there with them, had a chat. Not that she'd be wasting time! She was knitting a shawl and reckoning her money up. You could see her lips moving. It was a peaceful time o' day. I never wanted to go out a-nights, thought I never should. An old chap pottered in from the yard with the teapot. He'd been draining the water off. He tipped the tea-leaves on to the shovel and put it in the oven—ready for the next smoke. They was poor as church mice, most of those old chaps, but they was good company. We had some jolly evenings.

Three had been soldiers. God knows what war they'd been in. Gunner White was one of them. He was a sprightly old chap, with a white beard and one eye and a fine voice for singing:

> From Chatham I came back,
> I said, 'My dear, I'll marry you
> For I've *shiners*
> In my sack!'

He'd soldiered for the Queen for twenty-two year and been discharged afore I was born. He got a shilling a day off the army. There was a lot of old campaigners like him mooching about Stratford. They'd got parted from their families, couldn't find work when they came back to England or found their folks was dead. Neither Gunner nor the other two was Stratfordians. Like me, nobody *owned* them.

> 'Ere comes the young soldier
> Oo's money I squandered.
> 'Ere comes the young soldier
> Cut down in 'is prime.
> 'Is poor aged mother,
> 'Is poor aged father,
> 'Ad oftentimes told im
> About his past life—

—He died of the claps—

> For along wi the flash girls
> 'Is money e squandered,

Along wi the flash girls
Was his great delight.

I listened well to the old chaps' songs and I picked them up.

The fact was, old men on their own, they'd either end up in lodgings or go into the workhouse. Their sons and daughters couldn't keep them—or didn't want them. There weren't no old age pension then and, generally speaking, they weren't handy about the house like an old woman. You'd be surprised, some of the folks in Stratford as sent their Dads to Cal's, folks as would cross the street if they seen her a-coming! She didn't care, so long as she'd got their money! Phillips the lawyer for instance—he paid well—his Dad came.

Now there was an old cowman there about this time, he was rough as gorse on the common. One night he got drunk. I was a bit late. I'd started going out with my pals on Sat'day night. Cal didn't like it. I climbed through a back window I'd left open, took off my shoes at the bottom of the stairs. As I knowed well there was twelve vaulting stairs and a window at the top. Tonight there was no moon, I had to go by *feel*. I gropes about a bit and I takes hold o' summat bristly. Too late—it was the old cowman's beard!

'Caroline!' he shouts, loud enough to wake all Waterside. '*Caroline!*'

In she comes, candle in one hand, warming pan in the other.

'Caroline, I's seen a ghost!'

She saw the situation. 'You silly ole bugger! Look—I'll lose all me lodgers!'

Mr Phillips, the new lodger, stood at the top o' the stairs, and a couple of other old chaps, looking frit to death. 'It's a GHOST!'

'It's My Lad—*shut up!*—I'll wallop you wi this warmin pan if you don't stop blartin!'

It was no use. He was drunk as an owl. She turned on me. I'd come in a bit playful, I'd had a drop o' beer. I must have said summat. 'And you too!'

That was the nearest she ever got to clouting me.

Now there was four old chaps in the room where I slept; old Mr Phillips was one o' them and the cowman another. They was settling down nicely when I gets upstairs and I says: 'I ain't a-feared o' no GHOST!' I grabbed a leg in the dark and they all fell on top of each other in the bed, screaming.

It was all squared the next Sat'day. I didn't go out with my pals. I said: 'I tell you what we'll do!'

We had a bit o' fun. We got together and we put a candle behind a sheet, tied a cotton to it so's it moved about. 'Now e'll see the ghost!' we said as the old cowman came stumbling up the stairs.

Every day after breakfast they pottered up and down Waterside, sat in the Bancroft Gardens if it was warm. There was only one earth closet at Cal's, up the yard. It was in continual use. When the old chaps had been they'd creep out but they was never quick enough for her. 'You go an pump a bucket o' water out the well,' she shouted. 'Put it down!'

She didn't miss a trick! She started selling her own pop. She got powder from the chemist, put lemons in it, then she fermented it with yeast, strained it through muslin and bottled it. She sold no end of it to the trippers—penny a pint. It was very good pop too. She sold the shawls she knitted to folks as came to the second-hand clothes shop. They'd say—they was mostly babbies' shawls, shawls for when they was born—

'Me daughter's 'avin a babby. Ow much d'you want for that, Cal?'

She said: ''Alf-a-crown, that's all.'

She'd rig a woman out with underclothes for a bob.

If a neighbour went there for a petticoat: 'Ow much d'you want for that, Cal?'

'Fourpence.'

'That's a lot ain't it, fourpence?'

'Look!' she said, 'if you don't want it, I can sell it. Get out!'

She was good natured, but she'd stick to dealing. Her price was her price and she never lowered it. She went to the Sale, three times a week, to buy her vegetables. If it was bad weather and there weren't no work I minded the shop.

Folks said: 'Ole Cal's gone to the Sale! You wanna go down now! You'll get a better deal off George!' I used to give them a bit extra.

*

My first big job with Kennard was the new Co-op Stores on Sheep Street. There was twenty or so there—bricklayers, carpenters, painters and labourers. One of the older brickies would have one of the young uns with him, show you how to go on. I knowed them all: my Uncle Harry Hewins—he worked for Kennard all his life—Ned Bad, Jimmy Smith, Porky Savage. You had a labourer serving you; if there was three brickies there'd be two labourers. He mixed the mortar and carried it to you, put it on your mortar board, on the spot. And your bricks. They carried them in what we called the monkey—the monkey with its tail on. D'you know what the Irishman said?

'I've gotta good job now! I only 'as to carry the mortar an the bricks up to the bloke at the top and *e* does all the work!'

We was whitewashing the rafters of the new Co-op, hadn't got

14. Building workers posing in their Sunday best on completion of a job for a local church. George sits proudly with the other apprentices on the front row, far left.

the floor laid, slipping from joist to joist. And I fell! Right through the joists! I plummeted down into a big heap o' mortar, a cartload. The foreman runs down the ladder: ''E's killed! E's killed!'

It frit me, I can tell you—and it frit the old bloke down below, riddling the mortar!

The foreman said: 'You better go home—go home and 'ave the rest o' the day off.' He was white as a sheet.

So I went off and played football.

That was my first accident. There was some close uns with that old wooden scaffolding. One day we was having a bit o' bait and it fell. All the ropes gave in—we heard this *crash*! We'd stopped for a quarter so no one was killed that time. Blokes as was—or broke a leg or an arm, or got concussion—their families had nothing. How was you going to prove the gaffer'd been responsible? It was a risk you took, every time you went up in the air.

Each apprentice bought his own tools. I had a trowel, brick hammer, lump hammer and a chisel—and a level. I had a plumb rule too: a long straight stick wide as my wrist. There was a saw-cut down it and a hole at the bottom where the plumb bob was—a stone like a duck's egg—hanging from a string. Houses was built properly then. All the joints, all the *cross joints*, was solid. They had to be solid, and the lines level. We'd scrat a bit o' mortar out the front, to show off each brick. It was satisfying, building houses, mostly new cottages for farm workers. You could picture folks moving in, and what it would look like when the garden was nice and tidy and smoke coming out the chimney. I liked the work: it was in the open air, and we travelled about the villages.

We was at Grafton one day when the gaffer comes in the trap to check up. ''Ow you gettin on?'

'Alright,' I said. 'Workin 'ard as 'ell, if you wants to know.'

He looked surprised when I answered him. 'I don't want you to work hard, I wants you to work *fast*!'

He was a jew, Teddy Kennard.

I got my own back. He sent me to put the pony's collar back on. I put it on—arsy versy.

'This ain't right—summat's wrong wi this!'

'Please, I don't know nothing 'bout horses, gaffer!'

72

You'd a-thought that old pony gave me a wink! It flicked its tail and tossed its head! Teddy Kennard had to turn the collar round himself afore he could get started.

Sometimes we was home from work in minutes, sometimes we weren't home for hours. We'd walked to Grafton—five mile there, five mile back. When we went to Pebworth to put up some cottages me and another chap lodged with an old widow woman and her daughter. You heard that rhyme?

> Pipin Peb'oth, Dancin Marston
> Haunted Hillboro', Hungry Grafton
> Dadgin Ex'all, Papist Wixford
> Beggarly Broom an Drunken Bidford.

Well, they got it wrong, somehow.

This old widow woman and her daughter, they had a hard life. Bed and work, that's all they seen. They'd got work to do day and night to make both ends meet. They had no enjoyment, none at all. The daughter was in her thirties. She had a thing like you mend shoes on, she put kid gloves on it—'cut ready for stitchin, cotton supplied'—put the fingers on it, stuck them on and sewed them up and turned them inside out for a Worcester firm. After we'd had our meal she went on working by the light of a candle. There weren't nothing for us to do of an evening.

My mate says: 'Come to the pub, George?'

'Not tonight—funds is not great. I'll turn in early.'

I went upstairs to bed as sober as the day. Blow me if there weren't an old chap in white sat in the chair! She'd made no mention of another lodger—crafty old cow! I'd been looking forward to half a bed. I thought I'd speak up. 'There bain't enough room for three of us in this bed, Gramp!'

The old chap said nothing. I looked a bit closer. My hair went upright and I run down those stairs two at a time, maybe three.

The old lady said: 'You took ill?'

I told the daughter: 'There's an ole chap up there—e's *dead*!'

She went on working away at the donkey, never batted an eyelid.

'Er's balmy!' I thought. 'Or I am!'

'Don't worry,' she said. 'It's me Dad.'

I stared.

'S'alright, e died last Michaelmas. We often see im sat there. You don't want to take no notice—e won't interfere wi you.'

It served me right—I'd seen a *real ghost*! 'Course, I was too a-feared to go back upstairs, so I stopped where I was awhile. She was sewing up a long kid glove.

'Evenin gloves,' she said. ''Ere—I'll show you summat.' She got up and went to a dark corner of the room.

'Your hands clean?'

She held out a piece o' white tissue paper. On it lay seven of these evening gloves—the most delicate gloves you ever did see, fit for a princess. You couldn't imagine human hands fitting in them.

She could see I was impressed. 'Lemon an lavender's the colours this year. They 'as to be perfect,' she said, 'else they won't pay. I made five bob last week—it's 'arder when the nights draw in!' She gave me a funny look. 'I got to get on—the man from Dents comes to Bidford tomorrow.'

The mother was deaf. The daughter shouted at her from time to time as she stitched the glove—'Cabbages!' 'Turnips!'—top of her voice. I never knowed time go so slow. Suddenly she stops stitching and starts turning it inside out. 'She's done!' I thought.

Picture my astonishment when she whispers to me: 'I'll get into bed wi you if you likes—just for a bit o' company!'

'NO YOU WON'T!' shouts the mother.

There weren't time even to *think* about it! I didn't know where to put myself. I reckoned upstairs was the only place. I hardly dared to look—but the chair was empty! Was I glad to hear my mate coming up!

I was telling him about the ghost—it was dark, I hadn't got no matches for the candle—when in walks the daughter, in her shift.

He screams: 'It's a ghost, it's a ghost!'

Next morning on the job he said, 'I'll never stop in that house again.'

I didn't fancy it neither: I could see that old chap in white in my

74

mind's eye, I can still, to this day. So we walked back to Stratford and we hired a couple o' bikes, we biked it morning and night.

*

Cowardice won the day there! I weren't scared o' women, I'd knowed the facts o' life since I was a little lad, at Cal's. But watching is one thing, performing another. We'd got to be about sixteen, seventeen, and raring to go.

There was two whores we knowed of in Stratford. One of them was Half-Pint Ginny. You know the 'Anchor', bottom o' Bridge Street, and the 'Black Swan'—the 'Dirty Duck'—along Waterside? She had a bet with us, my pals and me.

'Bet you can't,' we said.

'Alright,' she said, 'bet me.'

We followed and she pissed all the way along from the 'Anchor' to the 'Black Swan', all along the path! She'd got a lovely husband, worked in the brickyard, he was a foreman, but all she wanted was half a pint. That's all she wanted. ''Ave you got three 'apence, Jack?'

One of my pals whispered: 'Er'd be alright wi a sack-bag over er 'ead, maybe!'

We couldn't fancy her, though. She was old. We fancied Poll. She lived on Meer Street and we used to go, every Sat'day night. This Sat'day night we had to hammer to get her out of bed and she shouts: 'You'll 'ave to wait! I got somebody's give me six-pence—and you lads come 'ere wi cocks like men for twopence!'

We had to wait till this bloke had done!

*

Sometimes we got into scraps. There was bullies in Stratford, same as anywhere. They made a lot o' noise in the pub, on the street, picked on a bloke who was smaller'n them. What we used to do was get three or four together, wait for him and set on him when he came round the corner. But my worst scrap was on the football field.

Since I was seventeen I'd played for Stratford Rovers, half-back. At Leamington I'd kicked a ball wherever I could, in the back streets, the playground, anywhere I could find a space, but there weren't no proper *field*. At Stratford there was the Rec! Thanks to the recreation ground by the river I'd got to be a handy little player—that's what the *Herald* said—handy and dirty.

We was playing Budbrook soldiers for a cup. Well, I pitches into this winger in my usual fashion.

''Ockle im, Leamington!' folks shouted—that's what they called me in footballing circles—*Leamington*. ''Ockle im!'

I hacked his ankle, sent him head over heels. We was a skinny team and not very tall. I was only five foot three and I weren't the smallest. When we'd played at home to Kenilworth St Johns the *Herald* said: 'The visitors had a striking advantage in weight and physique.'

Now you never seen such big well-fed blokes as these regulars from Budbrook Barracks! It was like being in with eleven bulls. Well, this winger picks himself up and he pitches into me. Was I a mess! I was covered in blood and mud.

Cal grabbed the edge o' the table when she seen me. But I deserved it. I never tried that again on regulars.

I was playing for the Rovers one Sat'day when the word went round: 'The touts!' The touts had come from Villa. They picked out Bertie Edge—he was our Captain, he lived on Mansell Street and his Dad was a white-smith, he made tins and frying pans—Harry Gilbert for another—and *me*! We couldn't believe it!

'The trials is at Perry Barr—we 'ave trials most Sat'days.'

We knowed!

'We'll lend you proper boots to play in,' they said, looking at our feet, 'and your expenses to Villa—*six bob*.'

We went by train.

After we'd warmed up and went to change a toffy gent came in. ''Ave you got your boots alright, lads?'

Yes, they's alright, we said. But when we put them on there was summat tickling. We pulled out half a sovereign from each boot! Well, we thought we'd landed at the end of the rainbow! But we daresn't say anything—we'd have been professionals then, wouldn't we?

After that none of us played well—we was too excited—even Bertie Edge, and he was a good player. I reckon they was disappointed with us.

'We'll be in touch,' they said.

Bertie and Harry wanted to go home. I thought I'd see a bit more of the city. I'd transferred my sovereigns to my shoes: I weren't leaving anything to chance in a place like Brummagem. I had a tanner tea in the Bull Ring, then I had a bit of a walk about. Everywhere there was cheap jacks, trying to sell you stuff you didn't want. It was a mucky place, sad; I didn't like it no better the second time around. I went in a pub for a beer. It was still daylight when I came out, and I spent my last tanner on a nice brooch for Cal. It had two hearts in gold and MIZPAH: *The Lord Watch Between Me & Thee When We Are Absent One From Another.* A girl stood on the corner of the street, watching me.

Hullo! I thought.

She said: 'You a stranger 'ere?'

'Yes, ow could you tell, could you smell me?'

'I am, I come from the country.'

'I come from Stratford.'

'I come from Bidford,' she said, 'and I've got to go to Stratford 'bout a job.'

So I said: 'You might as well come back wi me then.'

I left her in Stratford and told her to pick me up again at the public close to my Gran's. 'If you don't get the job come an see me.'

So she comes and she says: 'I'm too late, the job's took an me last train's gone!' That was the trap I expect. 'They tell me if you goes to Caroline Cook's, she takes in lodgers!'

Well, she only took in *men*! I said: 'I tell you what I'll do.' I was thinking aloud. 'I'm sleeping by myself at present, in the middle o' the buildin. Now I'll go on. When I've got in, knock on the door, knock it 'ard!'

She knocked the door fit to break it.

Cal cried: 'Oo's that? That My Lad?'

I said: 'No! Somebody knockin at the front door!'

'Oh,' says the girl, 'good evenin, sir—I 'ear you takes in lodgers.'

'Oh,' I says, 'we don't, only gentlemen. We don't 'ave no ladies.'

Cal shouts: 'Oo is it?'

'A nice young gal as came from Brummagem after a job and now she 'ears the job's took and the train's gone!'

'Well, you can't turn er away!'

I nearly dropped! I said: 'Come in please!' I'd give her the money to pay for her lodgings.

Cal said: 'Look 'ere, if My Lad likes to give up 'is bed for you, you could stay and 'elp me, give me a hand. I don't see much of im these days.' She says to me: 'There's room for you wi the lodgers.'

It worked beautifully. I went and fetched some more beer and we slept there for a week. Annie Salmon her name was—or so she said. She taught me a lot. We had to take a pillow out every morning, in case Cal went up. God knows who she really was, or where she went to. For a long time after when I saw a girl with that coloured hair—red like a fox's brush—and freckles, I caught myself thinking of her. She was a wild one!

At the end of the week she said: 'I should like to thank this kind young gentleman for givin 'is room up.'

Cal said: 'I wish you'd stop.' She'd really took a liking to her.

'It's nice in Stratford,' Annie Salmon said, looking at me from under her hat so's I wanted to laugh out loud. How easy it was to deceive! 'The truth is, it's the money, ma'am. It ain't enough.'

That shut Cal up. She never said no more about her stopping.

*

I played left-half twice for Aston Villa second team. I weren't good enough. From Villa I went and had a trial with Small Heath Football Club. Sometimes when I went to Brummagem I stayed with my mother on Barford Street. Joshua Farr was home, and he was a terrible man for whisky. Whenever I went to his house after playing football I never had a cup o' tea without it had whisky in it. I weren't a drinking man, I didn't like the taste. I left it on the table.

'Drink it!' my mother whispered. 'E'll not like it if you don't!'

You had to drink it, whether you liked it or no.

One night he followed me back to the station. He was drunk. He flings open the door of this cab, just one o' the cabs waiting for the trains. We both got a shock. There was a lady in the back, with pearls on.

15. Shottery football team, 1901–2. This dated and named photograph turned up in a job lot of old frames at a local auction. George is sitting on the left, middle row.

' 'Ere! Look! 'Ere's your bride!' he bawls.

I don't know who was more scared, me or her. She looked as if she was going to the opera—'opera and a late dinner' as they say in plays.

'She's got *bags* o' money!'

'I'll stick to country gals,' I said, hoping to shut him up afore the coppers arrived. In this mood he could a-done anything.

'Aw—bugger off,' he says. 'Never come 'ere again! Never come to my house again, you little bastard!'

I was pleased to oblige, I can tell you. Asides, something had happened to make me give up the notion of footballing as a career.

I got a-courting. This is how it happened. We was playing at Alcester: it was another terrible rough game. The Captain said when we went on the field: 'It don't matter oo gets the goals so long as they's got!'

Folks started jeering. They said: 'There's that dirty little bugger!' I'd had many a sock o' the earhole off a spectator when I came off the field, when the match was over. 'Take that!' they said. I'd been in many a scrap after the match, on the touchline when we finished. They'd set to and we set to, start on one another till somebody came and parted us, told us we ought to know better.

When we came off this Sat'day at Alcester we was all waiting for the fun to start. There was a big chap played for Alcester—Sabbo Bayliss his name was—his Dad was a bookie. He always ran the line for Alcester, his Dad did. Sabbo had been arguing with *our* linesman. So his Dad had said: 'Alright, after the match is over my son and you shall 'ave a scrap.'

'Righto,' our linesman said.

We nudged each other and grinned. You see, our linesman happened to be a boxer—he trained at the 'Shoulder o' Mutton'! Jimmy Curran, his name was. But Bayliss was crafty. As soon as he saw how he was situated he said: 'Master Bloody Curran! It's *you*, isn't it?' Sabbo went pale.

'Come on,' his Dad said, 'we'll all go and 'ave a drink!'

We all went up to the pub together, had a sing-song.

We came back in the brake. The driver worked for the man as owned the fire-engine horses. He was a card—he told us some tales! 'There's a gentleman comes one day to me cab,' he says, 'at the East and West, in a fearful rush. "I'm-a-commercial-traveller!-If-you-can-get-me-to-the-Great-Western-to-catch-me-connection-there's-half-a-crown-for-you!"' . . . 'So,' he says, 'I goes at a cracking pace through the town. It was "Oh! Oh! Oh!" a-comin from the cab. I opens the door at the station.

'Don't get so excited, sir, you've got quite five minutes to catch your train.'

"Excited be damned," he said. "The bottom o' the cab's fell out—I've *runned* all the way!"

'So,' he says, 'in about a week's time I sees this commercial come off a train. I says, 'Cab, sir?'

E says: "You know what you can do wi your cab!"

I says: 'Horse an all, sir?'

We laughed! We'd had some beer, we was a bit playful.

I gave them a song:

> I'll buy you fine beavers
> And fine silken gowns,
> I'll buy you fine petticoats
> Flounced down to the ground.
> If you'll promise you'll marry
> And be constant and true
> Then down by the green bushes
> I promise I'll meet you.

Now this is the girl—you sings this in a squeaky voice:

> I want none o' your beavers
> Nor fine silken gowns,
> Nor none o' your petticoats
> Flounced down to the ground.
> If you'll promise you'll marry
> And be constant and true
> Then down by the green bushes
> I promise I'll meet you.

We had some fun!

When we got to Stratford Tommy Tappin, that was the driver's name, said: 'Comin back for some tea, George?'

'Yes,' I said, 'don't mind if I do.'

And that's where I met her. She was his sister-in-law—loft tall, with shining hair, and razor sharp. Well, she had to be, she was a widow's daughter, only sixteen, but she'd learnt to be independent early, look after herself. She was servant at Henson's the farmer's, some three mile out of Stratford, and it was her night off.

Next time I saw her I was on the corner o' Sheep Street, by
Cal's, standing under the lamp. It was a naked light then, a little
gas light, a flame, and the lamplighter went round at twelve o'clock
at night and put them out with a long pole. My pals and I used to
stand under the lamp light *reading*, looking at the Sat'day *Sports Argus.*

''Ere they come!'

The cheeky uns would come over and look over you and say:
''Ave you won anything?'

She weren't cheeky like that, but she fancied me. I fancied her
and all. She said, casual like: 'You up?'

Well, with a couple o' bob you could go into the pub and treat
them. Thanks to Cal I weren't short of a bob then. They had two
pennoth o' gin as a rule. If there was a travelling theatre we might
take them to see that. We used to have one come to Stratford for
a couple or three month, down Cherry Street, in a field—a travelling theatre with players. 'The threepenny gaff,' we called it. We
had all the murders there was: *The Polish Jew, Maria Marten in the
Red Barn.* It was in a tent, with steps up the sides. We used to say
we'd dropped our caps, slip under the steps and give the girls a
poke with a stick! They'd scream! The villain he'd hardly done a
murder and the gaffer would call him; he'd run off the stage, come
over to us and chuck us out the crowd!

Then you walked them up the Weir Brake—over the water,
across that bridge. It was quiet enough there! At that time o' day
all the young girls they weared a flat straw hat and they got pins
that long with a black knob. That was *their* weapon! When I've
been performing I've had many a jabbing, I should think I have! I
shall never forget! All those clothes! They'd got near a hundred-
weight o' clothing to carry. Their dresses dragged the mowing grass,
and they had bloomers, two red flannel petticoats. You had to
watch the time. You didn't come again to the door if you kept
them out late! You had a good dressing down off the mother, and
she'd say: 'Hmmm! I'll strip er in front o' you—and *see* if there's
been any interference!' Yes, she'd say, 'Get out and don't you come
'ere again!'

And so we started courting. It took up all my time. I walked up to the farm after work, to meet her, three miles, brought her down to Stratford. We went and sat in the Bancroft Gardens when it was fine. One night we was a-sitting on a bench and *bang!* It was the chap from the liquor vaults, he'd shot himself, blowed his brains out not eight yards away.

'It could be a bad sign, George'—I mind her saying that—and she shivered.

There was more suicides then; self-murder the Vicar called it. They wouldn't give you a Christian burying if you'd done it. I didn't realize *why*. I'd never been short of a few bob. It was the worry—they couldn't pay their way. What could you do on a pound a week?

She liked to watch me on parade. I'd joined the Volunteers, most of my pals had, the Second Volunteer Battalion of the Royal Warwickshire Regiment. I was in the band. I had a scarlet tunic, a helmet with a spike in—oh I was poshed out!—five rows o' crowns, gold epaulettes hanging down, blue undress. It was a nice band, a drum and fife band; I played the side drum. We had an instructor from Warwick. Every year we took the Mayor to church and once a week we went to the Rec for the others to train, with their rifles. We played them to the Rec and played them back. If she could get an afternoon off she'd rush along, sit on the grass by the river with one of her friends; she loved to hear the selections. She told me once that what she would really like most in the whole world was a pianna. She couldn't play, but she'd have liked one. She was a fine-looking wench. She only had one fault: she was always late, never could keep time. Then one day she told me why. She only had one blouse and she always liked to wash it afore she walked out with me. She had to wait for it to dry.

'You won't 'ave to wait no more,' I said, and I got her one from Cal's: a pretty un with plenty o' wear in, still. It was a good fit. She dyed it pale blue, with ink, so's to be *different*, she said.

I always took her back to the farm. It was dark then, up that lane, across two fields. She lived in, looked after the kiddies, did the housework, helped to make the butter. He was a good farmer, old Henson, a chapel man. She was happy there.

Then one day she said: 'I've left me job. I didn't tell them why, but I'll tell you.' The bottom dropped out of my bucket!

I went to see Kennard: 'I got six months to do gaffer an I've got to get wed!'

'Oh,' he says, 'now I know why you lost so many quarters! Well I can't set you on as a journeyman,' he says, 'and I'm full up for labourers!'

I couldn't keep quiet after that: ' "Full up for *labourers*" and me six year in the shed? That's a bloody insult!'

'You better take your tools and go!' he said.

He sacked me. He couldn't a-done if I'd took it to law cos we'd signed an agreement. Anyways, the law was no good to me, was it? I wanted *work*. There was no union, nobody was in the union then in our trade. If you got dismissed nobody took no notice. It *wanted* unions, cos the gaffer done what he liked with you. There was nobody to defend you at that time o' day. Most firms in Stratford had only got about a dozen men in the building trade. There was dozens more waiting for your job, if you stepped out of it.

There was no labour exchange either. I went and I walked and I walked. It was something I'd never reckoned on. Cal was against me leaving or getting wed: 'After I'm dead,' she'd say, 'you can get wed then.'

I panicked! I thought: 'I'll go for a soldier!' So I set off for Budbrook Barracks, to sign up. All my life I'd had a hankering to see the world: now I'd got my chance! At Budbrook they gave me a number: 2012 King's Royal Rifles. They kept me a month or so, on trial, drilling and learning to shoot. Then I was called in to see the Sergeant. 'This is it!' I thought. They was getting ready to go to South Africa.

'You're not fit, lad,' he said. ' "Unfit to be of use to Er Majesty." '

'What's up wi me?'

He never said.

'I can do a good day's work!' More'n a day's work, I thought. Kennard could say what he liked—who could prove it?—but I'd never missed a quarter, only when I fell from the Co-op rafters.

'Take me!' I said, 'I'll be handy for you. I've been in the Volunteers.'

But there was no getting out of it. I'd got to go back and face Cal. And her. And her brother. He was a regular in the Old

Warwicks and he used to do a fair bit o' scrapping in the booth at the Mop—and out of it! I would sooner have come face to face with the Zulus 'n Harry Bayliss, just then.

Cal said nothing. That's what I liked about her. You never had to *explain*; she knowed already.

'You'd best find work—quick as you can. Pick up my taters from the Sale, first.'

I did, and as luck would have it I met Alf Bailey in the Sale Yard. 'Ullo, George,' he said, 'what brings you about at this time, you turned porter?'

I said: 'The gaffer's sacked me.' I told him all the truth, 'cept for the bit about the army.

He said: 'Me brother wants a brickie to build a wall five foot high round a rick-yard.'

I went to see him. 'Yes,' he said, 'you can start. Can you get a labourer?'

I thought: 'I'll get the Devil himself if needs be.'

That's how I met up with Tommy Taylor again. He was hanging about the brickyard. 'What's up, Tommy?'

'I'm a builder's clerk!'

'Oh aye.'

I hadn't set eyes on him for years, since the National School. He kept himself to himself, didn't go to the pub. His Dad had died early, left his Mam with six kids: five girls and Tommy. They'd come down in the world. Tommy was the eldest and he didn't look much good for carrying the books up the ladder, I can tell you. He weren't *fat* no more, but plumpish, with soft white skin like a wench and a clumsy way about him, as if his arms and legs was leftovers at the bottom o' the box.

I looked hard at him. I said: 'I'm lookin for a chap—but you'll 'ave to work!'

He blushed. 'I will!' he said. 'I need the money!'

'We're both in the same boat then.'

When we turned up at Walt Bailey's yard he didn't object to Tommy—I reckon he thought that was my look out—he was more worried about *me*! 'I wish we could stick a moustache on you.'

I was only nineteen, I hadn't got one. I looked young for a

brickie. Walt Bailey kept staring at me. I said: 'What else is wrong wi me then?' I was getting a bit touchy on that score.

He said: 'D'you know, I've seen you somewhere afore.'

I said: 'Yes, it was me as 'elped you downstairs wi the coffins at me Gran's.'

'Ah,' he said, with a crafty look. What's he got up his sleeve? I wondered. Not that I cared overmuch. I'd a sold my soul to him, half-price, to get work.

I hadn't told Cal about the trouble I was in. One night we was sat round the table and she says: 'They tells me that gal you's seein goes tater-pickin!'

My heart sank.

'I can't 'ave My Lad goin wi a tater-picker!' Well, we was above that class, with three shops. She'd started a sweetshop and all.

'She's got a widdered mother.'

'That's not all she's got, from what I 'ear,' she says. 'You go up the Tram and meet er. Tell er to pick er money up. She can come an make my beds. Tater-pickin! I've done it, I know!'

Well, it was wet, muddy . . . I sighted her fast enough, she was taller'n the rest o'them. She'd throwed an 'erden apron over her head. When I saw her out in the field there with the rain pizzling down her arms and her belly pulled out o' shape but a look on her face when I got near as said, 'I'll never give in!' I knowed that this was the girl for me. Cal was old: she was over seventy. She couldn't last forever—she knowed and I knowed that.

'Emma!' I shouted. 'Emma!'

*

And so we was wed. Tommy Tappin worked it so's he could pick us up in his cab and take us to the church. They meant seeing I got there!

> I'm a very-very jolly man
> That's the least that you will say,
> When I tell you ow like a lamb I went
> To be married the other day.

> We went off one very fine mornin
> Uncles Aunts an all was there,
> And as we walked down the street
> Ow the neighbours they did stare!

She wore her ordinary Sunday clothes; that was all you could afford in those days, no trains or veils—a long blue dress, a nice hat she'd had from Mrs Henson. She was just seventeen. We was wed in the Congregational Church; Harry Bayliss, her brother, was a Congo. He came in his uniform to sign, stood over me watching whiles *I* did. We was the second couple in the book. When I saw that book I panicked! I'd given my Grandad for my Dad. She was looking worried too. She'd given 'Joseph Bayliss'. Well, he'd deserted from the Warwickshires and been caught in Stratford long afore she was born. I took her hand and gave it a squeeze. She had his name; what did it signify?

It was relief to get out in the fresh air. Folks started to shout: 'They's comin down!'

She went blood red—being fair she coloured easily. She whispers: 'George—the safety pin's come undone!' And me trousers *was* a-coming down!

> Well sister Mary walked like this—
> Pitta pat, pitta pat, pitta pat, pitta pat,
> Then came Uncle stout an fat
> Oh aye oh aye oh.

> Uncle Thomas's wooden leg
> Fairly made the people roar,
> Someone at him threw an egg
> And that made them *laugh* the more!

We walked back to Windsor Street, to her sister's. Cal didn't go, nor to the church—no fear!

'I'm not celebratin,' she said.

There was Emma's older sisters there—Tommy Tappin was working—and her brother and his wife. Her mother was having stout; Widow Bayliss could knock it back! 'Go on George—'ave a drop! It'll do you good!'

16. Harry Bayliss, Emma's older brother. Harry, a marksman with the Royal Warwickshire Regiment, was also renowned for his pugilistic skills.

When I shook my head, she said: 'There'll come a day when e'll want more'n e can get!'

I've often thought since of her mother's words.

There was the neighbours from Sheep Street, my pals from Stratford—I asked Tommy Taylor but he never came—and four or five of my pals from Leamington, who'd been with me in the Minstrel Troupe. One of them had got to be a terrible drunkard. He was the last to be hanged at Warwick Gaol. He went to his mother one night, half drunk, and she wouldn't give him any money. He throwed the lighted lamp at her—and burnt her. He didn't mean to—but he burnt her. They hanged him at Warwick—but that's another tale.

They got me pretty drunk between them. I weren't used to a lot o' beer. On the way back to Sheep Street—we was going to lodge with her mother up Pimms Court till we could afford summat better—I fell down in a shop doorway. Emma went off, up the 'croft. She met the copper.

'Ullo—you managed it then?' he said, 'What you done wi George?'

She told him.

'You can't leave im like that! E'll catch 'is death!' It was September, the nights was sharpish. 'Come on!'

He picked me up and I put my arms round him and kissed him. 'You got the wrong un tonight, George!' He laughed!

That night I had to stop on the sofa. Next night I lit a candle about ten—we got no gas at Sheep Street.

'Where d'you think you're goin wi that candle?'

'To bed.'

'You 'ad your chance last night,' she said. 'Either you stops on the sofa or I stops!'

CHAPTER EIGHT

Monday morning, my suit went into pawn and *I* went off to work.
That was the end of the honeymoon. The pawnbroker lived on the
same side o' Sheep Street. He was from Brummagem. Folks said
he was the dirtiest bloke in Stratford—his sign was the three balls!
Well, Dirty Old Styles puts my suit in a white wrapper with moth
balls, labels it and gives the missus a ticket. From that Monday on
it was a regular performance. She took it in, got a bob on it, went
in Sat'day morning early to fetch it out for the weeksend. It cost
about a penny ha'penny or twopence a week—and he'd got hundreds like that!

I did complain the first time. 'We ain't that 'ard up!'

She looked surprised. 'Winter's a-comin!'

I could see it was a habit with her and her mother. Any rate, I
soon got into the 'out-a-Sat'day-back-in-a-Monday-and-on-wi-
your-ole-clothes!' routine: rubber bands round the trousers to stop
them waving about—they was cord—my cap and my hob-nailed
shoes.

I was glad to be out the road on Execution Day. Her mother
had been at Pimms Court the longest, so she and the missus had
the yard Mondays, the Whites Tuesdays, and so on till Friday. Then
Mrs White asked her if she could have a quarter at the pump and
a bit o' line? She'd got a big family, ten or eleven at that time and
always relations lodging with them—a brother or sister-in-law and
their families who'd got nowhere to live and was down and out.
Bogey had a regularish job, you see. He was the only bloke I
knowed who made more money in the winter'n the summer: he
was gravedigger at the cemetery. They packed into that cottage
a-nights like wrens in a hole.

The missus felt sorry for Mrs White. 'Alright then, just a dab.'

Her mother shook her head when she heard about it. 'Give em
an inch an they'll take a mile.'

17. Garrick Court off Greenhill Street, Stratford-upon-Avon *c.*1900

And she was proved right. The dab washing growed to a line or more. The missus's face tightened when she looked up the yard, Monday morning, and saw Bogey's shirts a-flapping in the breeze. We'd soon need that line ourselves! She'd have to get it back! *How?* As I said, I was glad to be out the road.

I never had my jacket nor trousers washed all the time I was wed; they'd a-took too long to dry. I weared them out till they was gone and then I had another lot. *She* went into a pinna. All the married uns weared un, you never seen them weekdays without it: a bib and a long white apron, white as snow. She'd be there to meet me when I came home for my meal with a white apron on, day in, day out. It hid everything. 'Coversluts' they called them, if the wench was slummocky. That was summat Emma weren't. She was clean as a new pin, swilled herself in the basin morning and night, all over, kept her hair smelling sweeter'n any wench I'd knowed. She had long, light-coloured hair—it fell down to her waist when she let it out a-nights—and tits like cooking apples!

We had to share a bed with her mother. There was us at one

end, and her mother's feet a-sticking in our faces! But I was lucky—the old lady generally dropped off fast enough after a day's charring and a couple o' stouts—and since that first night Emma had never turned me away. Plenty o' blokes' wives *did*: they talked about it in the pub, as we worked along the line.

'Er says "I's only middlin!" ' they said. ' "Feelin tired!" Bloody Sat'day night an all! Ole cow!'

I kept my mouth shut, don't worry!

*

The bottom stair at Pimms Court was the trunk of a tree. Her mother said a bloke had hanged himself at the top, once upon a time. I could see why. It was three hundred, four hundred year old, that cottage, smaller'n the Whites'—theirs was small enough!—

18. Old Court off Sheep Street, late 1890s

dark and dirty. Sometimes I thought it must have been there since time began. However much the missus scrubbed the flags, however much I limed the walls we couldn't keep it clean! Bugs and fleas, it was one long battle, and we was on the losing side. Those we catched was splattered on the wall, blood and all, like pressed flowers. There was one room downstairs with an open fire, where the missus did the cooking and the washing and the ironing, two tiny rooms upstairs—the one we slept in was over the passage. Outside in the yard was the well, and a double-handled pump. When we wanted our side we pulled the handle; the neighbours pulled it back when they wanted it. A score o' folks or more used that pump—men, women and kiddies—and the earth closet. I always went for a crap in the fields on my way to work.

One day a lady in a big white hat comes to do some sketches of our yard. 'It's just like Italy!' she said.

That gave us food for thought!

'*Italy?*' said Mrs White.

The missus said: 'Huh, er should come back Monday, see ow she likes *that* for a sketch.'

I guessed what had riled her, so did Mrs White, who was anxious to oblige on account of the line. 'Don't fret duck! Bogey comes in yesterday and e says, "Ey! I seen a *mushroom* big as a basin a-growin in our yard and I've only 'ad a couple!"'

We all laughed!

*

Four months after we was wed the babby started coming. They had them quicker then—they didn't stay in for long! She woke me in the middle of the night, and it was a mile and a quarter to the midwife's and back. I tears up the passage, I runs like hell up Sheep Street. I thought: 'What's that? It must be an echo!' I could hear this *pitta-patta, pitta-patta.*

I'd just got round Mulberry Street, by Great William Street, Mulberry Street corner, just got my hand on Granny Sutton's door and somebody says, '*Gotcha!*' The copper had been running after me, thought I'd been pinching!

'Oh!' I says, 'you's just in time to hammer at this door for I'm out o' puff.'

Whenever I met him after that he said, 'Shall we 'ave the run tonight, then?'

After all that commotion the babby didn't show up. I went to work and in the afternoon I played football. Well, her mother was there, and the midwife—she was in good hands. That night, about eleven o'clock—me and my pals had been to the 'Oddfellows'—we was stood about by the Fountain, still discussing the match, and the shop lights went out one by one. A couple o' chaps wobbled past singing 'We're soldiers of the Queen m'lads!' and a voice nearby said: 'Ain't you that bloke they call *Leamington*?' It was a chap who lived there, I recognized his face.

'Ah. What brings you 'ere?'

'I got no work. I'm up at the Big House.' His parents had died, there was nobody to look after him. He'd took to the road. 'You's lucky, bein wed,' he said.

'Yes, I reckon I *am*,' I said, feeling guilty. You see, I couldn't face going home, just yet.

I went to see Cal. I hadn't been since the wedding. 'Soon as you gets that babby into this world, My Lad, soon as it's fit, bring it down,' she said. 'Meanwhiles,' she said—she'd took no offence!— 'you'd best go back home. Er'll live! Er's strong—like me.'

Yes! I thought, she is! I dashed back up Sheep Street, up our passage. There was some kids outside in the yard—at that time o' night!

'Ullo, Mister Hewins,' said Hilda Rowe. They giggled. My heart was in my shoes.

Granny Sutton the midwife, she worked in the pub—she'd had ten herself so she knowed the ropes—she was an old-fashioned un. She shouts downstairs—I weared a leather belt—'Chuck your belt off Hewins, it's a boy!' and, ''ave you got the binder?'

The binder?

I'd got a son!

Her mother was doing summat mysterious with the goffering iron. There was a smell of scorch. I crept upstairs, and there was Granny Sutton cutting the babby's cord.

'Give Mother a penny, George,' said Emma. A penny? I hardly dared look at her; when I did she weren't as bad as I feared. She was smiling.

Her mother put a penny in the piece of white rag she'd been scorching and laid it on the babby's navel. It was screaming like a dillen pig. It looked like one and all. Then they was both bound up, Emma with an old bolster, so tight she could hardly get a cup of tea down her. She said: 'I kept 'earin "Come on Leamington! Come on Leamington!" a-comin across the river from the Rec. All afternoon!

'I'll try an get up later,' she said.

'No you won't!' said Granny Sutton. She turned to me: 'I'll be 'ere for a week, take er washin for a fortnight. Seven-an-six.'

'Did it 'urt?' I said, but she and her mother and Granny Sutton looked at one another and I knowed I asked the wrong question. Some things women liked to keep private.

'All I'll say is, Hewins, you's lucky it ain't a dead un nor gone the wrong way and 'ad to 'ave the doctor!'

We all knowed we *couldn't* have the doctor, cos you had to pay. We couldn't afford him as well.

On the seventh day, just afore Granny Sutton went, she took the two safety pins out the binder, let it come off on its own in the bed. It was like getting a human being back from the dead! Emma wanted to get up there and then, but her mother made her bide in bed for seven days more. As for the babby—it was covered with a veil for six weeks, never saw daylight. As soon as it *did*, as soon as it was fit, I kept my promise.

'Where you goin wi that babby?' Her mother was starting to get on my nerves.

'Me Gran's!' I said, and I was off, afore they could argufy.

The old chaps gathered round. 'E's George—after me. A fine lad, Granny Sutton says.'

Till then, I hadn't thought of him as anybody! Well, his looks had been against him—I'd seen prettier piglets—and the veil, and keeping him in a drawer. Gunner starts up:

> It does seem nice
> If a chap can say

I gotta look after the *babby*
So I can't come out today!

Cal gave him a big warm shawl. She said, low: 'You go up,' meaning the chimney in the second-hand clothes shop. ''Elp yourself, 'ave what you likes. Your kiddies'll not starve while I'm alive!'

*

I'd got a son and it was a new century! You felt it in the air, electric. We all felt the same: we was ready to scrap with *any*body, we could tackle *any*thing! Sir Arthur Hodgson—he was a big churchman and High Steward of Stratford—he dished out the prizes at the Volunteers' annual dinner. I'd won a couple o' rabbits for shooting. 'Fresh Clopton bunnies!' I thought, and I smiled to myself. I could picture Emma's face when she saw them!

Sir Arthur rumbled on. 'As Lord Rosebery said when England was nearly at war wi France over that stupid Fashoda business:

> We don't want to fight
> But by jingo if we do
> We got the ships
> We got the men
> We got the *money* too!'

Everybody cheered; we knowed what *that* meant! The old Colonel replied with 'a couple o' lines by Rudyard Kipling as 'ave just crossed me mind:

> Fear God, honour the Queen,
> Learn to shoot straight
> An keep yourselves clean!'

Fine words! We clapped and shouted!

Stratford was ripe for a riot. One of the shopkeepers, Bullard, he kept an antique shop opposite the Shakespeare Hotel. Well, somebody said he hanged a Boer flag out. Bullard said he didn't— and I never seen it, I'll say that. It was the time of the Relief of Ladysmith, and Sheep Street was being repaired. They'd just put all the loose stones down to roll them the next day. Some young toffs had come out of the Conservative Club; they was a-singing— 'We'll fight for England's glory, lads, we're SOLDIERS OF THE QUEEN!' and 'We'll allus be ready, steady boys, STEADY!'

They went and turned the gas lamps out so's it was all dark. I stood in an entrance and watched them. They got handfuls of stones. Then they went and smashed every pane o' glass in Bullard's shop. There was a lot of shouting and jeering and soon a crowd o' folks was milling around, shaking their fists and jeering too. They pulled out some of Bullard's furniture and started burning it at the top o' the street. You could see frightened faces at a window above, and the flames reflected in the glass.

I kept out of it. I didn't want to get into trouble. I couldn't *afford* to; asides, I felt sorry for old Bullard and his family, they hadn't done me no harm, but some of my pals who'd been in the pub joined in. The copper—he was a big chap this copper—he was a-running Charlie Jones. He'd got round the corner first, Charlie had, he was a bit playful, he got down on his hands and knees and as the copper charged round the corner he tripped him over, sent him head over heels! I didn't have the sense to shift. The copper picks himself up. Charlie had gone.

'You!' he says. I couldn't wipe the grin off my face fast enough. He was really riled. 'You'll be hearin from me,' he said.

The rioting lasted three days, off and on. The shopkeepers, business men, folks like that with money, started panicking: 'Stop these brutal mobs!' they wrote in the *Herald*. 'Where was the fire engine? Why was the police idle?'

On the second night gangs o' police came from all over Warwickshire. Thousands o' folks turned up, all punching one another.

'What *you* been up to?' said the missus when I gets home, a-Monday. 'The copper's been round!'

My heart sank. This is it! I thought. I told her then, all the truth. 'It's the truth!' I said. 'I'd best go an tell em!'

She was a bit flushed. 'I told im! I told im you ain't a drinkin man and anybody else as knows you'll say the same. You weren't a part of it. "Good day to you, Mrs Hewins!" 'e said. 'E ended up callin me *Mrs Hewins*!'

I looked at her in amazement. She'd handled em better'n I could! I told her: 'You *'ave* done it in a dish!'

Four of my pals was put in gaol. Charlie had a month, with hard labour, so did Billy Palmer, he worked at Wildmoor Farm. The Vicar was the only one who stuck up for them, he was the only one as did. Everybody else jumped on the wagon—even Parliament! Parliament called Charlie a *'dangerous ringleader* oo no doubt incited the crowd!'—afore he'd been tried! That was what shocked me. And they said that the other 'ringleaders' was being brought to justice!

The Vicar answered back, he weren't frit: 'They been left to bear their punishment alone, four men out of a mob o' five hundred!'

My opinion of old Arbuthnot shot up. Black George weren't the only name he was called in Stratford—but this time he was *right*! They hadn't been responsible. I knowed that, I'd seen.

'That the true ringleaders 'ave escaped punishment there is not a shadow o' doubt. They are a different class o' folks to the two half-drunken creatures oo was creatin a disturbance Sat'day evenin. But they 'ave been conveniently overlooked—their cloth 'as saved em. These are the individuals oo incited the more ignorant part of the mob to the destruction which was wrought...'

I met my Grandad at the top of Ely Street. Folks was looking at the damage, sheep-faced. Somebody said: 'Poor ole Charlie! E was up the pole, that's all!'

My Grandad said: 'There's one law for them and one law for us, allus was and allus will be while they's makin em, stands to reason. Some day,' he said, 'us'll make the laws.'

'What 'appens meanwhiles, Judy?'

'Lay low,' said my Grandad, 'that's my motto.'

They listened respectfully, cos my Grandad was well thought of, even if he was a skinny old bugger in some ways. There was a murmuring of 'Ahs!' and 'Ayes!' But to my mind he hadn't answered the question at all.

That winter and the next was terrible hard, terrible. The men had no work, no dole. The women couldn't go mangeling, they couldn't pull the mangels up, they was froze in the ground. They got chilblains on their hands; those as went washing or charring like Widow Bayliss came home crying where the soda had got in the cracks. Old folks died of the cold. The young uns like us with families growing had to scratch their heads to know how they was going to live.

To start with, our rent was three shillings and threepence. We'd

19. George at twenty-two

got a new landlord—Salt Brassington, he was Librarian at the Theatre—and he put it up from half-a-crown a week to *three-and-three*! If you didn't pay the rent you was chucked out. Folks as couldn't pay—if they was old or there was illness in the family—they ended up in the workhouse. Old Bill Hinton went in—Brassington upped his rent from three bob to five-and-six!—and the Rowe family off the street. They couldn't pay. It was a sad sight to see them go. The landlord sold their stuff—put the bailiffs in to get the money for the rent. Cal had two mats off them.

'Poor Bea Rowe—er near 'ad the clothes off 'er back!'

'It wouldn't a-been the first time er's done *that*!'

The missus joined in: 'It ain't decent!'

'The ole witch!'

Pulling Cal to bits took their minds off the Rowes. Watching the bailiff's men I vowed I'd never be in that position. I'd work day and night. 'Be sure of the rent bein paid,' folks said, 'and plenty o' firin—the rest'll take care of itself.'

I was doing a job at the workhouse, slating the roof. It was a bitter cold morning when we started, frost was in the air and I reckoned it could be my last chance o' work for a while. The door opens and the slummocky roadster woman they'd got for a nurse brings the babbies out, one by one. They'd messed themselves. She peels their clothes back and swills them under the pump like so many winter savoys. November and ice-cold water! They screamed! Those screams echoed round that square yard, hit the high brick walls o' the workhouse—and the roof, where I was.

The older kiddies starts to congregate. Who should I see but Hilda Rowe and Violet. They'd had their hair chopped off, weared long holland pinnas with big red letters: STRATFORD-ON-AVON WORKHOUSE. They did some sort o' drill, then they was marched in a straight line to the National School across the road. The babbies' screams and those red letters haunted me all day. If I weren't hearing the one I was seeing the other. When I got home I told the missus but she said: 'It's to *distinguish* em.'

'Oo from?'

'From kiddies oo's Dad's workin! Ow would you like our George took for a pauper?'

'Teddy Rowe *was* workin' I said, 'till e went to the Infirmary.' He'd got TB. They took you to the Infirmary to die.

I was angry: 'There's no need for them red letters! The pauper kids is distinguished alright! You can spot em straight away—they's up against the wall watching the others play! They ain't playin—and when they marches out a-night the other kiddies is callin "Workhus brats!" after em. "*Workhus brats!*" They's *distinguished* alright! If I ever catches our George callin like that...'

I could see she didn't think the same as me. She was wrong, the Guardians was wrong, and all of us, letting it happen. Why was you punished for being poor? 'Why do they part husbands and wives in the workhus, mothers an kiddies, tell me that? Some sent one way, some t'other, according? It's cruel!'

'Shut up, George,' said the missus.

And they didn't always wait till you was dead afore they buried you! One old chap I knowed, while he was in they made him orderly. He used to help the nurses if anybody died, and this day they called him up and he says: 'But e ain't dead, nurse!'

The nurse said: 'E soon will be, on that cold slab.'

That's how it was in the workhouse. Well, they hadn't got the staff, they hadn't got the wit.

*

The frosts came.

I'd been out of work for about a month. We was living on what I could make selling sticks at the door, doing odd jobs for folks and her mother's Parish Relief, that was two bob a week. Her hands had got too bad to go charring. Now the Corporation Surveyor, his name was Dixon, and while I was apprenticed he'd got to know me. He saw me at the top o' Sheep Street to'ards December and he says: 'What brings you up 'ere Harry?' He called me Harry.

I said: 'I got no work, none of us 'ave.'

'Ah,' he says, 'well you go up the Corporation yard. Tell em you're to start. Go down West Street and take both sides o' the street up, 'bout ten yards at a time, and re-lay it.' He said: 'I can keep you on till Christmas but no longer.'

'I thought you'd been lucky,' said the missus, 'When you didn't come back.'

She was in the fashion again.

*

That night the snow fell. Next morning it was still falling—big flakes swirling slow, settling. That was Dixon's job down the drain!

'There'll be cold crowdings,' said Widow Bayliss, 'afore this winter's out.' The light from the snow had woken her up too. Emma and our George was still asleep.

'The Nursin Home's got a flat roof,' the old lady said. 'It'll be a foot o' snow, leakin through. Just tell the caretaker you's my son!'

'I ain't!' I said—well she was an old scarecrow—but I went and I slipped up Sheep Street afore anybody in the town was stirring. I chucked the snow off the Nursing Home roof for them, early morning, and lo and behold the caretaker said: 'So you's Emma's lad are ye?' And he gave me a good bacon and egg breakfast. *Bacon and egg!* That's more 'n you ever got at home! I can taste it still.

That way I got my belly full afore I started snow sweeping. We went up the Corporation yard—plumbers, painters, bricklayers, carpenters, labourers, anybody who was out of work. Happy Prior was there—he was a gardener—wheezing and coughing away, he didn't sound none too good to me. The foreman picked out me for one and Tommy Taylor for another, and Happy scrambled alongside us afore he could argufy.

'Ullo Jack,' he said.

His face was the colour of ashes. My poor aunt and all those kiddies! Tommy and me was thinking the same thing.

We each had a shovel give us, four to a cart, and off we trundled. Those streets was all cleared of snow by nine o'clock and there was no traffic then! Without you went up Henley Street, then you'd see the brougham or Tommy Tappin on his hansom cab a-waiting for visitors, all you'd see in Stratford would be a farm cart passing through. Today there was nothing, the countryside was snowed up. The Board School in Broad Street and the National School, all the boys, all the schoolboys, had gone out, made snowballs. They was having a battle between the two schools, throwing snowballs at each other. It was deep snow. Walking past with my shovel and my broom—you could borrow a bass broom from the Corporation—I envied them, I can tell you. If anybody wanted their paths clearing for a couple o' pence they shouted you in: ''Ere! You!'

I'd touch my cap. 'Yes, ma'am!' 'Yessir!'

You'd got to do it, to get a living.

I took the missus what I'd made, then I picked up our chair and a spanner and I went down to the river, to put skates on. One year it was so cold the river was a foot thick, folks walked up from church, back to Stratford, on the river, roasted a pig on it. This year the canal was froze solid, and the basins. What you made depended on what skates they had. With the wooden ones you had to put a screw in and screw it round. Those as owned a shop, folks like the Mayor, they'd give us a bob a-piece, for show; the others gave from a ha'penny to twopence. Sometimes they'd put their own skates on, then you might earn a bit minding their shoes whiles they skated.

After a while they got it organized. All the money we made for putting skates on was put in a tin box, and the Mayor—well, him and Tommy Pargetter, he was a confectioner on Bridge Street—they came every night, got the money out, took it away with them. Sat'day dinner time they brought us all down, sat us at a big table. There was so many of us putting skates on, so many sweeping the ice. Tommy Pargetter had baked a big pie, a pork pie big as a bucket with a conker-coloured crust. The kiddies stopped sliding, crowded round to slaver and stare.

'Now,' he says, 'ow many's married? Right!'

He starts cutting. We could see the white paste and the jelly and rammed up against it big juicy gobbets o' pork! He cuts a piece for the missus too, then he says with a smirk: '*I'll* take the married uns' pie home.'

So we had nothing till we got home! The single uns took what was left; they ate it there and then—stuffed it into their mouths, 'cept those like Tommy Taylor who thought more of their Mam or brothers and sisters and started wrapping it up. We had to sit

20. Lucy's Mill on the river Avon at Stratford, 1900s

and watch them. I whispered to Tommy: 'Soon as you've got your money—clear off!' I could see from the married uns' faces what was going to happen.

Then the shopkeepers tipped the money onto the table. The married uns had a bit more'n the single uns—and then they took the missus's share home afore they'd give us our'n. They didn't trust us to feed our own families!

The most mysterious thing was Cal getting a piece of that pie. I dropped in to say hullo and there it was on her table—bigger'n mine!

'Ow d'you come by that?'

'Ah,' she said, 'I could tell you a thing or two about im, for all 'is grand ways.'

'What?' I was curious. I starts pressing. 'Oo?'

'All I'll say is, My Lad, there ain't as much difference atween some folks and us as you might think. E's what you might call a brother under the skin.'

And she laughed.

*

At nights when there was a moon we went skating ourselves. Some of us had wooden skates—I'd got steel uns! I'd found them! I *flew* over that ice, across the 'croft, towards the river. Two of us would catch hold of each other and skate, dance, on the ice. We could cut the figure eight! It took some learning—a good many toffs cut the one and dotted it! One stroke and sit on it! *We* was good, even Tommy, he'd practised so much. We could skate with one leg in the air, and if the mood took us we'd set off at speed along the canal. Under the arches we went—the 'Unicorn' rushed past, and a canal boat, hung with icicles. Afore us lay the road to a foreign country, white and mysterious looking, and the moon as big as a dinner plate!

'Look!' cried Tommy.

That winter the wind had blowed the snow into fantastical shapes across the fields and along the banks, like hundreds o' folks with a spell on them. When you touched them they was hollow, they crumbled away. We shivered and laughed.

'Come on!' I said, 'Else us'll be froze stiff'n all!'

'Let's go round the bend, under the next bridge—round the bend!' said Tommy, 'farther an farther.' I was surprised. He never put more'n two words together as a rule.

I said: 'Say "Ole witch use your power".' I did a little spin. ' "Get your besom and sweep all this snow off so's we can skate to *New Zealand*!" '

That name New Zealand stuck in my mind.

'Or Africa!'

I thought: 'It's only the lock gates round that bend!' I could see them in my mind's eye, heavy and black they was, shut ice-tight like the doors of a gaol.

'Or Australia, eh, Tom?'

You could never tell if he was enjoying himself, but that night I reckon he did. Skating, you felt as free as a bird. You forgot all your troubles.

No more snow fell. The roads was swept clean, every garden path in Stratford. There was nothing to do but wait for them to start skating again. Monday morning there was a worse commotion than usual up our passage. We kept a jackdaw in a cage on the wall—I left his door open but he never went far, came hopping back—well he was a-squarking, then our George started up.

'Ey, ey,' I said. I picked him up and rocked him. I didn't go out—it was a daft chap poked his nose into women's quarrels—I peeked out the window instead. The missus was there, with the dolly in her hand and a big pile o' washing on her arm. At first I thought it was the Relieving Officer come. He called at the houses with the money for the widows. He wanted to know where they worked and what they earned and what their character was—all for four shilling a week, or two if they lived with their children. Generally he was alright about her mother; well, he knowed the money wouldn't allow her to have beer much, although beer was only three ha'pence a pint. Then I saw it was Kate Rainbow from the Box Office. The landlord sent Alice or Kate Rainbow Mondays to collect the rent. She was moving back'ards, down the passage.

'I'm only doin my job!'

'Call that a *job*?'

Next minute the door busts open—'E wants to see you, George—Salt Brassington!'

Well, we was behind with it, but not badly.

'I'll make it up,' I said. 'Didn't you tell er? When I gets work.'

She plonked herself down on the chair. She was near her time. 'Er says e wants to see you now,' she said. 'I told er to bugger off. I knows it bain't er fault—but it made me feel better!'

We looked at each other and laughed, cos there seemed nothing else to do.

'I'll go an see Cal.'

'No!' said the missus. She and Cal didn't get on. 'There must be summat else. I could ask Kate.' Kate Tappin was her elder sister. They was well off, but they'd got kiddies of their own.

'I can see Tommy forkin out for our rent!'

I had an idea, so I said: 'If that's what e wants—I'll go and see ole Brassington!' I went to the Theatre and there was Salt Brassington sat at a desk with a pen in his hand. He didn't look up.

'Yes?'

I held my tongue—and my temper. It was an effort, I can tell you. 'There ain't no work at present—you can see for yourself—it's snowed up.' Still he didn't meet my eye.

'I'm a bricklayer by trade—but I can whitewash, and do odd jobs, plumbin an gas, set my hand to *anythin*,' (*to pay the rent*, I thought) 'and I'm good wi a spade. I knows I didn't pay last week . . .'

'No,' he said.

'...But I could make it up. I could work for you! I'd be cheap! Handy for you!'

That did it! Salt Brassington looked at me: 'Fit man, are you?' He looked long and hard at me, took in every detail. 'Alright!' he said. 'You can clean my windows—you knows where I live, up Rowley Crescent—paint my house for me inside and out. I want some frames for my plants and a gate makin so's to cut off a corner and when spring comes you can mow my lawn—'

He smiled: 'I'm writin a book,' he said, 'on the cottages of England.'

The river was still flowing under the ice; it kept washing it, you sensed it was there, and then one day when you weren't thinking on it, the river began to show. We got clay from the brickyard and plastered the doors up. That didn't stop it. We got the furniture upstairs when we saw the water coming over the Bancroft Gardens and over the coal wharf. On and on it came, up the drain, through the cellars. At Waterside, at Cal's, it was three foot six in her bottom rooms. I went to see how she was. 'Lower your basket then!' She had a rope and a basket. I popped the bread in.

She shouts down: 'Where's Lally? Is e drownded?' He was an old chap, one of the lodgers, a bit touched.

21. Waterside in the floods, 1901. Cal Cook's door can be seen beyond the tall building in the centre (the 'Wheatsheaf' public house).

'No!' I shouted back. 'But e's seen the fire bein put out!' He was sat there with his legs dangling in the water, waiting for his dinner.

I thought: I'll cheer er up! I shouts: 'They's bringing the collection round tomorrow!' They'd had a collection, the shopkeepers and businessmen, for folks like Cal as lived on Waterside, whose furniture and tack was lost in the flood. 'Clopton Bridge is still blocked—you can't tell *where* the river is—I seen a cow goin down this mornin. Er's called the new babby after the ole Queen—ELSIE VICTORIA!'

'Oh aye,' said Cal. She sounded pleased. Well, she was crafty: when we'd had a lot o' rain and the snow began to melt she knowed what was coming. She got stuff in, moved her furniture upstairs. She'd do well out of the collection, tell them this had been ruined and that, plead poverty!

The floods reached Pimms Court, but not to get in the house, just the tail end o' the wave. Oh the smell when it went away! The Corporation brought disinfectant and they got the Fire Brigade to pump the water out o' folks' cottages. The *stink*! But the thaw meant I could start looking for work again.

*

22. Waterside after the floods

It was all by word of mouth. There was a Brummagem firm came to work at Rowley Cresent, on a new house. All the toffs was buying land and houses up there—it was *fashionable*. Well, I was doing a garden wall for Salt Brassington—there was no end to the jobs he kept thinking up for me!—when the carpenter puts his head over and says: 'I'm a-goin to build two houses meself, up Vincent Avenue, will you come an bricky for us?'

When I was there he went to another builder and said: 'George will be finishin wi me.'

He said: 'Bring im to me!'

I was never out of work in the summer, hardly ever. I might see Whateley—he was another Stratford builder. He'd say: 'I hear you's a-goin to stop, George, and short o' work'. He'd tell me to come down to the yard, cos he knowed I worked well.

It was sixpence an hour for a good bricklayer then, and we worked fifty-six hours and a half when the weather was fine, from six in the morning to half-past five o' nights. The only summer holidays we had was when it rained a quarter and you went in the shed to dry. He'd book it, and then when you stopped again for another quarter he'd stop you half-an-hour. We had no holidays with pay, no tea breaks. If you had a bit o' food you ate it as you went along, kept putting it in your mouth. Sat'day was pay day. We didn't get our money afore one o'clock, and if the job was in Stratford the gaffer would likely keep you waiting at his house. Sometimes we had to wait an hour or so whiles he finished his dinner. We didn't get paid for that!

Then the Corporation started to fill in the Bancroft basin: the Medical Officer called it a 'death trap'. The toffs was against it going—it was safe ice for their kiddies to skate on in winter—so was the folks from Waterside. They chucked their rubbish in it: ashes, rotting veg, old bottles, all sorts. Cal dumped a lot o' things in there, I can tell you. With the stone from the basin the Corporation decided to build a river wall to stop the water, and that's where *we* came in!

They drained the water out of the river, right up to Hatton Rock, about three mile the water was emptied. We toiled and moiled all night, had flash-lamps, big arc-lights to work by. Calloway Brothers, they got the contract, they built that wall. We went Sat'days and Sundays, worked till Monday morning. All the builders let their men go, all day Sat'day if the water was low enough. We throwed in rubbish, tins, anything to sink the water should it still come. There was only a drop flowing down the middle. It was really quanked; you wouldn't a-thought it was the same river! As for us, they put boards all along but we was covered in mud. It was hard work, filthy. All the mud had to be carried up in barrows, day and night; we dumped it in the Basin. 'That won't stop it,' folks said. 'If the water wants to come, it will!'

But it was good money. We went to Calloway when we liked and picked our money up: carpenters, painters, plumbers, brickies, labourers, anybody who didn't get a good week's pay. We all had the same wage; three-pence ha'penny an hour a labourer was then, but Calloway paid extra cos we worked all night—*fourpence an hour*! There was eighty of us some weeksend. You got more in a weeksend than you got if you worked all week. Then we had to

23. At work on the river Avon

go back to work, back to our gaffers, Monday morning—clay from head to toe, dog tired.

*

The gaffer I liked best was John Roberts. He'd work by the side o' you, he was on the job. I used to work along the line with him; I was on one end o' the line by the wall, and he was on the other.

He was a bricky himself, a good un. He *knowed* if you'd done a good day's work. I'd sooner work for a chap like that—he was satisfied and you was. If you work for a bloke as takes the bill then don't know 'A' from a bull's foot about it, he don't know if you've done a day's work or you ain't. I'll give you an example. We was a-plastering some houses and there was a bricky at work outside. John Roberts weren't satisfied with what he'd done.

He said: 'Now I can do nothin 'bout you workin like this,' he said, 'but if you put your hand in me pocket an took some money out I could hit you on the nose!'

You could respect that.

He was a chapel man—we done all their work. Five of us was in the chapel on Brum Road, putting the heating apparatus in. I got up in the pulpit. 'I'm just goin to give you a few words from the Bible!' I said. I puffed myself out, cleared my throat like the Vicar—the others was falling about with laughing—when in walks the gaffer!

'Stop where you is! Let's 'ear it George!'

Our next job was in Meer Street a-tiling all the roofs. We got some plastering to do, and it was the house where Poll Davis lived. The women there used to go to the 'White Swan', wash up and that, bring the food back, the scrap food. I was there, and my labourer, and the gaffer.

Poll says: 'Would you like a few taters, Mister Roberts?'

He said: 'Ah, I'll 'ave one or two.' He helped himself from the basin.

She says to Tommy: 'Which ud *you* like, Tommy, some taters or a bit o' that?' She lifts her skirts up, high as they'd go!

Tommy went bright red. 'I'll 'ave the taters please, missus.' That's how he got his nick-name Tommy Taters.

24. Building workers, old Almshouses, Stratford-upon-Avon

Then, afore we knowed what was happening, the women'd got our gaffer down, got his legs, pulled his cock out—it was stiff and all!—and plastered it with lard!

He yelled! He said after: 'You two stood there! Never offered to defend me!'

Next day when he came to see how we was getting on they bawled half way down the street: 'You GETTIN ON alright Mister Roberts?'

He never came near those houses no more. He was a gentleman, John Roberts, a laughing man, but enough was enough.

Some gaffers you couldn't respect. Teddy Kennard was one; Jack Greenway was another. I never worked for him—thank the Lord! He was a terror with his workmen. We was doing a big cesspit at the workhouse when he was Guardian there, a man-hole for the drain all in white glazed bricks, just opposite the front door of the workhouse. He comes by and he says: 'You ain't a-gettin on very fast!' Likely he was upset cos he hadn't got the contract.

'Fast enough for me!' I said. I spat as far as I could. Tommy kept his mouth shut but I knowed he'd a-said summat if he'd dared.

Then there was Walt Bailey. He was a class on his own. He'd been the first to take me on when Kennard gave me the sack. As well as the building, he dealt with second-hand furniture, on Rother Street, left-hand side going down. He was a magpie. He'd got a big warehouse on the side of his yard; he'd got it crammed with furniture, pictures of all sorts, brass candlesticks. He sent me to buy some of it for him, from the Sale. He gave me the money: 'Do your best Georgie!'

He'd fetch it, after, cock his head all on a-side, have a good look at it, weigh it up. 'You done better'n *I* should there!' He gave me a tanner and off he hopped with his new piece o' treasure.

He was a carpenter by trade. 'Walter Bailey,' it said on his bill-head, 'Carpenter, Joiner, Coffin Maker and Wood Turner, New and Second-hand Furniture, Cricket Bats Repaired, Spliced and Bound on the Shortest Notice.' Now the workhouse coffins was all priced then, so much a coffin, and he'd got the contract. He said to me: 'If it rains don't go on the job, Georgie, don't lose time, come to the yard.'

He showed me how to make coffins, turn them and all. When I got through I could make them well. Then he gives me one of his crafty looks: 'I know you's a chap as ain't *pernickety*,' he says.

'Ullo!' I thought.

'I'll give you a packet o' Woodbines if you'll come wi me to the workhus and put folks in.'

'Done!' I said.

One chap hadn't been dead for long and he'd only got one leg. 'Busy about!' says Walt Bailey. 'Take 'is legs.'

I got hold of it as best I could. We sat him up and he went 'Aaaaaagh!' I thought of all the tales I heard tell of the workhouse. I never think my feet touched the ground I ran so fast.

'Come back, Georgie!' cried Walt Bailey.

I never stopped running till I reached home.

'The Devil after you?' said the missus.

'I rightly think e *is*!' I said. I told her what had happened. 'It was the wind!' her mother said. 'It was the wind ain't been worked out of im—that's all!'

Another time we went to put an old woman in at Binton—and she was a-laughing! She was winking her eye! Walt Bailey shouts downstairs: 'Does anyone want to see er afore I screws er in?'

'We's 'ad enough of the ole bugger!' they shouts back. 'You screw er in—us don't want to see *er* no more!'

But as I put the lid down I thought; 'I'd like to know what she's laughin about!'

And I had my wish.

We went to do up her cottage, and in the window sill, where the stone had shrunk, there was cavities.

Tommy says: 'Look George, look, there's some money!' It was a George shilling! We starts dabbing.

Walt Bailey says: 'What you two a-dabbing for?' He says, '*Oh!*' There was spade guineas, five bob pieces big as the top of a cup, thick too—silver! We shared them out and they sold for about three times their value.

Often you felt like telling a gaffer what to do with his job, but at that time o' day it was always the other way round. You worked for him and *he* ended it. He simply said on Sat'day when he paid you: 'Well, I shan't want you no more.' There was no money, no cards. If you hadn't got fixed up your heart sank. There was no union to back you up: if you got dismissed nobody took no notice—unless the other chaps on the job said, 'We's a-goin if e goes!' That was the only thing as kept you. It happened to me once.

*

I'd just finished for one gaffer. I'd got my bag o' tools and plumb rule on my shoulder and I meets a chap I knowed.

'Ullo, George! What, you packed up?'

'Ah. We finished.'

'Now,' he says, 'I'll tell you where there's a job a-goin—at Alveston, that big house, doin alterations: knocking a doorway out, y'know, puttin a new un in, bay winders an that.'

'That ud suit me down to the ground,' I said.

I walked to Alveston. It was white with kek along that lane, blue sky, the birds were singing their heads off. I kept my pace, I didn't linger: I was after work! It was a Brummagem firm—HARVEY GIBBS OF KINGS HEATH, the board said. I goes to see the foreman.

'You looks young. Can you lay bricks?'

'I shouldn't a–come else. I don't carry these tools about an be a labourer! I just finished a job.'

The foreman says: 'You can start now if you likes. Now our gaffer's a bit of a *devil*. E's a free masoner...'

I'd never heard o' them; master masoners yes, but not free masoners.

... 'E's a busy man. E's expected, so when e comes on the scene—dash about it. You can slack after e's gone!'

Tommy Tappin brought him from the station. The gaffer jumped out. He was a quick smart sort o' fella, a Brummagem tyke. His eyes was everywhere. He points to me with his cane. 'Oo's that?' He spoke Brummagem.

'That's our countryman! Country bricky! Damn good chap, sir, used to all these alterations!'

Harvey Gibbs said: 'Glad you started im!'

It was a lovely house, a mansion. It just suited my work. I was used to jobbing—putting a doorway in, bricking another up, bay windows instead o' square uns. We was supposed to start at six, but the foreman gave me walking time. I started from home at six and walked in their time. At half-past five when we knocked off I walked back in my own. That weren't bad, but the rate was. He paid me under what the rate was then. One of the chippies said: 'What's e givin you, kid?'

I said: 'Fivepence.'

He said: 'The bugger's twistin you! E's chargin the gaffer six-pence!'

He was getting a penny an hour out of me, this foreman. Well, I couldn't fall out with him cos the job would have went. You'd *got* to keep in with him, buy him a drink.

They was devils for drink, the foreman carpenter and the foreman bricky—Joe Davis was his name. They could drink some drink!

I thought: That's our rent's going down 'is gullet! But there was nothing you could do about it.

If the gaffer happened to swing a surprise and come, he'd knock his cane on the wall and say: 'Where's Joe?'

I weren't frit of him! 'E's had to go to the village,' I said, or 'E's been called away.' I stayed cool as a cowcumber. I couldn't say he'd gone for a crap cos I knowed he'd be away too long.

When the foreman got back he said: 'What did you tell im Harry?' He called me Harry.

'I told im you'd been called away—by telephone.' There was a *telephone* in the house! 'Your folks was middlin!'

He patted me on the back: 'You got out o' that one well!'

One day he says: 'We's gettin to'ards the end.' There was a big hall, big as a room—bigger!—to lay with Minton tile. 'But don't you touch it Harry,' he says. 'I'm a-goin to the pub to 'ave a drink, I shan't be long. Then we'll start an do this.' I thought: 'Alright!'

He stopped away till the pub shut at three. He'd given me the paper with the pattern on, all the tiles was there. I got about three yards done.

He rolls back. ''As the gaffer sent a bloke to do it? E said: "Don't touch that hall, Joe, I'll send a tiler, a proper tiler from Brummagem, to do that".'

'No,' I says. 'E sent no tiler 'ere.'

'But,' he says, ''oo done that?'

I said: 'I 'ave.'

'Well,' he says, 'you *'ave* surprised me!' He says: 'Go on! I'll serve you.'

He kept handing me the tiles, the colour. We got it all done. The gaffer came just as we finished it. He was dressed up to kill. 'Ullo!' Joe Davis muttered. 'I should a-guessed—it's the start o' the fishin season!'

Fishing? I couldn't picture anybody going fishing dressed like that.

I'd done all the laying. We'd put some sawdust on, to clean the cement off. It looked top-hole!

'Well,' says Harvey Gibbs, buzzing about like a hornet, knocking his cane on this and that, 'that bloke come then?' He always spoke as if you was invisible.

Joe Davis says: 'What bloke?'

'That tiler.'

'There's been no tiler 'ere,' he says.

'Well,' says the gaffer, 'oo's done that?'

'Harry here, our countryman.'

He said: 'Never!' He said: 'Put im some extra money in 'is packet this week.' Joe Davis's face fell. 'Give im the tiler's money!' I went home that night as happy as a cricket.

Then we went to build a big house on the Rowley Estate. Joe Davis got in the habit of slipping home early to Brummagem and leaving me in charge. I'd been with him for four months. A couple of the older chaps was jealous. This one chap, he was a labourer, he'd got a biggish family, he came to see me and he says: 'I've lost a quarter. I can't meet my payments—can you forget it?' I had to tell the foreman what times to book down, see.

'I will,' I said, 'for you. I'll let it drop this once, Tim.'

But when we came to be paid Joe Davis came to see me and he says: 'Harry!'

I said: 'Hullo'

''Ere's your back week,' he says. They always kept a week in hand.

'What *for*? What 'ave I done?'

He said: 'I trusted you! That bloke told me e lost a quarter!'

I said: 'The bugger's shopped me 'as e? E asked me not to put it down cos e was down-an-out and owed money.'

All the chaps heard me. They would stick up for you if they knowed it was a genuine case. They put down their tools. 'Joe! Harry stays or we all goes!'

So he had to have me back. Harvey Gibbs was in a hurry, and the other chaps backed me up. Timmy Sothern got the sack. He was worse off for the trick he'd done on me.

It was getting to be a struggle to find work, a struggle to keep in it. My wages were a penny lower'n they had been—and prices was rising! There was still some building going on in Stratford but not so much. You had to *scrat*. The boom looked to be over.

&❧ CHAPTER ELEVEN ❧&

'Our Dad! Our Dad!' George toddled alongside of us.

I daresn't turn my eyes. It was Christmas, and the Volunteers was playing Sir Arthur Hodgson from Clopton House. There was eight hundred soldiers followed: Warwick, Leamington, Rugby, Nuneaton as well as Stratford. We played him down Clopton Lane. The missus had took our George, and our Else in the old wooden pram; she kept up with us well, I could hear the pram wheels a-squeaking in the silences. The sky was like lead that day, there was a terrible chill in the air. Then half way down Clopton Lane it started to sleet. The sleet turned to rain and the rain bucketed down! Folks was a-shrieking, running across our path to reach cover. And the drums! Afore our eyes the drums turned into tripe—we couldn't roll on them, they kept going in! Water trickled down our backs, we was soaked.

At the end o' the lane we handed him over to the Battalion band—did they look glum! They'd got to play him through the town—the slow march. 'Good riddance!' we thought, and off we set at the double for the Swan's Nest Hotel that had been the 'Shoulder o' Mutton'—it was a 'hotel' now! Greenway, the builder, was in charge of the arrangements. But at the 'Swan's Nest' they put their arms across and they said: 'You Stratford chaps, don't come 'ere, there ain't enough room for all of you!'

We'd been promised a hot dinner—but we had nothing. We had to go home, soaked to the skin.

It took days to dry my uniform. The missus was upset. 'It's the gold,' she said, 'it'll never be the same!' It weren't like her to moither so. She kept going up to it and touching it. 'It don't glister no more!'

I couldn't a-cared less! My legs was like jelly, it felt as if somebody had took a hammer to my head. I was at low ebb, I can tell you, all overish. Her mother had talked me into having a hot shallot in my ear. I weren't used to being fussed when I was sick.

''Ere's a tale for you!' she said, laying down her end of the peg rug. I could tell summat good was coming. 'This'll cheer im up,' she said, cos Emma looked low too. 'They shoved Sir Arthur in so fast on account o' the weather folks is saying e didn't 'ave a *Christian* berrin! After them stoppin ole Bill Hinton an all!'

Old Bill Hinton had gone to the workhouse. Every week they let the old chaps get their baccy from the little shop on Mansell Street. One day he set off as usual but he didn't come back. They found him drownded in the river. We reckoned it could a-been an accident: the water was high and he'd used to potter about by the edge when he lived by us. The Vicar ummed and aahed, but the Bishop and the big Churchmen said it was self-murder, no doubt about it. No, they said, old Bill couldn't have a Christian burying. Well, serve Sir Arthur right! We had a good laugh over that!

The grin was soon wiped off my face. That night when her mother had fell asleep the missus said: 'I didn't tell you afore but now you's almost fit I will.'

I couldn't believe it! Nobody could have babbies that fast! Every year it happened—another un.

I was soon up and walking the streets, looking for work. Outside the 'Anchor' I meets Half-Pint Ginny.

'You looks down, Jack!'

'We's 'avin another un,' I said.

She said: 'Don't 'ave a load o' kiddies, Jack! Tell your wife to do what I did!'

'What's that?' She'd had no children. She was the only one I knowed as had none. Mrs White up our Court had a dozen or so, Mrs Onions on the street had a hell of a dose. I thought: 'This is my lucky day.'

'It'll cost you seven-an-six.'

I laughed.

'Five bob? 'Alf-a-crown? Well, if you buys me 'alf a pint—' Then she told me: 'I allus got slack, after'ards, fine slack, an *chewed* it.'

I told the missus. She pulled a face. 'Coal!' she said. But she had a go, she nearly made herself ill a-trying to eat the stuff. And she drank water that pennies had been boiled in.

*

It didn't work. They went on a-coming in that room over the passage: Edith Emma, after her mother, Jessie, Florence Beatrice, after the barmaid in the pub.

'Chuck your belt off, Hewins!' shouted Granny Sutton. 'It's another wench!'

Sooner'n you could have believed it we was eight, cos her mother was still with us. She weren't a bad old soul—she was a worker—but it was always Mother first. When we had meat at Christmas Mother had the first slice—she liked it well done—Mother had the best end o' the bed. That cottage was busting at the seams, and no chance of leaving now! I was in the one bed, with the missus and the new babby as wanted feeding; the old lady's feet was still a-sticking in my face! The rest of the kiddies was bundled into the old bed Cal had give us, next door. If one of them got measles or a fever the missus would say: 'In you go! You can *all* get it together and I'll know where you is!'

They had to go to bed whiles their clothes was drying too: they only had one change.

Clothes weren't the biggest problem: folks was kind, the under-taker over the street, Mr Bennett, his missus gave us their Hilda's old clothes. With a family like ours, when the one growed out of her clothes they dropped on the one below, whether they fitted or no, same with boots. We made do. But *food*! You had to find food in winter, same as summer, and all those hungry mouths to feed! They could eat—couldn't they! Our shopping list, for food and that, came to eighteen shilling a week! That was as much as I could earn some bad weeks in summer. In the winter we got desperate. The missus said: 'I don't know how we'll go on.'

The neighbours was good. At that time o' day we was altogether. If you'd got a neighbour come in dinner time, proper dinner time, one o'clock, and seen you'd only got the table cloth on, she wouldn't say nothing, she'd go back and fetch you summat from her house. 'I've seen the position,' she'd say.

If anybody died, if a kiddie died or a husband, all up that street they'd go collecting, so's they didn't have a pauper's funeral.

But in winter folks hadn't enough for themselves. They'd got no money—nothing. Then the kiddies was put in a home-made box,

a crate from the Co-op, anything. In the winter we went up Sheep
Street to a little shop there, the *strap shop*, for the stuff we had to
buy. Coal I got from the wharf: there was three wharfs near us and
plenty o' dark nights. The good uns—this shopkeeper would know
who was good payers, he knowed you was straight—he'd strap you.
He'd strap you all winter, in moderation. Then it took us all
summer to straighten ourselves out, paying so much a week back.

We bought a pennoth o' tea—he weighed it in front of you, then
rolled it up—and a penn'oth o' sugar. Bacon was about a penny a
slice, twopence for bits, and twopence for bits o' broken cheese.
We got skimmed milk for a ha'penny and sent one of the elder
kiddies to the Co-op with a pillowcase. The missus said to our
Ede—she weren't no bigger'n a bee's knee:

''Ere's threepence! Say "Could I 'ave this filled, mister? And
could I 'ave some change?"'

She came back with an old brown loaf, a currant loaf, lots o' tops
and bottoms of broken cottages, stale cakes and a bag o' broken
biscuits!

Out of the week's money I had sixpence for myself when I was
in work: threepence for the football match or a couple o' pints,
and with the other threepence a pennoth o' snuff, a pennoth o'
chocolate drops, a pennoth o' twist tobacco, or five Woodbines.
That was my pocket money in a good week.

This shopkeeper, if I said: 'I've only got a ha'penny!' he'd always
sell two cigarettes to me, and two to the next bloke. And I could
get more for a penny if I wanted: a pennoth of those bits o' twist,
to chew. He had a coil o' twist, it weren't done up in packets then,
and when a bloke went in for half an ounce he chopped it off, he'd
take a bit off if it was overweight, sell them to blokes like me who
couldn't afford nothing else.

The thing we ate most of was bread and dripping, or on Sundays
leaf lard, out the pig. Pure leaf! There's a big leaf in the pig when
he's cut open, about an inch and a half thick, width of his belly.
Folks rendered this down, put rosemary in it. We ate it like you
would eat butter: it was lovely on toast. When I was in work we
had meat and two veg on a Sunday, always stew cos we had no
oven at Pimms Court and it went farther. Two bullocks' liver was

enough for five, more at a stretch. I used to bring them home still steaming. Then the butcher's shop stayed open Sat'day nights, till eleven. We got cheap meat—a leg o' lamb for one and ninepence, a shoulder for ninepence, breast for twopence and threepence. There was nowhere for the butcher to store it, you see. 'Buy me leg, buy me leg!' he'd be a-shouting when we came out the pub. If he had any meat left it went to the Gas House to be burnt. There weren't no cats' meat in those days. Cats and dogs got their own living.

I got in with one of the chaps at the butcher's. He said: 'Ow's your circumstances, George?'

'Not grand,' I said.

'See me in the shop and it'll be alright,' he said. 'You'll 'ear me say "It's tenpence or it's a shillin." Allus 'ave a bob. If you 'aven't got a bob when you comes in the shop let me know,' he said, 'and I'll drop you one.'

He always shouted 'Elevenpence!' or 'A shillin!' but he only took about twopence ha'penny and gave me the change back out a shilling!

*

As soon as the missus had been churched after the last un—Granny Sutton took them to the Parish Church to give thanks to God for safely coming through, they daresn't go out the house till they'd been churched—she said, low: 'I'll get er off the breast and I'll look for work.'

I said nothing. Well, there was more work in winter for the women. So she went into the kitchen at the Shakespeare Hotel. It was the biggest hotel in Stratford. She left home about four o'clock; sometimes she was there, if they was busy, all day. She scrubbed the vegetables, swilled the pans. I got the food and when there was no work I looked after the kiddies. That's how it came about that they had more of me than they had of her.

First thing I'd do was send two of them up the Co-op yard, where the carts went, where all the boxes o' stuff was. They gave away stale bread at the back, and on their way out the kiddies filled their pockets with currants and raisins and sultanas. They came home with their pockets bulging! Well, they was no value then, twopence a pound. They helped with spotted dogs. The missus made big spotted dogs, a suetty roll with currants in. It stopped in them when it was there, filled them up. But some nights, *this night*, I made them biscuits, no end o' little currant biscuits! I learnt how to make biscuits at the baker's at Leamington. I cut them with a glass, pressed the dough, sprinkled them with sugar. We rowed when the missus saw I'd been using sugar!

'It ain't *your* sugar, no more the fat nor flour,' I told her. 'I've been round and about.'

I cooked them in a tin over the fire, and the kiddies had a blow-out. 'Keep eatin!' I said.

Another night I'd been on parade, and the kiddies came to meet me. We went on parade twice a week: our drill hall was where the Corn Exchange was, top o' Sheep Street. George led the way, busting with pride cos his Dad was in the band! He loved to carry the drum home—I kept my uniform and instruments at home, you see. He used to swank! On the way back I got a pocketful of horse beans, scooped them up from the sack outside the chandler's. They did them into meal for the pigs. I put them on a shovel and roasted them over the fire. They weren't all that ripe but the kiddies scrambled for them. In the rush one was shoved up the babby's nose instead of her mouth. She started to blather, she wouldn't stop, so in the end I carried her to the doctor.

The doctor said: 'If you'd a-waited till tomorrow she'd 'ave 'ad to 'ave er nose cut!'

The horse bean had started to chit! That cost a shilling! The missus was hopping mad when she heard: 'You let those kiddies do what they likes! You'll 'ave us in the workhus yet!' She turned to the old lady. 'And you's as bad as im—sat there sayin nothin!' She was tired, you could see that. She wouldn't have told her mother off, else. She was tired and cross. 'What'll folks *think*?' she said.

Me and Widow Bayliss laid low. That was one thing we both saw eye to eye on. Where was the sense in fretting about what folks *thought* when you lived from meal to meal, like us, from one week to the next?

Sat'day night I washed their clothes ready for Sunday, washed their hair. All the girls had long hair—you can picture how long that took to dry! Else helped me get the babbies to bed. She was no more'n six or seven but she was a proper little help, and crafty: crafty at getting things, and crafty at getting out o' things if she wanted. She knowed how many beans made five. George was like the missus—everything had to be just so—but when I watched our Else I thought of myself at her age.

I told them tales and I sang to them:

> In my ole lavender trousers,
> I stole our little Sammy,
> Booked for two, got right through,
> Me and 'is dear Mammy.
> But oh, that kid when the guard came round,
> E got me pinched an fined a pound,
> For e poked 'is nose through a hole e found,
> In my ole lavender trousers!

They shrieked with laughter, jumped up and down. I had to sing that one again and again, do all the actions. They liked riddles too:

> Underwater, overwater,
> Never touches water!

'*What's that?*' they shouts.

> Egg in a duck's belly!

I told them: 'I was a-goin over Clopton Bridge when I meets a man—stick in 'is hand and stone in 'is throat!'

'*What's that?*'

'A cherry! E was holdin the stalk!'

I'd tell them anything to keep them quiet. We had a houseful! They got a bit out of hand sometimes, but not one of them knowed the weight o' mine. I never tapped them. The missus did that—with the slipper. She let them know who was boss.

She came home praps eleven at night, often later. Through the 'Shakespeare' yard she came, down Sheep Street, and we was waiting on the steps, the old lady too, to see what she'd got.

Sometimes in winter the hotel wouldn't get many guests and there was a lot o' food left over that wouldn't keep. Nothing was throwed away there! If Miss Justins, she owned the Shakespeare Hotel, seen a weesil in the ham when it was cut open—they was round the bone, little white things—she'd say: 'Take it to your children!' It weren't properly cured see, they bred.

The missus got dripping too, and bones. She was a good cook, she could make a few bones into a good stew. Well, it's the bones as has all the nourishment. She brought home enough stuff to keep us all.

If I'd been on parade she said to the kiddies: 'Afore I gives you anything—where's them sticks?' They'd gone dead quiet, they always did when she came. They was frit to say anything lest she wouldn't let them get a spoon into the dripping. It smelt lovely. But she *knowed* they'd been on the drum: 'Where's them sticks?'

She hid them, till the next time.

∉ CHAPTER TWELVE ∌

It was summer, hot summer, June. One of our neighbours on the street, he worked at the bike shop, he got me a *bike*! He got me this bike for the day—with a wickerwork trailer hooked on behind!

I thought: I'll go an see Nance!

I could ride a bike well. I put our Else and our Ede in the trailer and I took them to Leamington to see Nance and the Middletons. The folks waved us off. In summer you couldn't see yourself for the dust in Stratford. There was no tarmac then, it was all stone and sand. It used to blow! When it came a wind you'd be stood half way down Bridge Street and you couldn't see the Cross clock! The Corporation had a cart with piping all round the back, with holes in: they had to water the streets cos of the dust. The kiddies ran behind, letting the water fall on them, shouting and laughing.

On the way to Leamington we met a chap on a bike, going the other way. I'd got my jacket off, my sleeves rolled up, no hat on. He shouts: ''Avin a good time, ain't you?'

We met him again coming back. We was all sat down on the grass, up that hill. We'd had a blow-out at Nance's afore setting off—cake and jam! Eight o'clock, and it was still too hot for comfort. The two girls had been picking flowers; they was dying fast.

He said: 'You'll be comin again next Sunday shall you?'

'Not me!' I said.

He said: 'I thought it ud quank you!'

They was hefty little girls, they was fat uns, I can tell you. What tickled me was when they got back, back to Sheep Street, the folks was stood on the steps a-waiting for us to come back—our Else and our Ede waved their flowers and cried: 'Me Dad's 'ad a ride! Me Dad's 'ad a ride on a bike!' They weren't thinking they'd had a ride, in that trailer.

I'd lost three or four pounds—did I sweat! The flowers fell to bits.

The missus said: 'You want your brains examinin, you do.' She was smiling, more at the Whites'n me. The sight of me and the trailer struck them dumb for a minute—they stopped rowing. Mrs White used to shout, 'Bogey! Bogey!' He'd shout back, 'Baaa-baaa, Baaa-baaa,' like an old goat. They was always rowing, but they was fond of each other, good to our kids and they'd had a load of their own. They'd got a Mother and Dad living with them then, an Uncle and Aunt and fourteen kiddies, *three families*! Bogey used to get all the wreaths, the wreaths on the graves, he took them to the tip, stripped them and sold the flowers back to the florist. The ribbons on the wreaths he brought home for the kiddies. This night our Jess—the missus always kept her nice, she had pretty hair—was smothered in red and white ribbons, *looked* like a wreath! Else and Ede thought they'd been missing summat: 'What you got Mister White, what you got?' Sometimes he got so drunk he ran down the passage and rolled down the steps into Sheep Street.

Old Mac was there and all. He was a farm labourer. He was in

25. Cyclist, Bordon Hill. The spire of Stratford Parish Church can be seen above the trees.

his seventies, a single chap, he lived on our Court. He went cherry-minding in summer, kept the birds off with a clapper, frit the birds away.

'I see you's been a-cherry-mindin Mac,' I said. You could always tell: it was littered with cherry stones, all up that passage. But he didn't hear me—he was too drunk already! He'd be that drunk o' nights he'd get out of bed, open the window and clamber out onto the roof. Then one night he fell down; he fell from the roof into the ash tin. He never got over that.

The chap as worked in the bike shop, Walt Matthews, he said: 'It's come back this time then, George!' sarcastic-like. You see, I'd nearly had a scrap with him once. It happened like this.

The missus had a relation who worked at Hatton Asylum. He boiled the skulls, boiled the flesh off so's they could examine them. I told him: 'I couldn't do that job for a gold mine! 'Avin' a bloke lookin at me whiles I'm boilin im!'

Well, Walt Matthews weren't supposed to let bikes out for practice, and I didn't know this relation couldn't ride a bike. 'Do me a favour, Walt!' I said, and this chap who boiled skulls, his name was Constable, he sets off up the Warwick Road. 'You needn't come George!'

Well, he couldn't fetch the bike back, he lost his nerve *riding a bike*! The hours went by. Walt Matthews comes to our house.

'Don't time fly?' I said. 'As the monkey said when it throwed the clock out the winder!'

He didn't laugh. 'What's the game, George?'

It looked black.

'Come on—outside!'

And just then Constable wobbled into sight—it saved the day! Walt Matthews thought I'd pinched it.

Everybody pinched. You had to pinch to make up your money. Going to gaol, that was a risk you had to take. I was careful, I was getting to be crafty. I'd had some good lessons off my Grandad: he was the craftiest chap I knowed. You didn't pinch off neighbours, but the farmers, the shopkeepers, they could afford it! I was building their new houses for them: every modern fol-de-rol, 'no expense spared'—'cept on our pay! I never pinched nothing 'cept food and firing—and gillies. They'd grow anywhere, gillies, even on top o' the Vicar's wall. It was a big wall on Southern Lane. Springtime, me and Tommy Taylor climbed on each other's shoulders to pick them, armfuls o' gillies! And every springtime Emma put her face in them and had a bit of a cry. They minded her of Henson's farm, she said. Old Mrs Henson had vases and vases of them—scented velvet gillies—on the sills, on the table in the living room. It was nice, there, she said, and the tears plopped down like big drops o' rain. Well, I had to agree—I'd been better off afore I was wed! Then she started to get jealous. It was no use me saying I'd got no time for fornication, she didn't believe me.

*

And so it came to peapicking time.

You could always tell when it was peapicking time: the roadsters turned up. Gyppos, Irish, tramps, they had a round, see, they knowed where they could drop into work. They went to the same farmers every year; the farmers knowed the roadsters would be there, they was relying on them coming. And folks like us. We *all* went peapicking. It happened this June I was bricklaying for a farmer up Tiddington Road and he gave me and Tommy a whole field!

'Now,' he says, 'you an your labourer can 'ave this field for yourselves! Get em off for me while they's green!'

We said: 'Yes we will!'

We had a lamp, a hurricane lamp, and picked all night. We picked them off quicker'n he wanted them. It was a marvel how fast Tommy could work. Same as the bricks, he kept up with me, row by row.

'It's a funny thing,' I said. 'I was goin to give you a bastin once, at school. I must a-found summat better to do when I got out!'

He never said much, you never knowed what he thought about things most o' the time. Anyways, I did enough talking on the job for two!

Five pence a pot that farmer gave us.

But mostly they started picking at five o'clock, the men had, and

26. Peapicking

the roadsters. The Stratford women wouldn't come till breakfast time, when they'd seen the kiddies off to school. If you was hard up the kiddies came with you—the school never troubled at pea-picking time—it was more hands to pick. They was alright at picking till they started to *eat* the peas. If the kiddies started to eat them they was eating them all the time—same with me! The missus took the old wooden pram, up the Loxley Lane, a mile and a half with the little uns. They paid you as you picked them. She'd drag a pot o' peas up to be weighed, about forty pounds, and if she'd got any left over the bloke'd take them out and give her them to put in her apron for the next pot. If they was wet, if the dew was on them or the rain, they weighed more. She'd got a little hand-kerchief pinned here, she used to pull it over and feed the babby when she cried. Our Flo hadn't took to condensed milk. The missus had to cart her everywhere, leave her by the kitchen door at the 'Shakespeare'.

A Brummagem bloke was weighing the peas. It was a Brumm-agem dealer who'd bought the field, off the farmer, and then he had to pick them, give you fourpence or sixpence a pot. Well, this morning a farm chap comes by and he looks under the scales and he says: 'D'ye know what this devil's a-doin?' He said: 'E's gotta two pound weight on this side o' the scales!' After he'd done the weighing he was taking this two pounds o' peas out and selling some himself! The farm chap had twigged it! Oh, those women did half give that Brummie summat! They beat him up—they *chased* him! He never came again a-weighing!

The Stratford folks and the roadsters got on alright: the Stratford folks picked in their rows, the roadsters in theirs. It was a picture to see those roadsters a-picking, with their clay pipes and their black cans o' tea. They didn't mix. You had a row each; they'd give you a row, up the field, then you followed down the next row coming back. The last pot they was a-picking, the women tucked all the big uns down here, a boiling, a good boiling. They saved all the big uns for themselves, put the thin uns in the sack. By the end o' the day they'd got full aprons—and tits as big as turnips!

I came up to meet her. It happened I'd fell out o' work. We'd built one side o' the street—my gaffer was building houses for the Warwickshire Building Society—and we'd got to wait for permission to build t'other. She'd sat the babby in the pram. Our Jess was alongside, not so smart today—she'd been through a few hedges.

'Put er in too,' said the missus, 'an geroff!' She was in a raring hurry. She'd got to get back for the 'Shakespeare'. I hared down to the gate with the pram, with near two bags o' peas under them and a stone o' taters Jess had got from the next field.

'By God Mister, those babbies 'as ris in the pram!'

The missus went red. But the women knowed what she'd been up to: they'd all been at it!

The roadsters had no home to go back to. I felt sorry for them. They'd go to the one farmer, set up their tents, finish his peas, then he'd throw them off his land, he wouldn't let them stop once they'd finished, even for a night. They'd move on towards Evesham or Alcester, fruitpicking for another farmer.

Next day I took the missus a can o' tea in the field and the women said. 'Let im stop and 'elp you, Bertha!' Her name was Emily, but at this time o' day she'd got it into her head it was old-fashioned. She told folks to call her Bertha. So I did stop—and

I done well. I got so's I could pick ten pots a day! *Sixpence a pot!* It was good money. Sometimes me and the missus got parted, she was three or four rows away from me. The women had a bit o' fun.

'How d'ye like it, Cooky?'

'Alright,' I says. They called me Cooky cos I still roasted at the Mop. They always called me Cook Hewins.

'Come 'ere Cooky!' they said when we went to the pump to cool off. After three or four hours your fingers was a-burning and so was your throat!

''Ave you heared this un?' They'd tell some jokes!

'There's a little gal sat on the rug a-lookin at 'er Mam. She says: "Mother! What a lovely pussy you got!"'

They all laughed!

' "Yes," 'er Mam says, "your's'll be like that my dear when its catched the bloody mice mine 'as!"'

When we'd stopped laughing, I said: 'Well, listen to this then. Teacher in a school: "Now you've all heard me ask you questions. I wants you to ask *me* some!" A little kid jumps up and says: "Teacher, can you eat candles?" "Eat *candles?*" she says. "Whatever made you ask *that?*" "Well, me Dad says to me Mam last night "Blow out the candle an let's ave a bit."'

We had another good laugh. Well, they didn't have much fun, once they was wed.

*

The farmer was what they called a 'gentleman farmer', Arlington by name. He was a big cricketer, played for Warwickshire. I was helping load the peas up after they was picked when I heard him say to his man: 'You know a chap oo can do whitewashin?'

I says: ''Ere's a chap!'

So I went and done his house for him, up the Loxley lane. I went to my gaffer, John Roberts, and asked if I could borrow some trestles and ladders.

He said: 'George, e's a terrible payer—e won't pay you. E don't pay nobody till e's summonsed.'

So I didn't buy the stuff; I had the materials booked to him at the Stores.

I worked up there for a couple o' months, whitewashed his house, coloured it and papered it, painted it. On the day I was finished he comes to me and says: 'I see you's loadin your truck up.' He says: 'I'm a-goin to Brummagem. I've got a cricket match on today. I 'spect you'll be gone when I gets back.'

'That's it!' I thought. 'George Hewins—you're a bloody fool!' I thought what the missus would say when I got home.

He says: 'So 'ere's your money!'

I bust out laughing! 'I never thought o' gettin this!'

'No,' he says. 'I pays them as needs it and lets them wait as don't!'

He paid me afore I'd loaded the truck up!

But his servant! He had a servant, a pretty wench, but ignorant, silly, didn't know 'A' from a bull's foot. They was kept under, see, they was never allowed out the house weekdays, never saw nobody near their own age from one month to the next. After I'd finished at the farm she comes one night to Sheep Street and she knocks on the door.

'Is my painter boy in?'

The missus shouts: ''Ere, lover boy—you's wanted!'

When I got to the door the missus took hold of my neck, put her face out first.

This young girl says: 'You 'is mother then?'

The missus got my head and hers together—knocked them together! 'No I ain't! I'm 'is bloody wife!'

The poor girl went down the passage quick—quick!

Then of course we rowed. 'That's a nice game you've 'ad up there!'

'Well, the farmer's wife was allus at home!'

And that was the truth.

I seen the girl after, in Stratford, on a Sunday. She'd been to chapel. She said: 'Why didn't you tell me you was married? I shouldn't a-come!'

'Well,' I said, 'it can make no difference. Come on, let's catch hold of your arm, I'll take you home, up to the farm.'

It was a mile and a half up the Loxley lane.

*

In the summer the hedge bottoms was dry as a bone. It was green and private in there, wide as a cart. You could lie in the hedge bottom all afternoon and not be disturbed. I got to know all the hedges, where the best wood for sticking was, where there was money to be made from them, come Autumn.

Sometimes I weren't there first! We'd got a job at Wilmcote, and as we went through the fields to work, early morning about half-past five, this one hedge was crabs, masses o' crabs. The mists was rising.

We stood and watched, quiet, and the hedgehogs came out of their holes with their bristles shut. Those crabs as had fallen, they was going mella, yella, and the hedgehogs rolled over on them, stuck up their spines, picking up a load o' crabs—and back into the hole! Yes, they went a-crabbing! We stood and watched them; you wouldn't think they could *do* such things, would you? They shut their bristles and off came the crabs, and that way they got a stock for winter.

But the old fox was the craftiest. I could have touched him one day. I was building a wall round a rick-yard, and the hunt was on, at Pathlow. I'd just got the wall about that high and was a-laying, when this old fox they was a-chasing he came, he hit my trowel as he jumped over the wall! He got into the building. They didn't catch him. They lost the scent and *I* never said a word!

There was fields and fields o' mushrooms; bags o' them we could get. They weren't worth cutting hardly—a stack so high would only make twopence when you got them home to sell them. Then in the Autumn we went nutting for wood nuts, and slanning. Banbury Road was good for slans. The women and all went; we sold them to the liquor vaults to make sloe gin. And blackberrying. Blackberries didn't fetch much—but sometimes you was lucky. One day I'd just picked a twelvepound chip—I'd got them in about half an hour, like mulberries, ever such big uns—and a woman comes out of her house, on the Banbury road. 'They for sale?'

'Well, I got to get summat to live!'

She gave me a shilling!

At nights when it was dark we went rabbiting, up the Tram, and bat fowling. We got a big net on two poles, held the net to the

27. Blackberrying lane, Luddington, near Stratford-upon-Avon

hedge, with a torch, with a light. Some chaps went t'other side and beat the hedge and the birds flew into the net. We only kept the best, that we could sell; we'd got our customers. Bullfinches and piefinches fetched the most. Sparrers was chucked back again.

The farmers set traps—for us! I was never caught, but some of the farmers, folks said, they still set man-traps. They drove a big peg in the ground, see, wired the traps to them, else those poor devils as praps got one foot in it, they could struggle to pull it out. Ah! They used to drive the pegs in too firm!

We had some bad scares. We was building a new farmhouse, up The Hill. He'd just got his winter taters up. They had *buries*—buried them in a heap, covered them with straw, let the straw go through the top to let the heat out, then covered them all over with dirt. When we went home we never reckoned to go without summat in our flag baskets. It was pretty dusk then, it was Mop time, you could hear the Mop down in the town. We routed our hands in the bottom o' the bury, started to fill our baskets with taters. Then we seed somebody at the other end! We thought it was the farmer dogging us! We put all our taters back—quick! When we gets to the other end it was a woman!

She said: 'Oo, you put the wind up me!'

I said: 'Yes—and us! We've buried all our taters again, now!'

She said: 'I thought you was the farmer!' She'd tipped hers out too!

Not all the farmers was tight: some was good. They'd say: 'There's an orchard over there—if there's no windfalls, pick yourself some!' or he'd give you a swede. If the farmer was good he'd say to us—there might be eight of us at work on two new farm cottages—'You can 'ave that field for yourselves, you can 'ave all that grows there, mushrooms and all. But don't let me catch you in none o' the others!'

We promised him he wouldn't.

There was some excitement in the 'Oddfellows' on Election night! All my pals weared the yellow: Warwickshire was a regular Conservative stronghold. The missus said afore I went to vote—it was the first time:

'They got the money, the jobs. You put your cross in the right place,' she said, 'and keep that on!', meaning my rosette. I'd been switching from the yellow to the blue and back again, according. I couldn't make up my mind.

Well, she spoke the truth: Liberal or Conservative, members o' Parliament had got to be monied folks. They went for the honour, they had no pay, same as the Mayor. I reckoned it wouldn't make much difference to us *who* got in. I watched the donkey cart go past—one of them had got a bloke to go round the streets with a donkey cart and a giant loaf—'You wouldn't starve if *they* got in!' and I thought: 'None of em knows what bein hungry is—or poor.' How could they?

It was a hard winter and I was out o' work. I went to hear Kincaid Smith speak, for the Liberals.

'Very few cases,' he said, 'is heard of steady an reliable men in need of employment. Only those as works *regularly* should get relief when depression hits their trade!'

'Hear, hear!' folks cried. 'Down wi shirkers!'

I was stunned! Any fool knowed that in the building trade you was never in regular work! None of us was idle—you couldn't afford to be!—it all depended on the weather and if you could find a gaffer to take you on. A gaffer might have forty blokes working for him one week, cos it suited him, three or four the next. How could you *save*?

That's what we should a-been doing, Foster, the Conservative bloke said,—*saving!* I went to hear him speak too. If we'd been thrifty, he said, saved for a rainy day, we'd a-been alright! Some folks was cheering, waving their hats in the air! Well, I got the last laugh. It happened a gang o' pick-pockets from Brummagem came to town that day, and those as was well dressed they stripped them of everything of value: watches, pocket handkerchiefs, money! There was some long faces after the speechifying at those meetings; there was a panic, I can tell you.

They gave the results out Sat'day night. We streamed out the pubs into the High Street—I'd never seen such crowds since Lady-smith and Mafeking—folks seemed to sense summat was going to happen, summat different.

A man called Eccles, a photographer, he'd put a screen up to show the results. There was a rumour going around that every bloke in Stratford had voted—those as could vote, o' course. It was midnight nearly. Two brothers stood by the missus and me. One was Liberal, with the blue rosette, one was Conservative, with the yellow.

28. High Street, Stratford-upon-Avon *c*.1906, the Guild Chapel in the background—an unwitting study of privilege and poverty.

'E's waved!' he said. It looked as if Foster had won, and he turned to his brother as if to say: 'There! What d'you think o' that, then?'

They argued like hell, and then Kincaid Smith came up and he'd got in for the Liberals—by over one hundred votes! A Liberal in Stratford!

His brother said: 'What about *that*, then?'

The missus was upset. She believed in the Conservatives, you see, she thought voting for them was the right thing to do. The Liberals had won! It was a landslide—they'd swept the country! Kincaid Smith preened himself, strutted about. There was cheers and hisses, up in the air went hats and tempers. Little did we know he was already planning to change his coat!

How did I vote? I'll tell you one thing, those speeches set me wondering about politicians.

*

When the nights got longer we couldn't do much at home: it was too dark. If the washing was dry and the ironing done the old lady picked up the peg rug, did a bit o' that by the light of the fire, long as it lasted. Else and Ede was making lavender bottles, to sell. They used scrap ribbon from Bogey's wreaths, those bits as was no use for nothing else, twisted them in and out, in and out. George cleaned the shoes. A small lamp stood on the table, that's all—just a flicker. Paraffin cost money!

I said: 'Bet you—!'

It was a game I played with them—'Bet you er'll bring'—You had to think what your favourite food was. George said: 'A veal an ham patty from Gibbs'!'

Else said: '*Faggots!*'

And Ede said: 'Cheese!'

You'd a-thought she'd be sick o' cheese! I'd sent her one day to the strap shop for a pennoth o' this and a pennoth o' that and they gave her a big lump o' cheese! Now our Ede never could resist cheese, she was worse'n a mouse.

She thought: I'll have a bit.

But just as she turned up our passage, a-nibbling at the edges, she fancied she seen her Mam, come home early! She panicked!

She crammed the whole lot into her mouth, gave a swallow—and it stuck there!

Else runs in. 'Our Dad! Our Ede's chokin to death!' And she very nearly did. I shoved her under the pump, tried to swill the cheese down her throat.

You'll gather from this it was one commotion after another. One night I was on parade, and the little un knocked the lamp over. That time nobody was burnt: their Granny put it out. On dark nights, soon as the missus came home, we went to bed. That way, you might think, we saved *more* trouble! But that's how folks like us got so many babbies:

> The night is long
> The sheets is short
> So cuddle up
> Me darlin . . .

You couldn't read the *Herald*, there was no lighting for football matches. There was nowhere to go, Sat'day night, only the pub. More folks drank. Well, it was cheaper: eight pints o' mixed beer for a shilling, three ha'pence a pint, a pint o' the 'Oddfellows' rhubarb wine for threepence. Two pennoth o' stout the ladies had, or gin. The 'Oddfellows' in Mansell Street, that's where me and my pals went, it was a home-brewed house. Billy and Teddy Eborall kept it, their father and mother afore them. The old man had drownded himself. He went in his apron up to the canal and he stood in it. It weren't high enough to drown in so he sat down. The Eborall lads both played football, and the Captain of our team, Bertie Edge, he lived round the corner, visited the 'Oddfellows'. It weren't really the beer, you see—it was wholesome and not so strong—you went to the pub for the company, to see your pals, for enjoyment.

The 'Oddfellows' had a pianna, it was well lit up and it was always warm and snug. There was sawdust along by the counter for you to spit your baccy in, and a footrail to put your feet on. We used to have a Dividend Club, paid a bob or tanner in when we was in work, what we could afford, had it out at Christmas. It was a help—one year I got more'n a *pound*!

When I walked in Sat'day night folks cried: ' 'Ere's George! E'll liven things up, e'll give us a song!'

Soon as I got in Billy Eborall drawed me a pint. It got him custom, see. If there was no singing, if there was no enjoyment, they'd go where there was! Chaps didn't go to the pub to talk o' work, no more the women of washing and dollying—they wanted to laugh about it!

> Now I'm a very handy man,
> To save a bit ups my plan.
> Last week I said to my wife,
> Our yard wants a wash,
> Upon my life.
> I'll go and I'll do that job,
> And I did so help me Bob,
> Made a pail o' whitewash,
> Set to work,
> The ole woman helped me
> Like a Turk.
> Slap-dab, slap-dab, up and down the brickwork,
> Slab-dab all day long . . .
>
> Now the missus I must now confess,
> She put me in an ole nightdress.
> A nightcap too she made me wear,
> She was dressed like me,
> So we looked a pair.
> And she held the pail so high,
> That I made the whitewash fly,
> Every now and then
> I could hear a squawl,
> I was takin the ole woman's face
> For the wall . . .

He locked the door when he'd got the room-full. It was packed, full o' smoke—some of them had clay pipes—enough to choke you! When the missus comes in, she'd been working, she said: 'I never heard such a row in all my life! Like a load o' cats a-squawlin!'

'Ullo missus,' Billy says to her. 'You'll 'ave a gin?'

'I will, thank you Mister Eborall,' she says. 'A-standin outside and listenin 'as got on me nerves!'

They laughed! But I could sing!

> Muffins an pikelets for tea,
> I never thought she'd a-sold me.
> While I was tryin to turn in a bob
> She would be 'avin a spree—
> And some other fella ud be on the job,
> 'Avin muffins an pikelets for tea!

The women started to cough. 'Uuuugh! Uuuugh!'

Somebody said: 'That's stopped the singin! Let's open the window!'

'I don't care what you says,' I said, 'wives *will* fall! They'll see somebody they likes better. Allus has been and it allus will be.'

And while the chaps was a-thinkin 'Ah, those two *is* a bit thick! I can see that!' I started up with the *Vacant Chair*. It's a good un for tears—

> There stands a chair, a vacant chair,
> The joy of once my life sat there.
> Twas my young wife, my all in all,
> Oo now is gone beyond recall.
> I see er now in mother's joy,
> Beamin o'er our baby boy.
> But alas! Death came an all things fled,
> An left me wi an empty bed—

The women joined in the chorus, they knowed all the songs, but they liked the sentimentals best. I said: 'The chap as learnt me that lost 'is voice.'

There weren't a dry eye in the house! But when I sings—

> We never speak as we pass by,
> Although a tear is in 'er eye.
> I know she thinks of 'er past life,
> When we was lovin man an wife.
>
> —And to the workhus door they went,
> Each one a different way was sent.

It's very hard all through this life,
To part a poor ole man an wife!

—they was a-shouting, men and women, one voice: 'Shut up! We don't want to 'ear *that*!'

They all knowed somebody in the workhouse.

I had as much beer as I wanted, I didn't buy none, and on Sunday morning when I went in he said: 'Go on! 'Ave that on me! I done well last night!'

*

One dark Sunday night there was a hammering on our door. 'Our Dad! It's somebody says she's our Gran!'

I went and there she was, like snow at harvest—my mother.

'Oh,' I said.

' 'Ave you gotta saw, son?'

A *saw*? I was thinking fast. I knowed we had to take her in. Well, she was my mother. Where would we put her? We was busting at the seams already. The missus would murder me! 'It's a poor hen as can't scrat for one chick.' That's what she thought of her.

But when my mother said: 'Er's gone to church!' I knowed she meant Cal. She'd gone to Cal's! Cal had took her in! It was a relief, I can tell you. Then I had a nasty feeling about that saw. 'What you done wi *im*?'

'E's restin!' she said, 'at the "Rose an Crown".' A make-believe look came over her face: it was the thing I remembered most about her. My heart sank.

'Well, never you mind. Come in for a bit, 'ave a warm!'

The kiddies stared: they didn't know her, neither did the missus. But they moved up, round the fire, made room. And so my mother told us her story.

'We've been living in a big new house in Brummagem! Our own house! Lovely it was,' she said—the kiddies was round-eyed—'with 'ot water come out a tap, servants . . . But we reckoned the air ud be better in the country, for *im*.'

Once upon a time, I thought, I would a-believed this tale. He was a good craftsman, Joshua Farr, I'd seen his work about the town, but he was a drunkard and times was bad in the building trade, even for chaps as stayed sober. He'd fell out o' work—why didn't she say so? She lived in a dream; my mother had lived in a dream all her life.

'Stratford,' she said, 'will suit us nicely just at present.'

'Huh,' said the missus. But I gave her a nudge and she never said no more, she let my mother whittle on about the big house in Brummagem and the servants and how they'd lived in the lap o' luxury. Emma knowed and I knowed what it must a-been like. If my mother wanted to make things seem better'n they really was, if she'd sooner have a dream than a nightmare, well, why shouldn't she? Who could blame her, wanting the sun to shine both sides o' the hedge?

'We've brought a bit o' stuff with us. A friend was lookin after it for us—e said er'd pinch it but er never—and a clock!' She said: 'You can 'ave it if you like, son. It goes.' Emma's eyes lit up. After a pianna it was the thing she wanted most in the world. The kiddies was always asking the time off folks in the street.

I thought: We better get that clock quick, or it'll end up at Dirty Ole Styles'! I said: 'Well, we could do wi it. What d'you want a saw for?'

The missus cut in. 'Our Else, go an fetch a bottle o' stout from Mister Thorpe. You can go an all, Ede.' George was old enough to keep his mouth shut. 'I'll be checkin on the label!'

That was a warning to our Else. Sometimes when she went for her Mam's stout she lifted the label and had a swig. Well, this night the girls pulled faces. They didn't want to go—it was cold outside, and they was frit of missing summat—but they knowed what they'd cop if they didn't!

My mother went on: 'There's an 'ole I know of be'ind the counter in the shop—and er's gone out!'

Then I knowed why she wanted the saw!

'For a minute there I thought—' What I was going to say was I thought she'd done him in. I could see the missus had thought the same.

I said: '*Ask* er for some money. Er'll give it you!'

'I daresn't. We've had plenty. Asides, I can't get round er like

146

you can. They tells me you's the favourite there!' She sighed. Well, when all was said and done she was my mother, though a pretty poor job she'd made of it. I knowed she wouldn't a-come to see me then if she hadn't wanted summat.

'For you,' I said, 'I'll do it.'

We tiptoed up Cal's passage—she'd got the key—into the front shop.

'Cut this piece o' board out for us, son.' I did, and lo and behold there was gold sovereigns underneath—all *gold sovereigns*, no halves! I whistled, low. She gave me one—well, I should a-been a mug to let her have it all and I'd done the work, a-sawing!—she had some herself, then we put the board back, and some dust on it, made it look as if it hadn't been moved.

But Cal was crafty, crafty as can be. She found out. How? That was her secret. I was up to most of her tricks. She kept her silver and her odd change in a leather bag up the chimney. The sovereigns she laid in rows, one just over the other, so's she could tell if they'd been disturbed. I'd been careful—but she guessed! Every week I went round to attend to old Bill Cook's feet, cut his toe nails. Cal said: 'You's as bad as er!'

I went hot and cold. I should a-known she'd guess! But the neighbours was right when they told my mother I was Cal's weak spot. All she said was: 'My lad, I've allus liked you—but you've one fault! You ain't greedy enough! Now go and get us two pennoth in this!'

She was a terror for gin. In my life I'd fetched her many a gallon. I took her blue bottle and I said to the chap at the liquor vaults at the 'Mulberry Tree', bottom o' Bridge Street: 'Put a *tannersworth* in!'

Never mind if the missus gave me a tongue banging; I'd done a dirty trick on Cal and I wanted to make it up to her. I knowed it only took a tanner to get her dancing!

'I got you an extra drop from that nice chap oo's single!'

Sure enough, she staggered a bit, then she began to dance! Round and round the clothes shop she went, up and down. I takes hold of an old jacket and I starts dancing too. 'E's a good chap, ain't e, to give you a bottleful like that! It ud cost sixpence!'

I thought: It *has*! I said: 'E *is*! And he likes you! I told im: "It's not the drink, it's not the rouge—it's 'er own rosy complexion".'

She was three parts and out o' puff. 'Now do you want any money?' I shook my head.

'I should think you do wi a family like that! Put your 'and up! 'Elp yourself, 'ave what you like. Don't let them kiddies go wi'out!' I took about six shillings from the bag up the chimney.

But the kiddies was frit of her. It upset me but I couldn't do nothing about it. Folks gossiped—their Mam did. Sunday afternoons when the work was done, the women sat on a bench in the Bancroft and gossiped. The kiddies picked things up. They thought Cal was a witch in her long black frock and her black bonnet. When they was playing on the 'croft she'd come out a-shouting, 'Little Hewins! Little Hewins! Come an get my paraffin!' They hid in the bushes, snook off home. 'Go and get it,' I said. 'Maybe er'll give you a penny.' She never did! or 'Er's not a bad ole soul.'

Every babby that was born I'd took them down to Cal's, and she'd give them a sovereign and their first shawl, a big long shawl. All of them had a shawl off Cal.

She wanted them to trot all over town for her. The neighbours helped too—well, they'd get their vegetables then, for nowt. But our Ede copped it most:

'Granny Cook says, "If they ain't got this bring that—if they ain't got that bring this!" '

'Er's old,' I said. Yes, I thought, Cal is getting old at last.

The missus, she said nothing. They never did get on.

Ede went for a pint o' paraffin in a can. It was teeming with rain. She slipped and dropped it and the top came off, spilt some of it. Just like a kid, she held it under a spout running from the wet fish shop, so's Cal wouldn't find out from the weight. When Cal filled the lamp it didn't half splutter!

'Where she get that oil from? Tell Tinker Freeman e could a-set the place on fire!'

'P'raps the wick wants trimmin,' I said.

Our Ede was terrified. 'Er'll put a spell on me!' she said.

I turned on her. 'Don't let me ever,' I said, '*ever* catch you sayin that again.'

She was shocked. I never told them off, as a rule.

*

The errands fell on Ede cos looking after the little uns fell more and more on Else. Mop night the missus was waiting for our Else to come home so's we could go. I'd been roasting the beast with my Grandad. Happy had died the winter afore—he'd gone and left my aunt with five more kiddies—and the old man got so's he relied on me and Will Blackford to do it. When I saw Will I thought: Yes, and I'd still be a labourer an all if I'd stopped with im. About seven we sawed the backbone off. 'That's for your Granny,' my Grandad said. He still bossed us about! 'And that's your piece—that's for you.'

I had two towels. I twigged which was his wife's and I changed them round. I'd told the missus: 'Now 'bout quarter past seven I'll 'ave the backbone. Be ready in the High Street!'

She was stood there; she'd got the evening free, for the Mop. I said: ''Ere's your'n!' and off she went with it. I left the other piece at Ely Street. When I gets home the kiddies was still picking.

The missus said: 'Leave some for your Dad!'

I said: 'No! I don't want no more—I'm full as a tick!' Whiles we was a-roasting I'd ate till I couldn't! What was left would be stewed up next day.

And at that moment in strolls our Else, mouth full o' mop rock. I'd given them a ha'penny pocket money. She'd forgot the time: she was supposed to be back at half-past eight. Well, she was only a kiddie.

'I'll tan the hide off er,' the missus muttered.

Else saw the situation too late; she froze. The missus got the hairbrush, I tried to stop her—and that's when the trouble began!

'It's alright for *you*!' she said—did our Else get a lamming!—'Sayin you won't tan em! *Somebody's* got to!'

She was half in a temper. Else was howling; the little uns whimpered, hid behind me. They didn't like to see Else beat. Why did her Mam do it? She was looking forward to going to the Mop, see, getting away from work and from all of them. It was her big treat. All the year round she looked forward to it.

29. Mop Fair, Stratford-upon-Avon, 1912

There was the ox-roasts and the pig-roasts, music and there was lots o' shows. One booth had in front 'PAINLESS EXTRACTION!' Folks was standing and watching this bloke having his teeth pulled out. He grinned and said, 'No! I never felt nothin!' Then those as had bad teeth went up to have them out. There weren't no dentists in those days, not for folks with no money. We watched a strong man lifting weights and tack. Then we went to the boxing booth. They offered a *pound* to anybody who could do five rounds with their bloke. Harry Bayliss, the missus' brother—he'd been discharged from the army and he worked in the brickyard now—*he* went on. He was a big chap, her brother, very tall, five foot ten or eleven! His pals was there, egging him on. The missus stood with clenched fists. Well, Harry did well, but he never did get the pound. But they came unstuck! They copped a boxer! The next chap up, he was from Stratford—an ordinary labouring chap—and he knocked their bloke out in one! We cheered and cheered!

Some of the shows was very rude. The coppers went round with the Town Councillors to inspect those they thought was vulgar. They came out laughing! At Mop-time the coppers was one of you. They joined in the sport, throwed confetti at us. 'Come an see me bare cock an arse!' one bloke was a-shouting. We fell for it—everybody did! Inside he'd got a bear, a donkey and an old cockerel!

Folks came out: 'We've been had!' But they soon fell a-laughing too!

*

The next one to die after Happy was old Bill Cook.

'They're startin to drop,' said the missus.

Poor Bill Cook, nobody noticed him much when he was alive and nobody noticed him die. Cal had always acted like a widow, dressed like one. But if folks could see no difference, Cal did! Now she was a *real* widow she made the most of it! She had everything that was going. 'My Lad, let me tell you, if you wants to beg, beg whiles you gotta crust in your pocket. It's no use beggin when you ain't—you won't get nothin!'

I went down every Sunday and sat on her bed while she went to church. She didn't trust my mother: 'Not while *e*'s alive,' she said. I locked the house up and I sat on the bed to mind the money. She'd got bags of it! It was hidden all over: under the mattress, between the sheets, little dabs, and a big box under the bed.

She'd got to be a regular churchgoer. She sat in the front row. She always sat under the Vicar so's he could see her, to get the Big Loaf. They doled out the Big Loaf to the widows as was poor. Now when old Arbuthnot retired, the new Vicar, Canon Melville, he had the idea of all the posh folks being at the front, with brass nameplates, his family in the front row. But Cal went on sitting where she was, in her old fashioned tats and her black bonnet. The Vicar couldn't shift her. Mrs. Melville tried. The Church Wardens had a go, so did half the congregation.

'Nobody's goin to shift me,' she said.

And in the end the Vicar said, 'Let er stop,' and he sent round a hundred-weight o' coal.

'Look!' said the neighbours. 'Er's gettin it!' meaning free coal. Cal just laughed.

Soon after Cal became a real widow, Joshua Farr was found dead in bed. He must a-died in his sleep, Cal said, and if it seemed a mysterious thing for a bloke to do, well, all I can say is, I've heard o' more mysterious things than that in my life. I shed no tears. I'd never had a kind word from him, only cusses. I dare say he had his good points, hopes and fears like other folks; he never shared them with me.

Both his brothers came to the funeral. My mother told me one was an Archdeacon, one was a Captain on a vessel. I couldn't go, she said, I had to stop away, cos they didn't know I was *alive*! But I went up at night after the brothers had gone. He was buried just inside the cemetery, it was a bought grave; he was the only one I knowed as went in one.

Back at Pimms Court my mother was a-sobbing. 'What'll I do? I can't manage on me own. What'll 'appen to me?'

The missus glared at her. I knowed what she was thinking: You ain't stoppin 'ere!

My mother said: 'Bring us two pennoth, son!'

She'd loved him—well she'd left me for him, hadn't she? I went and sat by her, gave her a bit o' comfort. She gave me a pound or two; it went a long way then, a pound or two! And she gave me his tools, little tools they was, like knitting pins.

'Look—I polished em up!'

Our Jess spread them out on the table—she liked bright things— played with them for a while till she lost interest.

'They done the bee-hive on Lloyds Bank,' my mother said, 'and the carvin on the Theatre. E worked in a top 'at you know.' And she starts sobbing again.

I thought: I could ask her now about me Dad, me *real* Dad. And then I thought: What does it signify? The Lord Mayor o' Brummagem is good enough for me!

Next morning I sold his tools to the stone yard in Guild Street.

Cal took care of her, but my mother never got over it. She ailed. Sometimes she cried out aloud: she must a-been in pain, the row she made. The doctor said she'd got tumours in both knees. He shook his head, 'She's been scrubbin,' he said, 'scrubbin hard—for years, I'd say. And she ain't got the constitution.'

Cal paid for her to have the tumours took out, but it left her a cripple, afterwards, with crutches. She growed thinner and thinner, got to be a bed case at Cal's. She whined and mewed like a drowning kitten. She just gave up. Very soon everybody but Cal lost patience with her. Life, as folks said, had to go on. Emmie Hewins had seemed to think it would stop, for her, that she was somebody special.

CHAPTER FOURTEEN

The missus came home one night from the 'Shakespeare', no basin, no nothing, and she said: 'I've got the sack!'

Our faces fell. 'What you done?'

'It's all on account o' that hearse!'

The hearse stood waiting for the folks with money in a big shed in the 'Shakespeare' yard. Black plumes the horses as pulled it wore, and the minute bell tolled.

'I catched May Twiney an a chap doin it in the hearse!'

In the *hearse*! We couldn't believe it!

'Well, in the hearse they was a-laying!' she said. You could see her dander was up. 'I'd half a mind to shut the door on em, lock em in! I never seed a sight like it in my life! In the hearse!'

I laughed. 'You wouldn't a-got me in there, if it 'ad been the Queen as wanted to go wi me!'

The kiddies giggled.

'Ow come that you got the sack?' May Twiney worked in the kitchen at the 'Shakespeare' but she was an old bag.

'I rowed wi er,' said the missus. She blushed, went red to her roots. 'It come to blows. Any road, I'd 'ave 'ad to a-gone. I'm in the fashion again.'

Two year breeders is never done. It was true! The next un was a lad. He came out fighting—you couldn't help but laugh! Granny Sutton said: 'This un'll be a boxer! Mark my words!'

I said: 'We'll call im after Jimmy Curran'.

The missus put in, quick: 'E's goin to be christened Reginald.' *Reginald!* That's a nice name to go to bed with! I thought: Reginald e may be, but Jim I'll call im.

But when she went and called the next un *Cyril* I thought: I give up! She always wanted to be different, you see, for us to *get on*. I could see no advantage in it. We was all in the same boat, we helped one another when we could. What was the point of trying to swim off on your own?

*

One day when our Jim was a-walking and Cyril in arms her mother said: 'It's time I went, Emm. There ain't enough room.'

We all knowed that. There was six in the bed next door now, with an old blanket hanging down the middle to separate the boys from the girls. Our George was nearly grown: soon he'd have to move in with us.

'We'll manage some'ow Mother!' I'd never seen her so cut up. 'Asides, it's your house!'

'So long as you keeps us out the workhus,' says Widow Bayliss, 'I'll be alright. There's plenty o' floors in Stratford,' she says, 'wants scrubbin.'

They'd just started to give out old age pensions, but she didn't qualify. You had to be seventy—*seventy!* A friend of hers tried to get it, altered her birth certificate. 'Course, she made a codge and modge of it. They found out, took her to court. 'You's lucky,' they said, 'we ain't sending you to gaol on account of your health!' Cal didn't get it neither, it was the only thing she never got. I reckon one of the neighbours ratted, told them she'd *been* to gaol!

When her mother said it was time for her to go, Emma bust into tears: she knowed she was right. And so we found her cheap lodgings with some other old ladies, up Taskers Passage. She went on charring, and the kiddies took her dinner round of a Sunday, ran up Sheep Street with it, along the High Street and round the corner, first slice and all. I missed her, and the kiddies did, but Emma missed her most of all. Many a night she'd be sobbing into the pillow, so's the kiddies couldn't hear. I lit the candle.

'Cheer up! And never mind about im!' I said, meaning Cyril. He was in bed with us, wanting a suck. I put my arms round her. 'Er's *nearby*. Er wanted to go—it was 'er idea. Now listen to this! John Roberts 'as given me a *character*! You knows the chief clerk at the Post Office? Well, e's gone to live in one of those Building Society houses we built.'

Yes, I thought, that's what we could a-done with. They was

lovely houses: they'd got four rooms and a scullery! I smiled to myself. There was more chance of us going to live on the moon! 'Well, when John Roberts lays me off today e says: "I seen Arden the clerk, I asked im ow e was settlin in?" "The Post Office wants some chaps wi good character, Johnny, for the Christmas mail, the rush." Arden the clerk e says to John Roberts: "Could you recommend a chap?" And John Roberts says: "I can." So e writ my character out and 'ere it is.'

I unfolded it for her to see. She started to show a bit of interest, leant towards the candle.

George Hewins as been at work for me off and on ten years or more and I can highly recommend im in every respect.
Signed: John Roberts

'Well,' said the missus, but she sounded pleased. 'Well!'
'So things ain't so bad, is they?'

*

I got the job—and I did well! I had a Post Office bike, painted red, and an armband—GPO in red letters—you buckled it. I never knowed where they was going to put me. If there was a postman ill, like on the Snitterfield round, they'd send me *there*, cos I knowed it. I did Clifford, took the bike an hour round Clifford, delivered all round Welford. It took me from seven in the morning, a Sunday morning, till eleven: a *shilling*! Ninepence to Goldicote, a bob to Bishopton, a bob to Snitterfield. I done all those rounds.

The lanes was rough. You had to pick your way. There was pebbles, great big pebbles. I was biking on one round and they'd been at mangel carts—the mangels they give to the cattle, big uns, like a football. One fetched me off, bruised all my face. And no matter what the weather, you'd got to go with the letters!

There was a house at Bishopton, just on the canal bank. I used to do Bishopton sometimes and the missus there would lock the front door and the back door, take the key out. The wenches opened the window—she'd forgot that!—and hauled me in, into the kitchen, for a bite and a sup. I was dressed well, trimmed up well, with a collar and a tie on! Well, I used to get a paper front and a collar for a penny.

You buttoned it on—a white front! It was worth it, the stuff I picked up, one way and another, on account o' that white front.

Sometimes I had a load of parcels to deliver. I followed the daily postman up to Goldicote with a great stack o' them—ninepence. That's about four mile from Stratford. At Goldicote House, I delivered there—the manservant used to keep me all the chicken carcasses, cos I'd told him I was married with a family. I said, hang dog: 'Ain't there a Christmas box for me?'

'The daily postman's 'ad that. But—you's a smart chap!—I'll give you summat! Wait there!' He was gone a long time, and when he comes back he was hiccuping! 'Here y'are!' he said, and he gave me half a bottle o' spirits! I drank some of it on the road, biking down to Coombe Farm. It was a rough path but I floated the last twenty yards or so. Sure enough, there was the farmer's daughter, waiting for me. She was a little minx. 'Right as the mail!' she said, and laughed. She used to write to herself so's I could deliver it. We had a cuddle in the passage.

'You needn't give us *that*!' she says. 'I wrote it—rip it up!' She smiled at me. The look said, 'They's not about so let's get on wi it!' She starts to unbutton her blouse. I had a peek and then I said: 'Blimey, I gotta get on!'

At Clifford where the Stour runs there was a big house. He was auctioneer at the Sale Yard; Barnard was his name. Well, what should I see when I gets to his letter box but two wenches in their shifts, waving to me from a window. I thought: 'These paper fronts 'ave amazin powers!'

They said: 'If you 'ave any letters for us don't put em in the box, put your hand up an we'll come!'

So they did. And I said: 'Why do you want this done?'

They said: 'The missus don't let us 'ave it for *days*!'

On Sundays they gave me a glass o' whisky when I got there, just after seven. They put the glass round the door; they was still in their shifts. I drank it up, wiped my mouth. There was a bit o' giggling going on. I could see bare pink toes on the tiles. I always said: 'Where's the missus then?' This Sunday, another half draught o' whisky comes round the door. It was my lucky day!

I said: 'Is the missus a-bed?'

'She's 'ere!' they cried.

I shall never forget it. It's a wonder I hadn't fainted! The missus opened the door and said: 'Drink your whisky all the same!' She said: 'Why do you do this?'

I said: 'Well, they told me you kept the letters.'

That done the whisky stunt o' course, but I reckon they got their letters on time from then on.

When I got home the missus said: 'Serve you damn well right!' But she had to laugh.

That winter the weather changed, got worse and worse, rain and wind. I was behind on my rounds. A farm chap shouts: 'There's a big flood at Clifford Mill!'

But however fast I pushed those pedals, however fast I wanted to go, I had to stop to empty all those little letter boxes on the gates—you know, that went to the farms, by the road. It was pitch black when I neared Clifford Mill. All the road was covered in water; I could sense it stretching on all sides for a hundred yards or more. There was only a little oil lamp on my bike. I thought: If I loses my direction, if I gets off this hard road into that river, under the bridge there, I shall be drownded. I could feel it rising. It was up to my knees. When I got to the dip, to empty the letter box at Barnard's, it was wet over the saddle. I was soaked in water. My paper front had fell off, my hair was plastered over my face. If those wenches could see me now! I vowed: 'This is the last time I shall come this way!'

I was three hours late, getting home. I said, 'I'm finished!' Asides, Walt Bailey had said he had a special job for me. Even Walt Bailey's idea of a special job was better'n this!

*

'It's a *pole*,' he said, 'needs carryin across town.' It was a pole and a half—a flag pole, fifty foot long! I thought: Where's e got this from? I'd got the butt end. We was going up the passage to his yard.

'Go on!' he says, looking about him. ''Urry up!'

And I shoved it off, the butt end. I couldn't a-bear anybody telling me to go fast. I worked hard; I reckoned that should be

enough, for anybody's money. Well, me letting go of this flag pole
bent the thin end and it hit him in the shoulder.

He said: 'You done that a-purpose!'

I said: 'I didn't.'

'Yes you did!'

'Alright, I'm off home!'

'Come back, Georgie!' he cried.

I thought: No.

*

Who should I bump into but Mr Doonan the postmaster. 'Ullo
George! Could you manage time off for the day?'

I tried not to look too keen.

'Somebody's gettin wed at Clopton House, the Reverend Hodgson's.'

I said: 'What's it a telegram?'

He said: '*Sixpence!*'

I couldn't believe my luck: they was nobility, there was *bound* to
be a lot o' telegrams! So—I runned backwards and forwards, backwards and forwards, from the Post Office in Sheep Street to Clopton House, back down to Stratford, up again to Clopton. I must
a-runned about eighteen miles that day.

Then Doonan says to me: 'Our caretaker's packed up. Would
you like to take the job till you starts work again?'

I said: 'Yes, I would!'

I took the job on, sweeping the Post Office up. I took the keys
home with me at night, the front door keys, and unlocked it early
morning, did all the cleaning and the dusting and the polishing.
The first morning I was there I was a-dusting where they stood to
write telegrams out. There was a bank note under the wadding.

I said to myself: The bugger! Well, I shan't 'ave it!

I went to the postmaster and I said: 'There was this bank note
under the waddin pad.'

'Oh!' he said. 'Somebody's writ a telegram an left it be'ind!
They'll come back for it, sure to.'

That's all he'd say. There never was another. They set all sorts
o' traps for you, at that time o' day.

They got me doing the last train. They took the truck up for me and I walked to the station and fetched a truckload back, about eight bags o' mail. If anybody got off at Stratford, a couple for the weeksend and the bloke said with a wink—'Could you recommend me to a hotel?' I directed them to the 'Shakespeare'. 'Just ask for Miss Justins. Er's very obligin.'

One night it was past twelve afore the train came. The next day I seen the copper. He says: 'Late last night, weren't you?'

I says: 'Ah. The train were late—where was you?'

He says: 'We watched you unlock the Post Office, put your bags in, put the keys through the letter box!'

'Well,' I said, 'I'm more happy now I *knows* I'm being watched—cos I used to get nervy, unlocking that gate,' I said, 'and goin right up that back. That's relieved me a good lot, I can tell you.'

'Ah,' he says, 'we watches!'

*

Well, it paid for the Christmas joint! We'd only got a Dutch oven, a three-penny tin affair. It stood on a couple o' bricks. The meat hanged from a hook and a tray at the bottom caught the dripping. It weren't big enough for the Christmas joint so I took it to the baker's. His name was Tyler, down by the East and West Station, College Street. I put a towel over our meat, wrote my name on the tin: HEWINS. About half-past twelve I went to fetch it—twenty or thirty folks was there! Tyler charged three ha'pence for cooking it. It was about a quarter of an hour's walk home—but I ran!

After Christmas, when the bad weather set in, we sent the kiddies for free breakfasts, afore school. Mr Pearce the jeweller organized them, in Wood Street, Derry's Room, for those whose Dads was out o' work. They went there about eight o'clock, between forty and sixty of them, and they got bread and dripping, as much as they could cram down them, and a hot drink. It had to last! Our Ede looked that hungry by the afternoon the teacher told her to stay behind. 'Sit down!' And she gave her a piece o' cake. 'Mind you don't leave no crumbs!' she said.

They was too famished to learn much. After school, to make a few pence, they got wood from the timber yard and went round

Stratford selling sticks, to anybody who wanted firewood. They did little jobs, like folks' steps, for a piece o' cake or pudding—they got a bit o' sandstone off the gravemaker. If the chem boats was in they went down to the canal. The chem boats stopped at Brummagem Road, at Kendall's, the brewery chemists. They dropped the hooks to pick up the sacks—and the chaps would chuck the stuff to the kiddies, from the boats. They loved it—I did too! It looked like Cotswold stone, dead hard. You gnawed it with your teeth. Sat'day mornings, our George did the knives and our Else went all day to Mrs Baum's, to help with the washing up and cleaning, for sixpence. Mrs Baum kept a grocer's shop on Wood Street. She was a Baptist; they had their Sunday dinner on a Sat'day, and dinner lasted till three o'clock. She was kind. She gave our Else tea and some days there was a roll of old carpet, a rug or a loaf to bring home! Our Ede went tater picking, up the Loxley lane.

I went eel fishing. Me and some other chaps set eel-ties at night in the river, opposite the church. We sat quiet a-watching the ties, to see if they went. We laid them on the bed o' the river, in the mud. You could tell when an eel had got it: it pulled your line. And then there was a struggle! We sold most of them to the neighbours: eels make a nourishing stew, just pop some parsley in with them. There was an old couple lived across the street. The missus would say, could she have a bit o' their parsley?

'Elp yourself, Emm!' they said.

It's a queer plant, parsley: 'sow on Good Friday, seven times down to Hell afore it chits.' These two growed lovely parsley; it went to show, folks said, what a God-fearing old couple they was.

But d'you know, the length o' the field away, over the field where we was a-fishing, there was a pond. And that night more eels crawled out of the pond than ever we caught with the ties! We smashed them on the head, clubbed them to death as they crawled from that pond across the field, towards the river. It was a slaughter. Poor buggers! I never went no more. I told the missus the eels had gone. She gave me a funny look. 'They tell me er's a-dyin.'

'Oo?'

30. The River
Restaurant (formerly
Cal Cook's cottage)
*c.*1912

Suddenly I knowed from her face she meant Cal. I rushed out, down our passage, down the street. One of the old chaps let me in. That was a bad sign. My heart was thumping. She was in bed—at this time o' day!—eyes shut, breathing heavy. 'What's up wi er?'

He shook his head. 'Old age,' he said, 'old age.'

I went and sat by her.

'I'll be raisin my price!' she muttered. She never said no more. I hardly dared look. A *tannersworth*! I thought. That'll cheer er up! Other folks might die—but not Cal. Cal *couldn't* die!

But she did. When Cal lay a-dying in the shop the Guardians took my mother to the workhouse; there was no room for her with us. Most of the old chaps went in too; it was the end o' the line for them. Granny Sutton laid her out. I heard her coffin talking with the missus and one o' the neighbours: 'Ah! Er *bust*! I' ad to sew er up in a bag.'

She had a quiet funeral. Well, now I'll tell you what I never told nobody else till this minute: she had a pauper's funeral. They pulled her along to the Parish Church on a bier with four wheels and a black handle. Nance said that's what her Mam would a-liked, she'd always acted poor. She was right, really: Cal reckoned to have the last laugh. She wouldn't be up at the front no more, but it had took God to shift her. I didn't go and see it: I daresn't lose the time. We was working on a cottage, by Bordon Hill. Twelve o'clock, I looked over the fields towards Stratford, and I did my mourning here, in my heart.

I don't believe in magic, but I know I seed a ghost once, at Pebworth. They don't mean you no harm; only thing is, if you sees this sight it frightens you, petrifies you. It's like Cal a-dying, knowing there's gold up there and she can't tell nobody—she's got to get back to it! Oh aye. Nance had all the money—all she could find, but there must a-been a lot more besides. Cal came back to Waterside: she wanted to tell somebody. But it was too late. Soon as she died workmen started ripping those cottages up to make a restaurant: the River Restaurant. I bet they had a haul!

'You was a fool, My Lad. You should a-took more when I was alive!'

I could hear her say it.

◆ CHAPTER FIFTEEN ◆

Here's a riddle:

Who builds stronger'n a mason, a shipwright or a carpenter?

A gravemaker! The houses he makes last till Doomsday!

I know *Hamlet* by heart, without a book. This is how it happened. Salt Brassington says one day: 'I sees you's in difficulties, Hewins, and can't meet your payments. Now I've got an idea.'

Ullo! I thought. What's e want doin?

'A job for your wife. Er's a respectable woman,' he says, 'ain't she?'

'Ah!'

I weren't sure. You see, she'd been so contrary lately—she went this way, that way, blowed hot and cold—I weren't sure if she'd take it. One minute she blamed me for sending her mother away, the next she was lamming one o' the kiddies till I had to pull her off, or said she'd seen me talking to some wench or other. I didn't know what to do with her. When I said, 'I've heared of a good job for you!' she flied at me. But when I told her it was dressing the ladies at the Theatre—she jumped at it!

She was dresser at the Shakespeare Memorial Theatre. It suited her down to the ground, she loved it. I was relieved, I can tell you. She had Violet Farebrother, Ethel McDowall (Ethel Carrington-to-be), Mrs Forster, and all their old hats. Soon she had a hat for every day of the week, and we couldn't see the tea caddy nor the clock for signed photographs! And there was perks for me. I'll give you an example: after matinées, if it was raining, I fetched the tea for the actresses from a cottage in Waterside. 'Keep the change!' they said, and gave me half a sovereign.

I prayed for rain!

After the play—it was eleven afore the play was over at night—the actresses got undressed. The missus helped them, packed the costumes in the wardrobe baskets. Sometimes she washed them down; if they'd been sweating badly she sponged them down and perfumed them. She got extra for that. If she was going to be late, sometimes she got home very late, I went and sat on the baskets, to wait for her. I was sat on a wardrobe basket one night and the barber, who made up the actors and actresses, gave me a funny look and said: 'You got anything to do tonight?'

I said: 'No.'

'Well,' he said, 'e's a bloke short. Ow would you like to come along?'

I said: 'Ah! Do me a good turn.' I didn't know *what* I was letting myself in for!

'You do an hour's performance,' he said. Blimey! I thought. 'And if you don't suit im the gaffer 'as somebody else—quick.'

Well, he must a-liked me! By two o'clock next morning the rehearsal was over and I was a super! A super with Frank Benson's Company! We had three bob a show, and if we stopped after the play at eleven, stopped till two sometimes or three, and rehearsed for the next night's play, to see what he thought of it, that was *another* three bob! Frank Benson would say at night: 'Now we've got some special guests a-comin, m'boys. I'll pay you extra if you'll stop an go through this play.'

I was in my element.

When Frank Benson's Company first started in Stratford they only had a week, then two weeks, then a month. Now they had two seasons a year! They came by train. We knowed what time the train would be coming: they generally arrived on a Sunday to open Monday. We went down to the station to carry their luggage up: you got a tip and they walked with you. Mostly they had digs up Rowley Crescent way. Mr Forster was the Agent-in-Advance: he came to Stratford a week afore the Company, to take rooms for them. When they went to London, anywhere, he had to go in advance to find lodgings for them.

The super master, he was a milkman: that's how he got the messages around. He liked to give us all a fair share, not make one do all afternoons and lose time. If I was out of work I used to tell him: 'I can come anytime you wants, Harry.' His name was Harry Megainey.

'Righto, George, I'll see what I can do!'

We had a happoth o' cow's milk then, of a morning. He brought it round in two buckets hanging from his shoulders. He got a ladle, tipped it into our jug and put us a little drop over—a happoth! We was careful with that!

Harry Megainey told us Frank Benson liked to think he'd picked supers out from Shakespeare's own relations! ' "Course," e says, "they'll be *bastards*, Harry—bound to be!" ' We all laughed.

One afternoon, it was an afternoon, Frank Benson—we called him Pa, he called us his Boys—said to the super master: 'I wanted Hewins this afternoon. Ow is it e ain't come?'

'Well,' he said, 'tell you the truth, what e picks up 'ere e loses more money from his work, e's a bricky.'

Frank Benson says: 'I'll pay the rest—get im!'

Harry Megainey comes up to the job, on the Rowley Estate. 'E wants you.'

'Ah,' I says, 'that's as may be. I can't afford to lose 'bout eighteen pence.'

'E says "I'll pay what e loses!" '

'I'll 'ave to see the gaffer.'

John Roberts says: 'You can go if you wants; it's only for 'alf a day. But you needn't 'ave told im *that*,' he said, ' 'bout losin eighteen pence. You could 'ave went, you could 'ave went and done a few hours 'ere at night and made your money up.'

'Oo wants to work 'ere on their own, nobody to talk to?'

John Roberts said: 'You ain't *supposed* to talk! By God, George, you's a cheeky bugger!'

Anyways, Frank Benson made it up. He said to the super master: 'Any afternoon I wants im, you get im, I'll make 'is wages up.' The play was *Hamlet*. 'E'll 'ave to 'ave that moustache off though.'

I nearly fainted. I'd been a-growing it since I was nineteen! He must a-seen my face change. 'Three shillin extra for losin 'is moustache!'

When the missus saw me she shrieked! 'You look like a babby!'

'I'm a monk!'

'You could a-fooled me!'

I was a monk with one of those skull caps on; four of us carried the bier when Hamlet's wife drowned herself. I said: 'Ow about us gettin *weeds*, gaffer, real weeds out of the river, look as if they's drippin off er?'

Frank Benson looked at Ethel McDowall; he stroked his chin. 'I *like* that idea! The river's handy! Fetch as much as you can, m'Boys!'

He liked things to go off perfect—and they did! It made a good scene. If Ethel McDowall weren't so keen on being covered with duckweed she daresn't say so—she was supposed to be dead! Drip-drip-drip! Just as they was going to bury her the curtain comes down.

The audience let you know what they thought. They would have booed if they hadn't liked it. They liked to see Frank Benson—he was Hamlet o' course—and if he was indisposed any time and couldn't do it they all went, 'Ohhhhhhh!' The actors had to be good. I played with Forbes Robertson, Oscar Asche, Murray Carrington, Harry Caine . . . Most of the expensive seats, they'd brought the book with them. When we was playing *Hamlet** they brought the book with all the words in, and if the actors and actresses said anything wrong these people published it in the *Herald*, where they'd slipped up! As I told you, I knowed all *Hamlet* by heart:

> A pick-axe an a spade, a spade,
> For—an a shroudin sheet.
> O, a pit of clay for to be made
> For such a guest is meet—

There was a time later when I was to mind how Harry Caine—he played the gravedigger—chucked that skull down: *pah*! But that's another tale.

We had free passes for the Theatre, we could go up in the gallery when we weren't on, or give it to the missus. I went up this night. I was up in the gallery a-standing by a piece and as they came on I started talking with the actor—I forgot myself!

She went, 'Shhh! Shhh!'

---

* This was Frank Benson's production of the 'Complete Hamlet' which he staged 1911 and 1912. It lasted 4½ hours, with a 'not unwelcome interval of ten minutes between Acts 3 and 4' as one critic put it.

I had to explain. I said: 'I'm sorry: I'm a super. It came natural.'

Sometimes I got carried away on the *stage*! I went too far. It happened I was a Roman soldier: I wore a skirt and crossed ribbons. And we had a battle. You knowed exactly where you'd got to go and when the other soldier came and stabbed you. Well, this soldier comes to floor me: he stuck his bayonet between my legs. It was supposed to go under my arm: it was *worked*. I said: 'Steady on Chalky.' But folks was cheering so I gave them a good death—only I fell a bit too far, into their lines!

Frank Benson didn't carry on at you, afterwards. He was a perfect gentleman. He'd say: 'I know in the excitement—folks was a-clapping an that—you could get excited. You got excited like they did' or 'you slipped up a bit there didn't you? Be careful!'

We walked home o' nights in our costumes, after the play. 'By God, the soldiers is small tonight!' said the copper, trying to rile us, and when that didn't work: ''Ere, Cook, 'bout an hour ago I seed a bloke comin out o' your house!'

We got him! We had beards after one play, black beards. We turns the corner into Sheep Street and runs into him. 'Oh!' he cries, 'Oh!'

We laughed! He went to report us; he stopped us going home in our make-up again.

The actresses was like no ladies I'd ever met afore. They liked a rude joke. One night, Violet Farebrother told the missus, they'd been playing *Don Quixote*. On this scene they had a donkey: everything had to be real at that time o' day. After the play somebody shouts: 'Oo's left a tap on?' Then they all starts a-laughing. It was the donkey pissing—it was coming through the ceiling!

The actresses got chocolates and flowers Sat'day nights, stacks of them. Folks brought them up and put them on the stage, labelled who they was for. I've pushed many a truckful o' bouquets and chocolates up to the actresses' lodgings on parting night. Sometimes a good un said: 'Take this lid for your children!' or ''Ere! 'Ave the ribbons!'

The trouble was, you didn't know where you stood with them, Mrs Forster, for instance. She was married to the Agent-in-Advance.

She didn't have the *best* parts. She'd got two young children, about five and seven, and she asked me if I could make a gate and hang it at the top o' the stairs, to stop them falling. 'My husband's gone in advance,' she said. While Frank Benson's Company was there they lived up Clopton Lane, in their own house. 'Course, when they moved to another town she had to lock it up, without she wanted me to do any papering or something, then she'd leave me the key.

Well, I didn't guess—but I was took to! I was hanging this gate, just shutting it, just putting the bolt into place, and she comes past me with a towel on her arm—start-naked! She was a big woman, near as tall as the missus, a great big woman, held herself well. You could see why they called her *The Duchess*! Ah! I slowed down with that bolt, I can tell you. She had a bath and I'd still got it in my hand when she comes back—the same!

She says: 'Don't take no notice of me, Hewins.' They didn't call you mister. 'We don't care in our profession *ow* we goes about!'

Well! I told the missus and she said: 'The madam! I wish I'd a-been there! I'd a-give er a piece o' my mind!'

I mean, I'd got excited! She could a-dropped the towel in front of her, couldn't she?

But the actresses was *genuine*. One day after Frank Benson's Company was gone we ran out o' bread. I sent one o' the kiddies up to the missus's sister, to see if she'd got a loaf. She comes running back, all of a flummox. 'Our Dad, Auntie Kate says, "I can't keep findin you lot bread"—an there's a *motor car* stopped on our street— a lady an a gent's got out—er's comin up our passage!'

And sure enough, I hears a cut glass voice. 'Could you tell us where Mrs Hewins lives?' It was Violet Farebrother—the prettiest of them all! The missus comes out.

'Emma!' cried Violet Farebrother. She called her Emma and she kissed her, then she shook hands with me. She *smelt* of violets, even her breath! When she smiled, all dimples, bright eyes, I thought: She's happy! You couldn't help smiling too. Everybody was smiling.

'I've motored from Brummagem with Fred. It's such a lovely day! E said "Let's go for a spin!" And I said "Let's go to Stratford! And the first thing we'll do is call on Emma!" Didn't I say I would?'

The missus went pink with pleasure.

'You know Fred—we're playing together.' Now he'd took his goggles off I could see it was Fred Terry. He was a bit sheep-faced.

'Oh! What a pretty little girl!' cried Violet Farebrother. She said to our Flo: 'I've got sixpence in one 'and—which 'and would you like?'

''Course Flo picked the one with all the rings and it was the other one. But Violet Farebrother gave her the sixpence. Then she darted here and there, up and down the yard: 'Oh! Can I 'ave a peek? Oh!' she said. 'Ain't it *old*? *Med-evil*! And just guess oo's the landlord? Ole Brassbound! Emma told me e keeps promisin to put a wash-house in—imagine! Nowhere to wash! Oh! *Plums*!' There was an old plum tree up our Court. 'I'll 'ave to try one!'

'Go an pick Miss Farebrother some plums!' said the missus, but the kiddies was dumbstruck. In any case Violet Farebrother had already picked herself one and was popping another in Fred Terry's mouth.

'Oh! What sweet ole cobbles! And a *rabbit*! What's 'is name?' She even had summat good to say about Walt Matthew's pigeons. I could see the missus was hoping against hope she wouldn't spot our door was open.

'Oh! Can I take a teeny peek?' And before you could say Jack Robinson she'd shot inside, and Fred Terry, and the kiddies; even Mrs White was there, craning her neck.

They saw the table. We'd got it laid but nothing on it. Violet Farebrother's face changed. ''Ow do you *manage*, Emma?' She looked at Fred Terry. 'Well, Fred, time is *flyin*!' And they slipped away, as fast as anybody could slip away with half the kids in the neighbourhood trailing after them.

The missus said: 'I could die o' shame!'

Ten minutes went by and from the Co-op came a big parcel o' groceries! Twenty more minutes, and a great big joint o' beef and a link o' sausages arrived! The butcher's lad gave me a quizzical look, I can tell you! The next person to turn up was her sister, Kate Tappin, carrying a big cottage loaf.

'Come on in Kate!' I said. 'That's just what we's short of!'

She stops dead in her tracks: 'God, Emm, where you got that from?'

It looked as if we'd all had three wishes. The table was piled high!

''Ere's me brought you a loaf all the way from Windsor Street!' And she throwed it at her!

*

Often it was very late afore the missus and me got home from the Theatre. The play weren't over till eleven. Then she had to undress the actresses, pack all those clothes up. I might have a couple o' trucks to push across town, or a rehearsal. It all helped. The kiddies generally made a bit too. They came home from school and they sat on the gallery steps to save the ladies' and gentlemen's places. They rushed home from school to get that job! Sometimes a lady came round to the house. 'Would you mind your little gal sittin for us tonight?' Would you mind! That would be a *tanner*!

There was parts going for them too. Our George got to be a page boy. Else was a fairy, but they didn't ask her again. She didn't laugh a lot now, our Else, more surly. She had to look after the others and she didn't like it. Well, it was a responsibility and sometimes I reckon she was frit, like the night the Gasworks exploded. *BOOM!* There was a blue flash and a noise like hundreds o' barrels being rolled across the sky. The lights went out all over Stratford. Our Else and the kiddies crept down the passage. Sheep Street was pitch black, glass smashed to the ground, slates and tiles was crashing, folks ran out the houses and the pubs, a-shouting, dogs barked.

Me and the missus was alright at the Theatre, it was electric, but in Sheep Street and Waterside folks panicked. Else daresn't go back indoors—she thought it was the end o' the world—she stopped outside with the kiddies, petrified, till we came home. And then, when she saw we was alright, she started carrying on about looking after them, especially Jim and Cyril—well, they was holy terrors. It weren't fair, she said, it all fell on *her*! By this time folks was flocking up Brum Road to see what had happened.

'Ten blokes' 'Twenty!' they said. 'Trapped!' 'Blowed to bits!' 'All of em wage earners!' I didn't go. Walt Matthews said to me: 'They been saying that plant was dangerous, for years.'

'Ah!'

Two men was killed that night, and more injured for life, not fit for anything but sitting by the fireside.

*

You'll have gathered our Else had the most to say—and that annoyed the missus, got on her nerves. Else had a book—I can see that book now, with a picture set into the cover and two girls' names—GERTIE and ADA, I think it was. She'd won it at school for an essay—the RSPCA prize!—and the lads got it and played with it, tore it up. Now Else had loved that book: she went mad, mad! She went for our Cyril—he was the missus's favourite, he could never do no wrong—and the missus went for *her*. She said: 'Just as soon as you've got your leavin certificate you can go into service, m'girl. That'll quank you!' She knowed our Else didn't want to be a skivvy. When she answered back the missus said: 'Roll on 1914!'

☙ CHAPTER SIXTEEN ❧

By the summer of '14, things was looking up. George was working as a printer's boy. The missus was thrilled. It was a nice career, she said, better'n the building. He brought home four bob a week. She'd got it all planned: when Else went into service Ede was to leave school and look after the little uns. I was building two villas at Welford. They was just past that public house the 'Four Alls':

> The King rules all
> The Parson prays for all
> The soldier fights for all
> The farmer pays for all

I reckon it should a-been 'the working man pays for all.'

It was the best job I'd ever had. I took it, win or lose, a pound a thousand bricks laid. I wore a bowler hat—I was my own gaffer at last! In two days me and Tommy had got the foundations out. I slogged as hard as I could: the more I done the more I had. Then Jack Wright the owner—he was a big shot at the Co-op, I knowed him well—came and told me. They'd declared war.

'What d'you think on it, Mister Wright?'

He said: 'You got seven kiddies: they won't take you! Asides, you're thirty-five!'

But that night I put my tools in my bag.

Tommy went white: 'What you takin your tools for?' says he, 'we ain't finished!'

'They'll call me up,' I says. I didn't tell him what was on my mind. You see, I'd signed a paper.

Jack Wright was there and he laughed: 'They won't take you. You'll 'ave to carry em in tomorrow.'

He was right: I did.

We got on with those two houses! I done the brickwork, Walt Clack done the carpentering. There was an architect named Knight looking after it. He checked me every thousand I laid. He'd come and open his pocket knife and *see* if the cross joint was solid. He seed that it was done alright and then he told the owner.

When it started to be bad weather, autumn, we lodged with a young widow woman, Florence, *Florrie* we called her, me and Walt Clack and the labourers. Well, Welford was five mile there, five mile back. I'd been a-walking sixty mile a week! I went home weekends, and I was going out the passage, our passage, of a Sunday, when I happened to see the postman stop on the steps. He said: ''Ere's one for you, George!'

I said: 'Thank you,' but my heart sank.

Well! It was a *picture postcard*! Of a couple! 'WHEN WE MEET AGAIN . . .' Those devils where I lodged had sent a postcard and signed it 'Florrie'. I shoved it in my pocket. That was a near un! I said to them on Monday: 'You could a-caused a big row! The missus might a-killed me!'

Tommy said: 'It weren't my idea, George!' The others laughed fit to bust.

The Recruiting Office was at the top o' Bridge Street, on the corner by Wood Street. It was a shop, a draper's shop: they had the bottom room for recruiting. There weren't no queues there— no fear! One Sat'day night when I got in the missus said: 'It's 'appened!'

My heart sank again. This is it! I thought. I can see her now, sat on that kitchen chair with her head thrown back.

'They got Harry.'

'Oo? The coppers?' Her brother was always scrapping.

'It's worse'n that! E an Benny Hutfield got drunk an went round to the Recruiting Office. They took em! Two drunks—one near forty-five, t'other a loony—an they took em!' We never said nothing for a minute. He was her only brother, he was a nice chap, the apple of her eye. They'd been *poor* together, you see, when they was young: widow's children. He'd been in the Old War-wicks—so had Benny—a regular soldier till eight or nine years afore. That's why they took them: thought they'd be handy, I suppose.

Benny was a bit touched, soft in the head. He worked for a firm taking gravel and sand out. He went up to the Hospital with his horse and cart. The nurse came to the door and he says: 'I got the gravel.'

'Well,' she says, 'you better come inside.'

'And bring the horse an cart?'

'You say *you've* got the gravel?* There's no one else 'ere?' she says. 'You *ain't* got the gravel? Oo's got it then?'

'Me.'

The gardener happened to see it and he told her, he says: 'E's a wee bit touched,' and 'It's alright Benny, tip it over 'ere.'

He could work, Benny Hutfield—he went with a horse and cart on his own—anything he could go at, like a bull. Well, now he'd got his chance. They put them both in the Pioneers.

'If they'll 'ave Benny I reckon they'll 'ave me.'

'*You?*'

'Ah.'

'They can't! They can't take you!' She got off the chair. She was near her time, she weren't so well as usual. She was frit. I thought: 'I never seen er frit afore!' I felt the ground shift under me. She said: 'Not wi seven kiddies and a babby comin!'

'That's what Mister Wright said. But I signed a paper.' Yes, when they disbanded the Volunteers and brought in the Territorials—we didn't fancy the Territorials, no end of us packed in—I was one of those poor fellas who signed the paper—'If my country needs me I'll oblige.'

'Get your coat on,' I said to our Ede. 'Fetch your Mam a stout—quick!'

*

I'd got the two villas at Welford plastered, practically finished bar the kitchen floor, when it came. It weren't no picture postcard this time: '*We've got your signature* . . .' Walt Clack had the same. He'd been in the Volunteers with me—we'd *all* been in the Volunteers, 'cept Tommy. His Mam hadn't let him join. Next thing I was having a *free medical*! It was a local doctor. We just walked by him: 'You're alright! You're alright!' he told us.

---

* *Pain while passing urine caused by kidney stones*

It was different from the Boer War: I'd come with no honours from there, quick, unfit to be of use to them. And then I'd *wanted* to go—that was the cream of the joke! Fred Winter the draper on the High Street swore me in, and afore I knowed what was happening we was being marched through the streets to the station. It was Christmas 1914. The missus had had the babby about a week afore—she was still abed. The little uns was waving flags, only our Flo was crying, and Tommy Taylor. He comes up to the train.

'Don't fret Tom, there'll be plenty o' work about now!'

He weren't listening: 'I asked for the Warwicks, George, but they put me in the RAMC. I've enlisted! I'm gonna learn to be a stretcher bearer!'

'You silly bugger! You can't stand the sight of a rabbit's guts, let alone a human bein's!'

I weren't so sure I could neither, but same as having kiddies—there was no getting out of it. The engine started blowing, and off I went.

*

I was in the Seventh Warwickshire Infantry. There was about thirty from Stratford in my platoon: Walt Clack, a barber, a butcher, two brickies, a chap as worked at the brewery. When they found out I could cut and shave they made me an officer's servant. We went to Nottingham first, in billets. We was billeted in houses: there weren't no room in the camps, they was full up. We made do. Each Company fell in, in the street—I was in D Company. There was two pretty daughters in the house where I was billeted: the Misses Linnet. I introduced them to two of my young officers; they took them out on the back of their motorbikes and they gave me a *tip*! The young officers had rich Dads and pots o' money! To top it all, none of them seemed to know how many beans made five.

Ullo, I thought, this is alright. There'll be some pickins 'ere!

Back in Stratford the missus was worried about me: I'd never been far from home afore, only once to Weston with the Volunteers. She sent me some of those effervescing salts, as fizzed, to keep me healthy.

'Now!' I says to my mate, 'watch! I'm a-goin to put some o' this stuff in the gals' chamber tonight!'

The Linnet girls was in the room above. All at once this stuff fizzed up, they screamed—and *bang*! went the pot on the floor, broke it! We laughed so much we was hugging each other, the tears ran down our cheeks!

That went off alright, but they reported it to the Sergeant Major. Next morning we was on the march—we used to have to go on marches every morning, they kept us going round and round the town, up and down the road—the Sergeant shouts: 'Fall out the two men oo broke the CHAMBER POT!' In front of the whole Company! They laughed, *did* they! ''Alf-a-crown stopped a-Friday!' said the Sergeant.

He had a job to keep his face straight! Well, you could have a bit of a laugh when you marched at ease along the by-roads, you could light up a fag. We marched with our rifles slung over our shoulders, anyhow, till we got back to the middle of the town. Then we marched to attention! There was a field at Nottingham where all twelve Companies went into one battalion, a thousand or so strong. We all marched together, then we came back and fell out and went back to our own streets, right in the town.

As I said, I was billeted with the Linnets. When I was took bad—I weren't used to it, being away from home—Mr Linnet wouldn't go to work. 'My chap won't go whilst *you's* 'ere,' says Mrs Linnet. ' "Lily!" e says, "I don't *trust* im with you, in bed or out of it!" '

Mrs Linnet laughed, but she gave me one of those hot looks that made me glad when Emma came over to Nottingham, to see me. I thought: 'You got 'ere just in time!'

I didn't fancy Mrs Linnet—she weren't the World Queen—but I wouldn't a-wanted to offend her. Emma came by train and she brought the babby. Lo and behold Mrs Linnet and her got friendly, she really took a-liking to the missus, they went boozing together! I gave my mate as slept with me a tanner to go and sleep next door, so's I could sleep with them.

'I called er Mary after the Queen.'

The babbies always slept between you when they was small so's they didn't fall out. This un had a sickly look, not like the others, for all she got plenty o' cuthering. 'I don't like the look o' that rash' I thought.

The missus had to feed her from a tit bottle. And the price o' food was going up, she said, every week. Army pay weren't enough to keep them.

*

Then we was moved to Danbury Huts, five miles from Chelmsford. There was no chance of seeing the missus there, and I'll speak the truth, it was a relief. She was scared of having another babby—so was I, I can tell you.

They watched us on parade. Sergeant Fife he'd be a-bawling: 'You broke your mother's heart but you won't bleedin well break mine!' I did it smart. Well, I'd been in the Volunteers. Stand to attention, doing the three motions: put my rifle on my shoulder, march in, take my line in, then come down at the easy.

Says the Colonel to Sergeant Fife: 'Oo's that man?'

'Sir,' he says, 'Hewins.'

The Colonel says: 'Put im in for promotion.'

I thought fast. I had ten bob a month for being an officer's servant, and sometimes I had three officers a month. That was thirty bob. And the tips. It was a lot o' money then. Normally you got four bob a week off the army. It was more'n that but married uns had to put four bob a week towards the missus—

> We only get a bob a day,
> The more we do
> The more we may.
> It makes no difference
> To our pay.

I should a-been paid more for being a Corporal, but I fancied the Officers' Mess. You couldn't have stripes *and* be an officers' servant. Asides, I couldn't have domineered the other chaps, especially some of my old pals—and they'd a-tried to take liberties, wouldn't they? They wouldn't a-*liked* me ordering them about.

I said: 'I ain't a-goin to 'ave the stripes.'

Walt Clack, for instance, I shouldn't a-liked to bawl at him: 'Stand to attention PROPER!' I couldn't have done. It would have stopped my friendship with the chaps.

They weren't all from Stratford. We had a chap in our mob from Brummagem. We called him Roachy. We sat round the table playing cards.

He says: 'Any of you goin into Chelmsford tonight?'

We said 'Yes!' There was several of us going.

'Well,' he says, 'you ain't got no money.'

We all said: 'I know *I* 'ave!' We put our hands in our pockets—he'd picked them! He gave us it all back. Then he showed us how he did it and he said: 'Now I'll show you ow you can stop anybody pickin your pocket. Put a dozen or more Barcelona nuts in. E can't find the money, e'll keep pickin the nuts!' He says: '*That's* the way to stop em pickin your pocket, put some nuts in!'

We soon got friendly with the locals. The woman I took the officers' washing to, she was about thirty, a smart piece o' goods. She thanked me well for getting her the washing, I can tell you! I was starting to *enjoy* being in the army. When we was marching along the country lanes we sang at the tops of our voices—

> We are the Warwickshire lads,
> We know our manners,
> We spend our tanners.
> Marchin down the Danbury Road,
> Doors an winders open wide,
> We're the boys of the infantry,
> We don't care for the ASC,
> We are the Warwickshire lads!

The officers joined in—ah! I had some good officers. It happened there was no place for two of us to sleep with the men and we had to go and sleep in the hut with our officers. Lieutenant Kirby—he was from Coventry, his Dad was a motor-car manufacturer—says to his mate: ''Ere! Look out! My servant *walks* in 'is sleep!'

That was me! I used to! The other chaps was frit to death I should get my rifle.

Lieutenant Kirby says: 'E *might* get his rifle—but e'll step over you alright!'

His mate complained to the Colonel, but the Colonel said: 'E's

just the chap we wants at the front—we can send im out o' nights
when e's walkin in 'is sleep—to get information!'

One morning the Provo Sergeant says: 'Come 'ere kid, I wants you.'

'Yessir!'

'Ow many wives 'ave you got?'

'Sir?'

'This is six you've took out o' camp.'

Well, Lieutenant Kirby he brought them in of a Sat'day night
and he looked to me to get them out on the Monday. He'd make
out a pass: 'PASS PRIVATE HEWINS AND WIFE'. 'This is the *sixth*
wife you've took out.'

I told him then, most of the truth. Now he was a terrible
drunkard, the Provo Sergeant: all of us had to treat him to two
pints. I said: 'You shut your mouth, come up to the hut. E's gotta
big carpet bag, there's whisky and brandy and rum in it. You can
pull this bag open at one end,' I said, 'and drink 'alf a bottle.'

'I'll come!'

Later: 'Christ!' he said, 'That were good weren't it?'

I said: 'E won't know, e gets drunk, e won't know but what e's
spilt it.'

Now Lieutenant Kirby had got a rubber bath as he bathed in. I
had to get this rubber bath and some hot water for the piece as was
stopping with him for the weekend, Sat'day and Sunday. He'd say:
'Leave the water—you needn't stop!'

The wenches often gave me a tanner when they left. ' 'Ere, ' they
said, 'we done well out of im.'

And they winked at me.

Another officer I had was Teasdale, Lieutenant Teasdale. He was
a farmer's son. He took me haymaking in the summer. He said,
'Could 'is servant go along and look after im while e was on leave?'
And he paid me, too! Poor chap! When he said 'Attention!' he
couldn't say it smart!

The Colonel said: 'Say it like this—"TEN-shun!"' '

But he'd got a country drawl, I can hear him now: 'When oi
says "bayonet" you don't fix, when oi says fix, you whips it out an
whops it on.'

He weren't smart at all, he couldn't get out of that country way of talking—or thinking. 'Ey! Hewins! It's moi duty today to fetch the money from the bank!' He looked worried to death. 'You better come wi me!' We had a regimental guard, both sides o' the door. I'd never seen so much money! I can tell you, I wouldn't a-left it with Lieutenant Teasdale. He was an easy touch. He says: 'We's a-goin to the station now to pick up Missus T.' When we gets there I says: 'God, she's altered ain't she?'

He nudged me. 'Mum's the word, Hewins.'

That was another tip.

I never got a tip out of Captain Edwards. He was different. For a start he didn't bother with women. He didn't hate them—not like our Company Captain, Captain Bethell, *he* was a confirmed bachelor, a terror!—Captain Edwards could do without them, that's all. His father was a parson, Malvern way. He was a plumpish, nice sort o' chap. His mates called him Jumbo—we didn't, o' course!

One day he says: 'You've been a servant to me for some time, Hewins.'

Ullo! I says to myself. 'Yessir!'

'I likes you, Hewins.'

'Sir!'

'I don't mind you 'avin a cup o' tea, but you might 'ave asked me.'

'*Tea?*'

''Ere's the bill—Captain Edwards an Hewins.'

'I'll take my oath I've 'ad no tea,' I said. Well, I could get it free. 'Come on,' I says, 'let's go down to the cook house.' We sees Sergeant Cook and Captain Edwards says: 'This lad says e's 'ad no tea.'

Sergeant Cook says: 'Well e ain't!'

'What you got it down for, then? *Hewins?*'

'That new officer in your hut, that one from Evesham, '*is* name's Hewins.'

Captain Edwards apologized to me. He was a gentleman. 'I'm sorry,' he said.

Between times I kept their clothes nice, cleaned and pressed, and their belts polished, and their revolvers clean, and their buttons shiny.

31. A 'before embarkation' photograph of the officers of the 2/7 Battalion, Royal Warwickshire Regiment, published, rather belatedly, in the *Tatler* 16 July 1916. Officers mentioned by name in the narrative are: 2nd row (sitting) second from left: Captain Edwards; fourth from left: Captain Bethell. 3rd row (standing) seventh from left: Lieutenant Kirby. Lieutenant Teasdale is missing although listed amongst those officers who embarked for France.

They got so's they depended on you. It was jolly at Danbury Huts. We all had a shock when we got our marching orders—to France!

*

First we had a week's leave. On the train from London I stood in the corridor. Somebody said: 'There's plenty o' room, Tommy! Why don't you come in?'

I said: 'I'm crummy.'

I *was*. Somehow I'd got crummy. You catched them off the others. I kept myself clean as a new pin, and my officers, but I'd got crummy.

'Never mind, Tommy!' they said. 'Come in!'

When I got home the first thing the missus did was put a good iron on them. 'I'll get the little buggers!' she said. It was the only time I got relief, the war through. 'Pop! pop! pop!' they went. The missus would have got Jerry and all, if she could. She was a fighter—all the Baylisses was—and she'd had some battles since I'd been called up.

For a start, they'd got a *new house*! It happened like this. We'd put in for a Council cottage years afore, but we was turned down. When I went in '14, the missus had another go. Well, we was overcrowded, there weren't enough room. George was almost a man. He had to sleep with the missus and the babby, he was too grown to sleep with the girls. Asides, you couldn't keep the place clean! She told them! An Inspector came and the landlord panicked. He built *two* wash-houses up our yard, put in a tap with an earthenware sink! But the Inspector agreed with the missus: our cottage was 'unfit for human habitation'. So—the Councillors gritted their teeth and they lashed out! They built new cottages on Brum Road and Park Road: the first new Council houses in Stratford!

Most o' the big families from the old Courts was moved. The missus said she wanted one of the new cottages—her chap was fighting for King and Country weren't he?—and they said 'Yes!' There was some chuntering amongst the neighbours.

'Look at er!'

'Movin out o' one slum to make another un!'

'They say the Corporation'll 'ave to *burn* em down on account o' the bugs!'

But for once in her life the missus didn't give a tinker's cuss *what* they said. She got a hand cart for all our stuff; they pushed it through the town, up the Brum Road, and the little uns each carried summat.

When I gets there I looks round: 'Where's Bogey? Where's Walt?' It was like a foreign country. The Whites had been moved to Brum Road, the Matthews to Old Town. We was in Park Road.

There was fences between the yards—and a long garden! It was really modern, three bedrooms and two downstairs—a nice front room and a kitchen. The coalhouse was inside and the toilet was up the yard, but it was a good toilet. You didn't have to share! The missus loved it, she liked being private! I weren't so sure. One thing was certain, she was better off with me in the army! She had money coming in regular, now, for the first time. It didn't matter that the rent was seven and six; with my officers and the allowance they'd started giving for the kiddies, she got two pound, ten shilling a week—more money than a lot of us had ever brought in! Mind you, she'd had trouble a-getting it.

They'd set up a special office for the allowance; you had to go there and *apply*. A bloke sat on a stool and gave the allowance out. Well, this bloke starts umming and fussing about handing it over— you'd a-thought it was *his* money! He gives the missus a nasty look and he says: 'EIGHT children! Was they all born in wedlock, missus?'

She felt herself going red. She said: 'What d'you think I am?' And she dropped him one on the jaw. She knocked him out! She knocked him out in one! And so the bloke who gave out the allowance summonsed her. She had to go to the Police Court. But times was changing. The Magistrate was on her side! He told the bloke as he should have said: 'Now this is a very nasty question I've got to ask you, Mrs Hewins, but I've *got* to ask you—' He dismissed the case.

Park Road came too late to do the old uns any good. Her mother had died in Terrets Court, up Taskers Passage, four years afore, charring till the day she died. And my mother: soon as I got home I went to the workhouse infirmary to see her. She'd been there six years. The bones was coming out of her skin; there was no fear of her getting well.

'I wants to be put aside *im*,' she said. 'There's room.'

I gave my word. And I promised I'd get back.

'I shan't see you no more, son,' she said.

I thought: And that *is* the truth. I'd never loved her like I loved Cal, or Nance, well I never really *knowed* her, but I was upset.

What's more, I was upset about going back this time. So was the kiddies. I'd been telling them stories about the army—the women and the jokes—singing them songs. They didn't want me to go. Our Flo was a-crying at the station. Well, I thought, they weren't *dragged* up. They're all clothed nice, they're fairly developed children. There ain't one wi rickets.

The missus said: 'I wish you weren't a-goin.' She gave me two bottles o' the 'Oddfellows' rhubarb wine—''Ere!'—and a photograph she'd had took of her and me and the kiddies. She'd writ on the back:

From a Loving Wife
to
A Loving Husband
—Emma.
Will the finder kindly send to
Mrs G. H. Hewins,
20, Park Road, Stratford-on-Avon,
Warwickshire,
England.

Even then I'd no thoughts of *not* going back. There was a chap in Stratford who'd knocked a saucepan o' water over him and scalded both his feet. He said: 'I'll suffer the agony!' They found another chap hiding in a bunker on the golf course. But *I* hadn't seen, you see, I didn't know. If you'd asked me why I was going to fight I'd have said: 'To save the country'. If the Germans won we would be slaves!

We was travelling to Salisbury Plain, the whole battalion. At one of the country stations, the platform was crowded with Cadbury's wenches. They was on an outing. There was a long line o' them. They shouted: 'Tommy! Tommy! Chuck us your number an name an address!'

I chucked mine. Winnie Walderviss picked it up. And then she got into the carriage! She was going home, leaving the others to go home for the day to see her mother. She was foreign by the sound of it. She *looked* like a foreigner, dark, very dark. She had a funny face. I didn't want to make a fuss of her—well, I'd just been home for a week! She didn't know 'A' from a bull's foot, you could see that.

'I'll send you slabs o' chocolate,' she said.

'Righto!'

Well, it was summat for nothing. The carriage was packed with folks; I never went but two yards with the wench. I never dreamt where it would lead to. I'd got other things on my mind.

32. The Hewins family, 1915. Top row: George senior, Else, George junior. Middle row: Emma, with Mary on her knee, Ede, Jess. Front row: Cyril, Flo, Jim.

We was rushed up to the front in camouflaged trucks. It was like the Cattle Market on a Tuesday: they shoved us all in, quick, a-shouting and a-cussing. I thought: 'We might as well be dumb creatures!' There was one thousand in our battalion: nine hundred and sixty of us and forty officers.

It was worse'n anything I'd expected. For a start our dug-outs weren't above four foot six inches high; you couldn't stand upright in them, you touched the roof. They oozed water, they was never dry. A piece of wet sacking flapped at the entrance. That was your front door. We crawled in and we scrobbled and we crouched. We fell asleep crouching. It were bad enough for us and we was mostly on the short side—but the officers!

Lieutenant Kirby gets the cramp, he stretches himself, puts his head up—he was a big tall chap, six foot four—and a Jerry sniper hit him in the head.

Said the Sergeant: 'You'll be in 'ere for a fortnight if you's lucky, maybe three weeks, so you might as well start usin your brains!'

We learnt fast.

'You could be two 'undred yards from Jerry, you could be only fifty. When e's that close keep your mouth shut and your head down! E ain't *dead*,' he said, meaning Lieutenant Kirby—he didn't have much time for the young officers—'but the next un could be! Never underestimate Jerry!'

We didn't! We was sitting on the firestep one day, looking through the periscope. ''Ere! Look at this!' We didn't know what it was: it looked like the sea a-coming towards us, yella, six inches from the ground. I thought it was water, going to drown us. Then somebody shouts: 'GAS!'

There was a panic. Those as couldn't get their masks on in time, those as was away from the trenches, it got in their eyes and it blinded them.

We daresn't sing or play cards or have a chat in case Jerry catched us napping again. We was that bored we had a tune for one of the snipers. He had a machine gun and we used to hum it under our breaths: 'Pom-tiddle-om-pom-*pom-pom-pom*!'

In the finish we had him, but the silence was worse. Now there was only the sound of the rain. It rained and rained. We was drenched to the skin, day in, day out. Even when we knowed Jerry weren't planning to come over—you could always tell when he *was*, the Sergeant said, cos he started to shell—we was jumpy. We crouched on the firestep all night, *just in case*. Our clothes dried on us next day. But the thing I couldn't a-bear, the thing that turned me up, was the rats: swarms o' rats, rats with yella eyes and big fat bellies like old ladies' cats, running all over, after the food. One squeak or a rustle—that was enough for me! I didn't give them a chance to get nearer. I kicked out and they'd hit the roof.

The food—well, it was fairly good when you could get it. Often it was more'n we was used to, but it was a funny mixture! Captain Bethell comes round one day and it was bloaters. Now I loved a bloater, but they hadn't got enough, we had to cut them in half, for two. He said it weren't enough for the men. He sent for a big jar o' jam—

> Plum an apple, apple an plum
> Plum an apple, apple an plum
> The ASC gets strawberry jam
> An a ration o' rum,
> But all that we poor devils gets
> Is apple an plum!

Jam and herrings! How about that for a diet? I thought: It's better'n *nothing*! Sometimes if Jerry was shelling heavy we couldn't get to the food dump. We had nothing to eat for days on end. One day a couple of our chaps was sent down to fetch the food. We watched through the periscope. We saw the Pioneers drop it outside the latrines and start arguing.

Our chaps said: 'We're not 'avin it '*ere*!'

They said: 'You bleedin move it!'

The Pioneers came up to the front with the food bags, sheets of corrugated iron for the dug-out roofs, emptied the toilet buckets. They didn't hang around—they was in and out! I watched out for Harry and Benny but I never saw them. There weren't no time: you never seen blokes work so fast! 'Cor Blimey,' said Sergeant Fife, 'they shifted em! That's the way to work,' he said. 'I bet they never worked like that at home!'

'No,' I says. 'They means to get away from the shellin.'

This day they left it a bit late. Jerry heard the argument: he dropped a shell and he scattered them *and* the food. We cussed!

The officers didn't eat the same as us. We had to fetch the officers' bags from the food dump. Each one was labelled with his name on it. Now there was a big fella in our platoon. He was awful coward. You should a-seen some of the chaps from Stratford, bully sort o' blokes they'd been in the pub, lost it all when they got to France. Well, fool-like, we was a-going down to the food dump carrying our tin cans, hoping for some pickings. When this big fella gets down by the dump somebody whispers: 'Push im!' He fell and his tin cans knocked together. Jerry heard it and blowed the food to hell. It served us right.

Then they sent us carrying shells to another regiment. I'd found summat to eat, I was eating. I only dropped two or three crumbs. The officer starts shouting at me above the noise of the shelling: 'We got pride in this trench you dirty bastard. I'll report you! Oo's your Colonel?'

And I hears a voice behind me. 'Get out of the road!' It was one of his men. He pushed me aside and he shot him in the head. It was an awful sight. But it was no use that officer thinking things was the same as they'd been at home—they weren't. *Nothing* was the same in the trenches. A lot o' bullets ricocheted in there, I can tell you. You had to treat your men proper, and most of them did. There was strict discipline in our platoon but no snappiness; our officers didn't snap.

Afore there was going to be a bayonet charge the top brass came up the trenches: we could *sniff* them coming. 'Ullo,' we said, 'there's summat comin off.' Then back they'd go, right behind the lines, miles away.

Afore we went over they gave us rum—*rum*! Those who was 'in' with the Sergeant had above their share. Sometimes we'd had no food in us for over two days: it took effect, naturally. You wouldn't a-done such things otherwise. One night, *this night*, we was waiting to go over on a bayonet charge. It was shelling like hell all around. There was no sleeping. I was touring the trench with my officer and a bloke whispers in my ear, 'Hewins!' I jumped round. I didn't know he was behind me, I didn't know he was *there*!

'Ow should you like to be on Clopton Bridge now?'

'Bleedin nice,' I said.

They was shellin us terrible heavy. In the flares—Jerry used to send flares to light us up—I saw his face. It was Harry Caine—one of Frank Benson's actors. His real name was Lieutenant Hawkins. He was the gravedigger in *Hamlet*.

'Harry Caine!' I said, but I'd gone chill to the marrow.

When you went over you was in No Man's Land. You can laugh now, but if you got behind a little twig in the ground you thought you was safe—you know, as long as you'd got a *bit* o' shelter. Shells was a-dropping all about; our artillery didn't lift their barrage high enough and *they* shelled us and all. In No Man's Land if you got held up you started to dig. That's why we had little shovels, about six inches long—entrenching tools, we called them. I'd had good practice at digging; ah, more'n some poor buggers. We scratched and scratched, scratched out a little channel as you could lay in and you thought: Shall I be the next? and when the shell bust and went over you, I'm alright now, or: I'm still alive!

It was terrible. There *weren't* no cover. The first sight I saw in No Man's Land was a bloke without a head. Then you saw bodies everywhere, where they'd left them: they couldn't pick them up, see. You sensed your pals there aside of you, lashing out at it, digging away to get just enough to cover them, about a foot deep, to lay in. I tell you, there was no working to time then, it didn't want no-one to watch you. Your life depended on it—and my main thought was to keep alive. I weren't much use to no-one dead, was I?

We *crawled* forward. When we seed the shelling had stopped a bit we got up and run, rifles at the ready, bayonets fixed. We could see Jerry. I reckon I did kill one: my bullet zipped the wire, I saw the sparks fly. I may have killed him—God knows—I needed that rum inside o' me. And the noise! Talk about a prize fight when we charged! 'Come on, you BASTARDS! Come out o' your TRENCHES!'

We weren't drunk, we was just in that mood when we could have fought the Devil. But when we got to their trenches most of them had gone. There was only a few stragglers there as had been braver than the others. They was crafty, the Germans: if you got them cornered they upped their hands in a tick, chucked you their rifles. They didn't make a fight of it.

Then we had five nights 'rest'. Well, *rest*, it weren't a rest cos Jerry followed us, he shelled us where we was at night. We was in billets—*houses*—and I always tried to get under the stairs. We slept five or six together, it kept us warm against one another; we slept in our clothes, with our blankets round us. When they buried you, you was only wrapped in your blanket, there was no coffins.

We met the next lot coming out the trenches when we went back: all wounded, torn up, some on stretchers, moaning, screaming. And the dead. It was a dreadful sight. My blood froze. They buried them by the roadside, anywhere. I went to one funeral. It was a young kid, about nineteen. The padre there, he was a Frenchman—you didn't catch ours hanging around at the front, no fear!—he said:

'E's only a boy' and 'May you sleep well in ze rich soil of France!' It was rich alright.

I never went to another.

That night I toured the trench with my officer. A chap comes round the corner a-bandaged all over his face in white, a-moaning. It made us both jump.

'Christ!' I says. 'You give me a fright, mate!'

He mumbled summat—he was a German prisoner! He could speak English. He said: 'Why you done this to me, Tommy? I didn't want to fight you! I got nothin against you, you got nothin against me!'

I kept my mouth shut, so did Captain Edwards. But I thought:

Yes, poor bastard, you an me 'ad to come, didn't we, there was no option for *us*!

Sitting on the firestep I thought a lot about that chap. He was right. *I'd* got nothing to fight for.

*

Then it came about that we had near a *fortnight off* ! The rain pissed down, just as it had in the trenches, but there weren't a single shell dropped—and no dug-outs! It was Heaven, a place called La Gorgue.

The first thing they did was give us a shower bath. Well, we was mud from head to toe, crawling with bugs. We filed in, one at a time, like a lot o' sheep—

> When this bloomin war is over,
> Oh how happy I shall be.
> When I gets my civvy suit on,
> No more soldierin for me.

Some got scalded, for some it was icy cold. They chucked us each a vest, shirt and pants—

> No more goin home on furlough,
> No more goin home on pass.
> We will tell the Orderly Sergeant
> To stick 'is passes up 'is ass . . .

I had a shirt as touched the floor. We got together, big uns and little uns, and swopped. They was hard as a board, never washed, only fumigated.

'What you gonna do, George?'

'I'm gonna find a nice French gal!'

They all laughed.

'To do me washin.'

It was like waking up after a nightmare. All we did was mooch about, never had no parades, no mass together. I polished my officer's belt, his shoes, shaved him, helped lay the table for their lunch—and the rest of the day was my own. We had nothing to do, only eat, sleep, go for walks. We still got paid! And to top it

all, in the regimental bag came a stack o' parcels: 'Hewins!' 'Hewins!' 'HEWINS!'

I thought: This is too good to last! and What they got up their
sleeve? It was the sort o' feeling I used to get when Walt Bailey
gave me a couple o' Woodbines for nowt.

The parcels was full o' chocolate from Winnie Walderviss. The
later ones had socks and things in too. The letters got ever
so friendly. The last one said: 'From Your Loving Sweetheart
WINNIE'.

Me and some of my pals was billeted with a French family: they
had a shop, sold vegetables and that. The *French*! He'd leave the
shop, do what he wanted to do in the gutter and walk back in. It
was a shock the first time. They did have toilets in La Gorgue: in
a row, in the street, with just a band so wide covering them. They'd
sit there and laugh as we went by. A courting couple would go in
together, arm in arm, taking no notice. And they was crafty too!
When we went to the pump they'd creep up—'You do pump well,
Tommy!' They got us pumping their bloody water for them.

Now this bloke I was billeted with, he had a young daughter. I
said: 'Where's Papa?'

She said: 'Mama too big, she give im money to go ze brothel.
Papa go zare regular. E got what you English call ze cock stand!'

My mate looked at me. 'Did you 'ear what that bloke's got?'

'Yes,' I said, 'I reckon I've got it an all. Come on!'

We went down the street and we saw a long queue. At first we
thought it was an electric picture palace. They was a-queuing
outside! We waited and waited. As soon as we got inside two
women showed us photographs: you could take your pick from the
photographs on the wall, for half an hour. Then you went upstairs.
Each o' them was naked—they didn't look much like the photographs, I can tell you—and each had a little table with souvenirs,
trinkets, embroidered postcards with 'MOTHER' on them and
flowers. You tore off your pants but they kept you fussing round
the table. 'Christ!' I thought, 'I can't hold onto this much longer!'

'Buy a souvenir, Tommy!'

I took half the table in the end, so's she'd get a move on, put my money down. That's when I seen it: gob on the floor—all over it, now I came to look—no sawdust!

'No-no,' she says.

I weren't used to their money, it was all francs and paper, but I weren't *that* slow! I asked for my change.

'No-no,' she says.

That did it! I lost all my interest. I weren't going to be short changed by nobody. A lot o' the young uns *was* and they got the claps into the bargain. It was a lucky escape, I can tell you.

My mates and I decided to try the estaminet over the canal bridge. There was some French soldiers patrolling; we started singing our version of *Mademoiselle from Armentières* and they shook their fists at us. We laughed! *We'd* got a fortnight off! The wine at the estaminet was a penny a glass! Penny a glass! The chaps was drinking them down faster'n they could draw them. The landlord gave me the nod. 'You wants to come at dinner time—'bout fifty mamzelles comes from the factory! And we got a *gramophone!*'

So I did. I gave the Mess Cook a slab o' chocolate. Being an officer's servant I was supposed to stop and help Mess Cook lay the table for lunch. Me and my mate slipped off but the others followed us. Word got around. Well! We got the gramophone a-going, and the girls arrived, just as he said. They worked in a big factory nearby. They'd got that frightened look on their faces: when a plane went over they crouched on the floor, they'd been bombed so much. I picked me a wench. We danced and danced, and I tried a bit o' deaf-and-dumb language.

'See!' I said, 'I made you smile!'

She was shy but she guessed what I was after. 'If you *likes*, Tommy . . .' she said. It was 1916. They'd picked up some English by the time we got there . . . 'If you likes, I'll do your washin for you.'

We had a card, a big printed card given us, what French meant, so's we could learn to speak it. *Du pain* meant Bread. That weren't much use. So I kissed her.

I fixed up to take her for a walk. I thought: I'll surprise her! and I went and bought her a fancy pinafore, pretty it was, wrapped in a parcel. She took one look at that parcel, squealed like a rat in a trap and run! I catched hold of her. 'It's alright! It's a *present*! It's a pinafore to put round you!'

She apologized. 'I thought it was a bomb!' And she smiled. When they smiled it was like seeing the first swallow. We'd left the town, we was walking through this field, hand-in-hand. I'd given her a bit o' my chocolate when who should we meet but Captain Bethell. I cussed! As I said, he hated women.

'Oo's that?' He points his stick at the wench. 'Oo's that?'

'Sir! I'd lost me way, sir, I was just talking to this young lady, askin er if she could direct me back to the war.'

He says: 'That's alright then. Come wi me, I'll show you!'

In the end I ran out o' chocolate and the Mess Cook shopped us. We was at the estaminet. Somebody had found a piano accordion and we was all a-dancing. I jumps on to a barrel and starts beating time. And in comes Captain Bethell. He says: '*You*, Hewins! You's old enough to know better! I'm disgusted wi you.' He gave us all a good dressing down, then we followed him back like a lot o' ducks, one behind the other. The girls waved. We never saw them again.

They closed the canal, put a guard on it, so's we couldn't go over. It was made out-of-bounds.

Captain Edwards said: 'Why did you take the risk?'

'I might be the next to go under.'

'Don't talk so foolish,' he said. 'Nobody knows oo's goin to be the next.'

*

We walked back to the front through fields o' red poppies. They was that bright they affected our eyes—we could see red for days.

> I don't wanna go to the trenches no more,
> Where the Jack Johnsons they beat on your door.
> Take me over the sea,
> Where the alleyman can't snipe at me.
> Oh my, I don't wanna die,
> I wanna go home.

We knowed where we was a-going. The sound of the war was ahead of us, like summer thunder, and the flash of shells.

We went quieter through the villages; we didn't sing. We marched to attention with bayonets fixed. And so we came to the brick fields. They'd got a big place dug out, like a cellar, underneath the brickworks, the brick kilns. There was a lot of brass about, a-telephoning to the front and that.

Good! we thought, Jerry won't 'it us 'ere! But no sooner had we settled down when he started to take the brickworks off, the kiln off; row by row he kept chucking shells. I hears a shout: ' 'Elp me! Somebody 'elp me!'

I dashed up the steps: 'What's up kid?'

'The buggers 'as blinded me!' he cried. 'I can't see!'

It was the blast from the powder, when it hit the kiln. Jerry knowed somebody was there, right enough: it was hot at the brickworks, hot shelling. He got information—from *French spies!*

Yes! We was all agreed about that! You couldn't trust the French—they was crafty, by God, craftier'n Jerry! We swopped stories about them. I said: 'You remember soon after we got to the front an we went over in a bayonet charge?' They all nodded. Well, none of us was likely to forget *that!*

'An six on us got strayed from the regiment? Well,' I says, 'there was a little cottage in a field. Roachy an me sees a gal, a French gal. She comes out and says summat, we couldn't understand it all. 'Course, we thought we was alright!' Everybody knowed what I meant. 'So—we starts talking an showing photographs. I showed her mine. Then, all of a sudden she cries: "Mama! Papa! Picanninies! It can't be you! Run, *run!*" She ran like hell, so did I! And VROOM! Up went that cottage with the other five in it, Roachy and all. This photograph saved my life!'

'Ah,' said one of my pals, 'that French gal was spyin for Jerry. No doubt about it.'

*

There was going to be a big battle. We could smell it. We could smell the ammunition coming up, the shells being brought up to the artillery. We knowed summat was a-coming off, and as soon as they started to bring up jars o' rum for *us*, we knowed that we'd be in it. The old Colonel appeared. He said: 'It'll be a walk over lads!'

Our front line trenches was like a horse-shoe and we was in the middle of the U. Two minutes afore half-past-five we was to crawl out; the flanks was to wait. Half-past-five under cover of a barrage, we went. It was a summer's afternoon*, through a cornfield, lovely sun shining—but it didn't shine on your buttons cos you never cleaned them! No use polishing yourself up so's he could see you. But the flanks did see us. Soon as they seed us crawling out, *they* came out—Jerry saw them and that was it!

It came like chucking gravel out a cart. It was busting everywhere. There was only about a hundred yards between us and Jerry. I stayed close to my officer. Those who had cutters on the end of their rifles tried to cut through the barbed wire so's we could get through. It was all planned out, who was the cutters. One got about six or seven yards o' wire and cut it and pushed it down, so's we could get over it. My trousers and my puttees was ripped. I moved quick. It was hand-to-hand fighting. We wasn't *drunk*, but we was awkward. They'd given us enough rum to make us awkward. I would have done anything to anybody. I wouldn't a-done it sober.

And all the time I was thinking: I must get shelter, and if I can get into their trenches I'll be alright maybe. But I never got the chance. A shell bust on top. It was only like a donkey kicking me. I looked down and I was bleeding. I put my hand on it, to jelly the blood. It seemed I was hit in the hip, Captain Edwards in the knee. I got one of my puttees off, thinking to bind his leg somehow and a German came for me from behind. They was coming from *behind*! Captain Edwards saw him and he shot him with his revolver, shot him from where he lay. He fell dead on me. But not afore he'd stuck his bayonet in my arse.

When did I open my eyes? I don't think I ever shut them. I wish I could a-done. I heard a chap saying: 'I'm done! I've been carrying the f——g wounded all night—it's no good!'

It was midnight. We'd been there six hours!

Another voice said: 'Shove im on my back! Put your arms round me, mate.'

* *19th July 1916*

They took it in turns. Two hundred yards back was a first-aid station, where they patched you up. Walt Clack runs up. 'George! You got hit?'

'Ah,' I said.

He was an officer's cook. He said: 'I'll go an get some whisky.'

Next thing I knowed, they was carrying *him* in. 'What's up Walt? Where's the whisky?'

He says: 'I don't bleedin know. I *got* it for you,' he says, 'and Jerry hit me! You won't find it now!' He whispered: 'I wonder if we'll get to Blighty?'

They sent us further down, by ambulance. But news travelled fast. It had been a slaughter. Eighty of our battalion was left standing—none of the officers in our Company—and we was over one thousand strong. In the field hospital a chap laid next to me. I thought: I'd know that voice anywhere! It was the Sergeant! Sergeant Fife.

'In and out an up an on the left—SHIT!' he shouted, over and over again. He'd had both his arms blowed off.

The last thing I remembered was two blokes whispering to each other: ' . . . Funny, after that charge! Ole Bethell was missin—never found im. Ah. Nobody ever found im in No Man's Land. Maybe,' said one to the other, 'e bust.'

*

When I came to there was a face bending over me, trying to say 'George'. It was a nurse—and she was black as night!

'Ullo,' she was saying, 'Ullo, Judge.'

And so I got friendly with her. Some o' the chaps weren't so keen. 'Er *smells* pecoolier!' Coming from them that was a bit of a nerve. Well, smell she might a-done—it was a funny frowsty sort o' smell, like Cal's clothes shop—but she walked like a Queen. You never seen anybody walk like that wench, and carrying shit pans and all: head high, tits and hips a-swaying. You'd a-thought she owned the world!

They was always teasing her: 'It comes from balancin all those coconuts an tack on her head—don't it missus?'

'Where you *from*? Zululand?'

'What's er doin *'ere?*'

I had to agree. It did seem a mysterious thing: a wench as black as night in the middle o' France!

She smiled at the other chaps, or laughed. The only one she ever talked to was me.

Now it happened that this black nurse was fascinated by my hair—it was thick and strong—she couldn't keep her hands off it. She comes up to my bed one day with her hands cupped together and she says: 'Judge! See!'

On her palm—she had shell pink palms! 'You pink anywhere else?' I said, and she laughed—was a clutch o' wild birds' eggs.

'For hair!' A funny look came into her eyes, almost as if... She broke the wild birds' eggs into a basin and she set to work. 'Keep doin it wi this, Judge, rub em in,' she said low—in perfect English! I could a-dropped! 'English eggs'll do—and you'll never lose it.'

The other chaps stared. Then she said, loud: 'Now—visitor! My friend de WITCHDOCTOR!'

You could almost hear the eyes a-popping! He was black and all, a little wiry chap with a big grin. Well, he starts tapping my head and mumbling and muttering.

'You's the first white man e's visited.'

'E's—a nice chap!'

'E's a friend o' mine. E likes you. You won't die now—you'll live to be a hundred!'

'Ow'd e get in 'ere?'

All she'd tell me was he went about with her, from hospital to hospital. 'Afore I was a nurse,' she said, 'I was in a circus. We went all over the world, north an south, east an west. I danced on red hot irons.'

'What did *e* do?' He'd finished with my head, he was playing on the back wall with a shut-knife. 'Tell im e'll dub the point o' that knife on the bricks,' I said.

She weren't listening. 'Look!' she said. She lifted one of her feet up. The sole, *it* was pink, was a mass o' blisters!—then the other.

'You a married man?'

I thought I'd show her the photograph—well, it had saved my life. But when she saw it her fussing wavered and went.

She never came again. The other chaps made out they couldn't remember her. 'Oo?' they said. I could see they'd ganged up together: they was jealous, I expect. So I asked one of the other nurses about her. She shook her head and smiled and said: 'You been very, very poorly.'

That's all she would say.

The witchdoctor weren't the only visitor I had. Captain Edwards came to the hospital, he was on crutches, to see how I was.

'I'll show you this telegram,' he said. They'd sent a telegram for me to get leave! 'MOTHER GRAVELY ILL'.

'I'm afraid,' he said, 'I've got another un.'

I can guess, I thought. 'Well, she's out er misery.'

'Ows the wound?' he says. 'You know what Shakespeare said?' 'Course, he knowed I came from Stratford, we'd had many a chat in the trenches. "Take off thy coat and show thy scars!" He said: 'You'd look well a-takin off your trousers and showin your'n!'

'Yes,' I said, 'I'm glad I had some fun at La Gorgue.'

The Zeppelins was dropping bombs, we could hear the shrapnel a-rattling against the building.

Captain Edwards said: 'It's followed us.'

When that shell bust by the trenches it had cut my thigh, made a wound eighteen inches long, three wounds in the back, ripped one leg open to the knee, and blown the top of my privates off.

It was a Blighty one. When they was carrying me on to the boat at Boulogne I vowed to myself: Here's an end of it for me. Nobody will get me to no war, never again.

They said: 'What you got there, under that blanket?' It was my tin helmet. I wanted it. The Sergeant used to tell us: 'Don't be seen DEAD wi'out your helmet!'

They said: 'You can't take that. Come on!' I wouldn't let go. 'Give it to us. You won't need that no more.'

We set off for England. All of a sudden there was a shudder and a boom. We'd been torpedoed!

'This is it!' I thought. I was blowed into the sea, strapped to my stretcher. Somebody was shouting: 'Raise yourself up! Don't keep your head down!' Waves rushed over me. *'Raise yourself up!'*

Next minute I was out the water: the navy had picked me up!

If I'd had my helmet on I could a-drownded.

*

I was in hospital in London a year, with a weight on my leg. I was wrapped up same as babbies in the old-fashioned days, and a pair o' rubber knickers. It was a military hospital, but there was plenty o' ladies fussing about. The Colonel's lady—Colonel Lodder—she was a fine looking woman; her daughter was the same age as our Jess.

She said: 'Any news from home?'

'My daughter's bein confirmed.' The missus had said in her letter: 'I got a veil for our Jess off the Church. I've altered it so's she won't be took for a workhouse brat but she ain't got a decent dress!'

Well, me mentioning that was a lucky stroke! The Colonel's wife paid the missus's fare up to London! She smiled and she said: 'You can keep this dress! It was *my daughter's*!' It was a lovely white dress—silk. 'Take it!' she said.

'Thank you ma'am,' said the missus. She was pleased but she made no fuss. It weren't her way.

The nurse said: 'Shall I show you 'is wound now?' She took the bandages off—and the missus fainted! They had to keep her in hospital overnight.

In the morning I said: 'Cheer up. It's not so bad. I could a-been dead.' I gave her a piece o' copper they'd took out o' me, big as a penny it was, to make a locket.

'Yes!' she says. 'I wishes you *was*!'

It was a nasty shock, I can tell you.

She throwed a letter down on the bed, in front o' me. I saw 'Your loving—'

Well, it seems that when I got wounded, instead of sending Winnie's letters and chocolate to the hospital, they sent them to the Regimental H.Q. at Warwick. Warwick found my address in Stratford and sent them there! To our house!

'Read it!' she said.

'*You'll be pleased to know I got a better job now—I'm a lady bath attendant.*'

The missus said: 'I wishes you was both at the bottom o' the bloody bath, drownded together!'

I thought fast. It was no use me telling her I'd never been but two yards with the wench. 'It's George Sprowson,' I said. 'It's that chap over there.'

When she was out I tipped him well. He said: 'Now it weren't your husband as had all those chocolates an socks off this wench. I'm a married man, missus, and I asked George 'ere if e'd let me 'ave it sent in 'is name—and all the letters I opened, an the parcels.'

Emma gave me a funny look. Then she pulled a pound note out her breast. ''Ere—you better 'ave this.'

That was a narrow squeak! I said to myself. I thought I'd got out of it!

I told her: 'I don't want it.' Well, army pay had been five francs a week. I'd got a tidy bit left: the nurse kept changing it for me into English. 'It'll do you more good.'

That's the only time I ever refused money!

*

I used to sing the old fashioned comics for the Colonel's lady. *Another Little Drink* and *The Donkey Ride* were her favourites—that surprised me.

> She got on to the roundabouts
> And a lot o' things beside,
> But the best o' the fun was when she begun
> 'Avin a donkey ride—

One day two of us, me and Charlie MacDonald, was took out for tea. She said: 'We could use a song or two, couldn't we, Alice?' Alice was the young girl who took us.

Well, I got pally with her. We was in this Hall; the Colonel's lady and her friends was sat there listening. I took the girl's part:

> Oh George isn't it nice,
> I like it—it seems to go throo-oo yer.
> Never before have I had it I'm sure,
> The feelin's most pecooliar.
> Makes you feel 'all over' like,
> It really is sublime.
> Oh do let me go for another un George,
> Is it only a penny a time?

Then I sang in a deeper voice—

> She 'ad about a dozen rides,
> I thought she'd never stop.
> She whacked that poor ole donkey,
> Till they thought that e would drop.
> But the more e made to chuck er off,
> She caught hold of 'is mane,
> And she shouted 'Oh Neddy! Oh steady boy steady!
> We'll 'ave it all over again!

I tell you, it surprised me, her choosing *that* one, and I touched this girl's elbow, this young girl called Alice. She was stood by my wheelchair. That did it! I never saw the Colonel's wife no more! The matron put a card on my bed with 'MARRIED'. As fast as I kept turning it to the wall she turned it back.

'I've got my orders,' she said.

The nurses was on our side. They throwed details as to who was in what ward, how bad our wounds was, out of the window. The factory girls picked them up and came of a Sunday. They'd say to me: 'Where's the bloke with the big un?' We had a laugh! Two sat on my bed, two on Charlie MacDonald's. He was a sheep shearer, from Australia; we was good pals. He said: 'Why don't you come to Australia, George? It's the Land of Opportunity.'

They brought us fruit. Matron said: 'Come on! E's married!' She pointed to the notice. They said: '*We* don't mind, missus!' and laughed. Those Cockney girls were full o' cheek.

Matron got her own back later. She'd sniff. 'I can smell fruit.' And she'd take it all off us, all we hadn't ate.

Then the Colonel came round. He made a beeline for me. He said: 'It's about time this chap went out of 'ere, ain't it? Lets have another look at 'is leg.'

And so I was sent to Ireland. They'd got a hospital at Stratford but they had to send me to Ireland for my next operation!

It was Christmas Eve 1917. It was a very hard winter, and snowing. They put me in charge of five more chaps cos I was the oldest soldier.

They said: 'Can we 'ave our travellin warrants?'

I said: 'It's all in one.'

'Oh,' they said.

The train stopped at Cheltenham and a young Captain from the Regiment came round to inspect the wounded. He looked hard at me and kept staring. He said: 'My God, it ain't Little Jack?'

It was Bert! Bert Middleton, Nance's lad. He'd done well: he'd got a commission in the Warwicks! He was the only one I knowed as had. He talked posh. I thought: Well, she done summat wi ole Cal's money!

He was keen on the army, you could see that, keen as mustard. I didn't say nothing. It weren't no use me saying what I thought. He'd got to find out for himself.

He said: 'I'll go and see the Colonel, Jack.'

He comes back. 'No luck! E says, "My orders is all these cripples 'ave got to go to Ireland." '

And so I lost touch with him again.

When we gets to Cardiff these five chaps who was with me says: 'We're a-goin to the buffet. We shan't be a tick!'

And they all went *home*! Brummagem chaps! They all went home. I looked the other way; if I could a-moved much I'd a-gone with them. I was the only one with two crutches. Months later I met a couple of them. They nudged me and said: 'Ey! Ain't you the chap oo was in charge of us?'

I said: 'Yes! Ow did you get on?'

They said: 'Only a month!' A month's pay stopped.

It snowed and blowed on the boat to Ireland. On the deck there was an officer with a telescope. He kept saying he could see a submarine. 'There! There!' He was a bag o' nerves—so was we by the time he'd done. When we landed they said: 'Hewins an Party?' I had to tell them—the Party had missed the train.

There was a gang of us, about two hundred, all sorts. I was put in the married quarters at the camp, with some Irish troops. We'd only got one blanket apiece for the night. They said: 'E can't sleep on the floor wi nothin on im. It's freezin. E'll be dead be mornin.' And they all gave me their blankets.

The next day they put me in hospital, at Cork, and I had an operation.

*

When I came back from Ireland they just gave me a note for the Colonel in London saying *Finish the job you started on*. I had to travel with an officer. I saw him give his servant my warrant to travel. There was a lot o' ladies in the compartment. They kept saying to the officer's servant: 'Go on—*give* it im! The chap wants to go home an see 'is wife! *Go on*!'

The bloke says: 'I daresn't.'

I went to have a shit, at Cardiff. Shitting was like having the bayonet up me, all over again. I was at low ebb, I can tell you. I thought: 'I'll escape now! 'Ave a week at home!' But I couldn't run, I was a cripple. Asides, I was in the blue. They put all the wounded servicemen in blue. They'd have spotted me and catched me.

I reckon that officer *knowed*. He watched me like a hawk after Cardiff: he took me on the bus, right up to the gates of the hospital, he seed me in and shut them. He didn't mean losing me, ah! And it happened that the Colonel was there and he said: 'Oo's this?' He didn't remember me.

Says the officer: 'Just returned from Ireland, Sir, and this is what e wants to give you.'

It was the note: '*Finish the job you started on!*'

'Oh,' he says, 'well, I'll 'ave to 'ave a look at that leg, I suppose.' And he had a look at it. 'Course, it was bound up.

He said: 'I'll 'ave to 'ave the bandages off to show the rest of the jury. E can't go with them on.'

I says to the Corporal after they'd gone: 'D'you reckon there's any chance of me getting my ticket?'

'If *e's* put you on the Board,' he says, 'the *Colonel*, you'll get it!' I didn't take no chances! I watched that leg. There was only skin over, sealing the big wound, where the ragged bone was. I used to bend down and do up my shoes, split it open. I knowed what that chap had meant: '*I'll suffer the agony*'.

I had to go afore the Board, show them my leg. There they sat, a load of old Colonels. You'd a-thought I was guilty o' summat. I started to wonder what I'd been pinching, to *feel* guilty! They fussed and they ummed and they aahed.

'Alright,' they said, 'e can go.'

I was given a paper—

> *Private George Henry Hewins of 7th Warwick-*
> *shire is discharged on account of being no longer*
> *physically fit—*

—and a suit. The cap they gave me had inside it 'WANDSWORTH WORKHOUSE'.

*

I was free! I got as far as the top of Praed Street, and there was a public there called the 'Load o' Hay'—well, it *could* a-been called the 'Load o' Hay'! I went in.

This publican—cos I'd got my kitbag, see—he says: 'Let me shake hands wi you! You got your ticket?'

I says: 'Ah.'

'Where d'you come from?'

'Stratford.'

He says: 'This is a Stratford pub!' It was a Flowers' house, owned by the brewery. 'Go on!' he said, ''ave what you like!'

And he got me drunk. Then he took me outside to the copper. The copper says: 'We'll see you aboard, mate! It's only 'bout fifty yards onto the platform, onto Paddington Station!'

Who should we meet when we gets on there but our padre! I thought: 'E couldn't be much farther from the war'n *this*!'

He looks me up and down and he says: 'E's in a nice mess.'

'Ah,' says the copper. 'E 'appened to go to the "Load o' Hay".'

'Where's e got to go to?'

'Stratford.'

The padre says: 'I'm goin to Hatton Asylum!'

'Blimey!' I thought.

'I'll see im to Hatton: e'll 'ave to change there. E ain't got above eight more miles to go—likely e'll be sober by then.'

*

The kiddies ran home. They said: 'Mam! We seen a man! We was a-goin into school this afternoon an we seen a man wi a kitbag an crutches a-comin from the station. 'Is face weren't 'alf black—e kept fallin down—e was drunk!—but it looked just like our Dad!'

She said: 'It was. E's upstairs.'

CHAPTER NINETEEN

Next morning I woke and I thought: I'm home!

The sun was shining. I said: 'I'll go and see the grave.'

The missus said: 'Your mother ain't there.'

'*Ain't there?*' It was a double grave, Joshua Farr's, it had been bought.

'They said it ud cost a lot o' money. They'd 'ave to open it, turf it.'

I couldn't believe it! 'There's a vacant grave there! She 'ad an insurance!'

The missus shrugged her shoulders.

'Where is she then?'

She was in a common grave! After all that, she'd been shovelled into a common grave with folks from the workhouse. We rowed! I went to see Bogey White, at the cemetery. He told me how much it would cost to get her out—I *couldn't* get her out. I hadn't the money, it had all gone. I'd got to leave her in there with strangers: a little girl aged five, an old tramp—

I was shocked, shocked. 'But—'

'Don't fret, George,' said Bogey White. 'Emm's right—the money'll do your kiddies more good. It only cost ten bob to put er in.' He said: 'You's *poor*, George!'

He spoke the truth, but that didn't make it no sweeter. I stood there and cried like a babby.

We was a-getting into bed and Emma says: 'I'm sorry.'

'I'm sorry an all,' I said, ''bout Harry.'

She'd had a tidy go. She buried my mother, I got hit, and Harry—all in the same month. The Germans used to drop three-cornered steel spikes, from Zeppelins, to cripple the horses. Harry Bayliss hadn't got his helmet on; one hit him in the head, went straight through his brain, killed him.

She said: 'You know ow the postman allus knocks on the door? Well, that mornin e didn't knock. E opened it an throwed it in.' She said: 'I wondered why e didn't knock.'

I said: 'What's 'appened to you?' There was a lump hanging out of her stomach, big as a rugby football.

She tried to cover it up. 'I could ask you the same.'

I said: 'Well, you've got no belly, I've got no balls. That's one good turn they done us—we can't 'ave no more kiddies! Hop in,' I said, 'let's 'ave a cuddle.'

She'd got it hay baling with the Forage Corps. While the war was on the women went hay baling, at the East and West station, down by the racecourse. It was hard work after having a babby and she'd gone and ruptured herself. You couldn't have an operation for summat like that, not unless you got a ticket. You had to pay or get a ticket signed by a local businessman, a big shopkeeper. She was too proud to go a-begging.

I thought: I'm not! Tomorrow I'll see what the pickins is! I told myself: You weren't brought up by Cal Cook for nothin!

*

'Wait there,' said one bloke. I thought I was in luck.

He gave me a book: *The Complete Works of William Shakespeare*. A *book*! Somebody had writ inside: 'It is hoped that this will always keep you in mind of the true greatness and glory of the cause for which you have fought and suffered.'

Then I went to see the Vicar, Canon Melville. He looked me up and down and he said: 'I ain't got no ticket, but we gives a pound a year to twelve *deservin* cases. You 'as to come to Church to qualify, spend a morning in Church every Sunday for a year. 'Course, I won't *guarantee* it,' he says, 'it's all *depending*—'

And then I had a letter from Malvern. It was from Captain Edwards' Dad. He writ and said: 'My son is dead!' And a ten bob note fell out! 'Jumbo',—*Jumbo!*—'went back to the front and was hit,' he said. There was pages of it! 'E thought a lot o' you,' he said, 'missed you when you went—the *company*. If you writes back I'll send you another un,' said Captain Edwards' Dad. Writing never came easy to me, but I did. I writ back and told him what a nice chap Captain Edwards had been—well, it was true!—and got another ten bob. Then I got tired of answering. He never sent no more.

'Never mind,' said the missus, 'I wouldn't a-let em cut me anyways. Look,' she said, 'you got one from the *army* this morning!' She always opened the letters. 'Maybe it's the Medical Board.' They kept calling you for examination, to see if you'd got better—some hopes o' that—then they could dock your money. The first Board I'd been to I'd done alright: they gave me *extra*! I went to Budbrook Barracks. There was a sergeant there I knowed: Sergeant Sanders. He shouts across the square: 'Ullo Hewins! Ow you gettin on?'

There was two young officers on the Board; he went to them. 'I knows this chap well. E is an intimate friend. You keep on wi your tennis and I'll look at 'is leg.'

I had a five bob rise on the pension they gave me for being disabled—and they never seen me!

'Sergeant Sanders is a good chap,' I said.

'Huh,' said the missus, 'listen to this!' I could see her dander was up. The letter was from the Recruiting Office: 'If you don't report to this Office by eleven o'clock a military escort will be sent to fetch you! Just let them come!' said the missus.

Two soldiers obliged.

'What do *you* want?' she said. She stood across the door with her arms folded.

'Read this, missus!'

'E's been out this twelve month, wounded.'

'Ah,' they said. They had a think. 'You gotta son George Hewins?'

The other un said: 'That's it, missus, we'll 'ave *im*.'

She said: 'E's been six month in the Flyin Corps. 'Ere—where's *you* a-goin?' She thought I was going to the pub. She was getting fed up with me drinking. Many a night I got a bit groggy and a couple o' chaps would say: 'We'll take you home George! We's a-goin your way!' But today I weren't after rum—

'I'm gonna find a *Magistrate*,' I said.

They told me I better get a Magistrate to sign me off. I went to

Fred Winter and he said: 'I'm a very busy man. You go to Boyden at the *Herald*.'

I told him! I said: 'You weren't too busy when you signed for me to go in!' I felt better after that. Then I went to the Recruiting Office. I'd got the silver badge on and the two wounded stripes.

'I'm George Hewins,' I said. I chucked my badge on the counter. I'd a-chucked the stripes and all but I couldn't get them off, they was sewed on.

'Good God,' he says. He could see I was a cripple. 'This must be a mistake. We'll apologize. I'm very sorry.'

On the way home, I met an Irish girl by the workhouse. 'You can 'ave this,' I said. And I gave her my silver badge: 'SERVICES RENDERED'.

'What you done that for?' said the missus when I told her. 'I could a-*pawned* it!'

*

And so I pottered up and down Waterside—I had crutches at first, and then two sticks—sat in the Bancroft when it was warm, with the old men. We talked about the days afore the war, and women getting the vote. They should never go to Parliament, I said. We didn't want no petticoat rule—'We got enough o' that at home!'

'That's the way, George!'

Stratford seemed to a-changed as much as I had! The streets weren't *tidy* no more—well there weren't the blokes to do it—and there was queues everywhere: queues of women waiting for food, queues of wounded soldiers from Clopton House waiting for God knows what, there was even a queue for bloaters at the corner o' Meer Street! Who should I meet on Meer Street but Jack Wright.

'Ullo,' he says.

I asked him if he knowed of any work? He shook his head. 'You's a-goin to be a gentleman, George,' he says, 'for the rest of your life. Ey!' he says, 'I 'ear that nancy boy Taylor's copped it. Best thing as could 'appen if you asks me.'

I couldn't hit him; I could never do no more bricking neither. Ah. I could only do what was on the floor, I couldn't go up in the air, or bend, come down the ladder. Nobody would take me on to do the

33. Wounded soldiers queuing at the Town Hall, Stratford-upon-Avon

bottom; you'd got to take your share, go up with the rest. The army had given me a character—Character Certificate Number 3733:

Description: 5ft. 3 ins. Complexion: Rather pale. Eyes: Blue. Hair: Dark, slightly greying.

Somebody had added 'Scars' and 'His conduct while serving with the colours has been very good. Civil qualification: Bricklayer.'

There was a big queue outside the Stores: the margarine cart had come! Margarine and butter was rationed and tempers was a-running high on account of the notice: 'RATION CARDS AIN'T NO GUARANTEE OF SUPPLY'. A rumour was flying about that folks with money had got their cellars stored high with butter and marg, to say nothing of tea, and the Stores was supplying them! The manager comes to the door, adds fuel to the flames:

'There ain't enough to serve you all!' and 'To see this gang out 'ere you'd think we was givin summat away!'

A woman shouts: 'They am! Up at the Recruitin Office! Khaki suits!'

Things start to get nasty. The missus was in the queue too and she shouts: 'If you'd like one go up an get one!'

They all cheered. 'Ah!' bawls another, 'we knows the breed an seed o' *you*, Artie Finch!'

I laid low. But I thought those women shouting about khaki suits should go and see for themselves, then they'd *know* what war was like. They wouldn't even wish it on Artie Finch then! But what was the point of saying we was wet through, sat on the firestep all night 'case Jerry came over, and the clothes dried on you next day—would they a-believed it? And there was your pals blowed to bits aside of you—like Tommy Taylor, who wouldn't a-hurt a fly—legs, brains, fingers, splattered about. I was still upset 'bout Tommy. I'd seen one of his sisters in the town; not to speak to, the Taylor girls was always a stuck up lot—poor, proud and pretty as they say. There was Tommy splattered about in a foreign country where they didn't even speak the language—for *what*?

*

That was a time when I couldn't abide being shut in. Rain or snow, I didn't stop in the house if I could help it. For a start there was the silence. So silent it was you could hear the clock a-ticking—*tock! tock! tock!* It didn't matter to me that the war was over. 'I'm not celebratin,' I said. I weren't *handy* no more. I got under the missus' feet.

The older kiddies was at work. Our Ede had started at Asquith's of Old Town, skivvying. She stopped one week—and walked out! The missus said: 'You're supposed to be at work! I'm takin you back!' They always reckoned to go to the missus if they wanted to ask about a job, or anything. The last word was hers.

But our Ede said: 'I shan't go. I'm not 'avin that, even if I don't 'ave nothin. Why should I go cleanin other folks' houses out? The Asquiths is no better'n us—worse! They owe money all over the town, my Dad says so.'

The missus says: 'You'll lose *two-an-ninepence*!'

'And for another thing,' says our Ede, 'there's four servants over you, reportin. I'm goin to the Guffin.'

So she and our Jess went to the brewery, at the bottling end. It was hard work, lifting cases o' bottles—yes, I reckon it was hard work for them. When they started they was underground and up to their ankles in water all day, wearing clogs and 'erden aprons. They called them 'the Guffinites'.

'Never mind,' said Ede, 'you knows when you's a-goin to start an when you's a-goin to finish. And you gets your money on Friday night.'

They kept half a crown. The missus had the rest: seven and six apiece. Ede was like her: she was strong. Poor Jess died of it, but that's another tale.

*

Mornings was the worst time. The pubs didn't open till dinner time now; the younger kiddies had gone to school, all but our Mary. She kept shrinking from me. She didn't know me, she howled for her Mam.

The missus said: 'Put er down an stand over there by that door.'

'Oo? Me?'

She said: 'What about this gal? It's a lie! It ain't George Sprowson on the letters! It's a lie!' She'd had another letter from Winnie Walderviss. It *was* a lie!

'Oh,' I says, 'it's the truth.'

'I'm goin to Cirencester,' she said, 'to see er mother—now!' And she stuck her hat-pin through her hat.

I reckon she frit Winnie's mother to death. She wrote after and told the missus: 'I still can't believe it! It can't be! He *can't* be a married man with children! My daughter would a-*knowed*—why, he'd be betwixt thirty and forty, with eight kids!'

Poor Winnie! Her mother said she kept saying: 'It *couldn't* be im, Mam!'

I got out of it, but it was a struggle. I hope *she* did. She might a-been funny looking—I could hardly picture her now—but her chocolate gave me a lot o' pleasure, one way and another.

'She's earnt 'er seat in Heaven,' I said. It just came out. The missus looked at me, sharpish: 'What's that s'pposed to mean?' But from that day forth she was softer to'ards me. Plain words she always used, that was her way, but she never lashed me with her tongue again, not after going to see Winnie's mother.

*

Things were starting to look up! The next excitement was—I heard
about a *job*! I couldn't wait to tell the missus.

'I met Sanders up the town.'

'Oh aye.'

'E allus asks after you.'

'You didn't buy im a drink did you?'

'No.' It was another lie.

The war was over, but Sergeant Sanders had six months to serve
of his time. The missus didn't like me mixing with him: she said
he was a *rapscallion*.

'Sanders says they wants a night watchman at Clopton House.'
It was turned into a convalescent home for soldiers. 'E reckons I
might get it on account o' my wound.'

I *did*! It was all night, at the top of that lane, and very lonely left
propped against the gatepost there in a wooden sentry box—but it
was a job! I kept the box locked. I daresn't look out in the dark:
chaps shouted their names and I crossed them off. I took their word
for it! 'Bannockburn' was the army password. The wounded had
got to know it. 'Bannockburn!' they sang, 'Bannockburn—'night,
George!' And off they went, down to Stratford. Who could blame
them? I didn't! ' 'Night!—'Night!' I never said a word more. If I'd
a-argufied they'd a-pushed me over, box and all!

In that coffin up Clopton Lane I started to have dreams. I fancied
I was still in the trenches, with the rats running all over: swarms
o' rats with yella eyes and big fat bellies. You could a-told me it
was only the branches of a tree a-squeaking and a-scratching across
the top o' the box—it wouldn't a-made no difference. I used to get
off the seat and crouch underneath it, eyes shut, hands over my ears.

The Reverend Hodgson from Clopton House, he was Sir
Arthur's son and a parson, he comes to see me. 'All those wounded
as stands along the rails—clear em off!' he says. 'They've caught
some pushers up 'ere,' he says. 'You're not doin your duty!'

'I got two sticks—I can't give em much of a hand.' I thought: I
wish I could!

He didn't like me answering back. 'A soldier gave a Stratford gal
'is coat last night. Didn't you notice e 'ad no top-coat when e come
back?'

Course I hadn't! I never looked out!

'And they's drinkin till all hours. They's comin back *drunk*!'
I pulled a face.

'I'm goin to the Colonel 'bout you,' he said.

So I got the sack. And I got a paper come to go to another Medical Board. I went and they knocked me a quid off and I'd only been earning five and twenty bob! They knocked me a quid off my pension.

'You's workin,' they said. 'You must be alright!'

I couldn't believe it. That's what done me—starting work! I thought: Yes, it looks as if they're goin to stop it all!

'God help us,' said the missus.

*

I had an idea. I put in for the lump sum! Everybody swallowed it: you gave up your pension and you got a lump sum. Well, it was enough to buy the kiddies new rig-outs and a couple o' dozen fowl, to start a poultry farm in the garden. The trouble was, I couldn't move fast enough. The neighbours had the eggs—three for sixpence and a fowl for a bob—but I couldn't get the money off them.

I bought a game cockerel. One morning, I was on my hands and knees checking to see if there was any chicks born and he got on the back of my neck. The neighbours had to come and rescue me—from an old cockerel!

Even the dog got the better of me. We had a dog I'd found by the canalside; somebody had tried to drown him. I put the eggs in dozens and they kept disappearing. The neighbours said: 'You's misjudgin us! Look in 'is mouth!' It was the dog!

Then we had a lot o' ducks. They'd get out of hand, kept coming in the back kitchen, catched hold o' the missus' stockings.

'You flamers!' she shouted.

And a pig. He'd come in, flop himself down in the kitchen. It took three or four of us to shove him out! He'd squeal his head off! We mixed a bowl up to tempt him, he knowed it was wash, and he'd follow us back up the garden with a smile on his face.

Beasts as well as folks, they all took advantage. Even the budgigeers. I bought a few budgigeers—I liked to see them flying free—and they started laying, faster'n the fowl. Soon I had fifty! They settled on my ears, kept pecking me round the chin. I couldn't sell them.

I said: 'It's no use. We's losin money on this!'

We *was*.

*

And then it happened I got the surprise of my life. It was winter again. I was hobbling up Windsor Street, going careful cos of the ice, when what should I see but—*three performing bears!*

Ullo! I says to myself. It ain't the drink—it must be shell shock!

They were making straight towards me! When they gets close the biggest bear throws up his arms: 'Jack lad! Little Jack!'

It was George Cook, come all the way from Canada with the butcher's widow and their daughter Bertha. They was in fur—*fur!*— from head to toe. He'd made his *fortune* in the war, selling dubbin for the troops!

'I reckoned the army had gotta march on its boots, lad. Remember, if you don't speculate you don't 'cumulate!'

They was staying in Leamington, at the Regent Hotel! 'Look us up, lad, look us up.'

'You seen Nance, then?'

His face changed. They'd had a row. 'Bertha ain't used to sharin a room.'

He wouldn't stay with his own sister! That shocked me. But I was thinking fast. He'd got money—bags and bags o' money by the looks of it. I told him I was out of work. 'There's nowt about. Those as does get fixed up, it's only for a week or a fortnight. Only job I heared of lately's caretaker at the National School. E ain't left yet but folks reckon Vicar'll make im cos e's gone and deserted 'is missus.' Yes, I thought, poor bastard. 'It's the kiddies suffer most, George, when you ain't got no money . . .'

'Get *confirmed*, lad,' said George. 'That's my advice to you. Get confirmed!'

' "Bertha ain't used to sharin!" Well!' said the missus when I told her. 'I thought I'd heared everythin!'

I could see she was upset about the money. She didn't like me begging—it weren't respectable, whatever that was—but she thought George might a-given us a bit. I said: 'Maybe they's stayin at the "Regent" on account o' Maggie.'

Nance still had Maggie: she'd always had her. Poor Maggie! She was a grown woman now, in her thirties. I heard afterwards that Maggie kept on saying: 'Why can't *I* 'ave a fur coat? Why can't *I* 'ave one?'

'George said e'd seen me Grandad. E told im e was down an out.'

'I bet e did,' said the missus. 'The crafty ole bugger.'

'George said the neighbours told im me Grandad ain't been the same since e heared 'bout Will Blackford.'

Will had been killed in the war. 'E won't last long, they say.'

'Huh.'

But my conscience was pricking me. I hadn't given the old man a thought for donkey's years. I went and I looked him out. He was by the Fountain in Rother Street. He says to me: ''Ave you seen our George? E's come to 'ave a tombstone made and e give me some money!' He did a little skip and a jump and I thought: 'Blow me—e got it!' and 'You'll live for ever, you ole devil.'

He was craftier than me, by far.

It seemed George Cook had come all the way from Canada to make arrangements for a *stone*! He'd bought the grave his Mam and Dad was in, bought the other folks as was in it too, and left the money with Mattie Wing. He didn't trust none of us to pay the gravemaker. Mattie did it and sent him a photograph of it, all the way back to Toronto. It's a big stone, with big letters, past the chapel towards the railway—

IN LOVING MEMORY

OF

WILLIAM

&

CAROLINE

COOKE

I smiled to myself when I seed it. I knowed what Cal would a-said about *that*. She'd got an 'e' and all.

◆ CHAPTER TWENTY ◆

I decided to take George Cook's advice. I put in to the Vicar. 'I got through the war wi'out bein *killed*,' I said, 'and I'm very grateful to God.'

'Well,' said the Vicar. You could see he was surprised. 'Well,' he said, 'I wishes there was more about like you.'

Maundy Thursday, a Bishop came to the Parish Church and done me. About thirty to forty kids was there that day, all in white; just me, with my medals, in the middle of them. It made a pretty picture. That day I wished I'd kept my silver badge. The church was packed. Afterwards the Vicar sidles up to me: 'The Bishop came an whispered in your ear. I should very much like to know what e said.'

'Well,' I said, 'e said "I think you've been a very brave man, Mister Hewins, wi a family o' children like you got, an no money an no work—"'

The Vicar said: 'D'you reckon you could do our school job? Our caretaker's gone an left 'is wife.'

'Oh, ah.' I tried not to look too keen.

'You got a wife,' he said. The missus was a-waiting in the porch. 'A big strong wife an grown children. They could help. The money ain't much—eight pounds a month—an you'll 'ave to wait a month for it.'

'We'll manage some'ow, your Worship,' I said.

*

In the church I'd caught the eye of two old maids, the Misses East. They lived by Narrow Lane. They went to the Vicar and they said: 'A rest ud do that poor chap good! Could we send im to a Church *home* for a month, to build up 'is strength afore e starts work?'

And so it came about that the Vicar wrote and got me in to Clewer Green. The Misses East came to the house and asked me when the rent was due. They said: 'We'll pay it.'

The missus glowered at them.

There was yards of paper to fill in, what I'd got to do. I'd even got to take the return fare in case I misbehaved myself!

The missus said: 'You're goin away again.' She didn't want me to go.

'I'll soon be back this time,' I said, 'and likely it'll be no trouble for me to be TT either. I've 'ad to *sign*!'

'Hmm.' She was trying to cure me of drinking. When I'd drunk too much and a couple o' chaps brought me home she'd be waiting. 'I got a bottle o' beer 'ere. You'll be wantin one shall you?'

She *knowed* I couldn't drink no more! And many a night I stayed downstairs. Drunk or sober I was afeared to go upstairs in the dark. When I did sleep in bed I had dreams about the trenches, with the rats running all over me. I tried to kick them with my feet. It was no use. I'd get out o' bed and hide underneath it, all night long, or till Emma found me.

*

Clewer was a mournful place two mile from Windsor. My heart sank when I seen it. This was their idea of a home! It was like a big barracks, with a wall fifteen foot high, big iron gates with spikes on top and a Chinaman holding them ready. Somewhere a bell tolled. It made me shudder when that bell sounded. The Guild Chapel bell was bad enough—but that! Then *bang*! The big gates shut behind me.

It was run by the Sisters o' Mercy. There was all sorts at Clewer: mostly folks who'd been sent out their villages by the Vicar, as weren't in good health. Asides the patients, the only blokes in the place was the Chinaman and a Vicar. There was even a lady doctor! I woke up in the night and she was bending over me.

Blimey! I thought.

It was the best experience I had in there.

It was all religion: three times a day to prayers, communion every week. We sat in rows for food—it was lovely food!—and the Sisters o' Mercy was watching our *eyes*! That was a job in itself cos they had hundreds o' young girls there, who they'd rescued. We never spoke to them. The Sisters walked between, dished out the dinners, so many to the girls, so many to us. I often wondered...

It was prayers, prayers, prayers. We sat in a circle afore we went

to bed. It was communion for me: the Vicar had told them I'd took
the Sacraments and did they give me some too! Then the bloke on
one side o' me, he kept me talking for hours, all about *Shakespeare*.
He worshipped Shakespeare. When he found out I was a Stratford
man he haunted me, drove me balmy. On the other side there was
a discharged soldier. I'd got pally with him. He whispers: 'If I stops
'ere another night I shall go crackers. You comin wi me?'

'I gotta stick it. I got no work, see, not yet. They're payin the rent.'

'Well I'm off!' he says. He climbed out of the window, over the
wall—and escaped!

I envied him, I can tell you.

There was a little Post Office in the village; I went there to post
a card to the missus:

ITS NICE ERE GRUB GOOD A BIG KISS X GEORGE

I meets a cabby there. I'd seen him afore, coming in through the
gates. Funny thing was, whenever he did this the bell would start
a-tolling. He says: 'Would you like to go out wi me? Any afternoon
I could take you round the village, round the town if you likes,
for one-an-six a-piece. I got some peppermints and I knows some
pubs.' Four of us went. He showed us the tree in the Park where
King Teddy and the Kaiser got arguing over summat and Teddy
knocked him down. Then we stopped at a pub.

After a couple o' pints I spoke what was on my mind: 'Ain't it
marvellous as the Sisters don't come wi you!'

'Ah,' he says, 'they trusts me.' He said to me: 'You're a-goin
home soon ain't you? Would you like to come out wi us tonight?'

So I sneaks out with him after we'd ate, in this hansom cab. We
gets up a dark alley. He shouts: ''Ere's one!' There was a young
girl stood there. 'You lost?'

'I must earn a few shillin, mister!'

'You poor thing.'

'I 'ad no food today.'

Then it was off to Clewer with them! He told me he'd picked
up more'n fifty girls like that, for the Sisters. He says to the girl—she
weren't above nineteen—'You wants to stop! It's a lovely place.
They'll 'ave a lovely meal for you.'

'Ah,' I said, 'I'll vouch for that'.

'What'll they *do* to me mister?' You could see that she was frit.

'Well,' he says, 'they'll strip you, give you a sackcloth shift, bath you. Then you'll 'ave a nice calico nightgown!'

She turned to me. ''Ere mister, if you finds the bloke oo owns this, will you give it to im?' She handed me a little stone.

'Oo is it?'

'The *Devil*.'

'Oh,' I said, 'well, I'll keep a look out.'

The Chinaman was there with the big gates ready. When he sees me he points at my wound, then points at himself and says in a squeaky voice: 'Bang! Poof!' He said that whenever he seen me. Those was the only words I ever heard him say. I reckon he'd been in some war himself and the blast had taken his wits away.

The young girl agreed to stop. Then they tolled the bell to let the village know they'd picked up another stray and she was a-stopping. I'd still got her stone in my pocket.

*

'Well, you been a teetotaller for a month!' said the missus when I got back. I didn't tell her I hadn't! 'Let's 'ave a good look at you!' She was pleased to see me. 'Go an give your Dad a kiss!' she said, but our Mary never would.

The Vicar sent for me. I'd got to tell him what it was like at Clewer. I laid it on with a trowel, you can bet your life I did. Then I went to sit for half-an-hour with the two old maids. We exchanged flowers. I told them about Clewer too, and about the Sisters. 'We made our own fun', I said. 'We played cricket most days—'

And I promised I'd call again, next weeksend. We became friends. I did their garden for them, gave them some o' my plants. They was nice old souls: they gave me many a pound, the Misses East.

*

The Vicar had been right about the school: it weren't one chap's work. I could see now why they'd wanted to build up my strength at Clewer! It took all of us, the missus down to Mary, to do it.

There was wood to chop, coal to heave, fires to make, floors to scrub, desks to polish, toilets to swill, fifty or sixty towels to wash a week, and dusters. 'Will you fetch a mop? A child's been sick!' Kiddies was always being sick at that time o' day. But the fact was, it was better'n nothing. The money weren't much, but there was blokes about Stratford still looking for work.

We was lucky four of our kids was earning. When they'd finished work they got their tea—all but Else, she was away in service—then they came to the school, to help us with the cleaning. We was finished by eight o'clock. Then Ede and Jess, they tidied themselves up, ready to go out, to meet the young chaps under the trees, up the Brum Road. Yes, they was courting age! The missus said: 'Don't you be no later'n nine o'clock! I don't want you two in the workhus!'

The workhouse was the big threat. I'd whisper to them: 'Well, I'm a-warnin you, come quiet. If she's locked up I'll let you in!' Many a time I let them in. All mothers was strict, by God. You'd see Mrs Windsor arriving, nine o'clock, for her Beryl. She'd be armed with a big stick. And her Norman—he had to sleep in the pigsty if he got in late—a grown lad, earning!

Our Else was lonely for home. Every week she wrote letters to the missus. She hated service. She was away at Kenilworth—up at the crack o' dawn, did the washing, cooking, ironing—just her, and looked after the kiddie. It never mattered if she was middling—you was never ill! Then she used to help to do the Midland Bank at night, till ten or eleven o'clock! He was manager of the Bank. She had to say 'Yes'm,' and 'Yessir', and 'Miss Joyce'. She was only three, that kid—*Miss Joyce!* The missus never said nothing. But she put her hat on and she went to Kenilworth and told our Else that the cook at the 'Red Horse' wanted help. When she came back she said:

'Never mind a reference for skivvies—they should 'ave a reference off the last un, to find out what sort o' missus they're goin to 'ave—if er's mean or bossy!'

Sunday dinner we sat down together. We always waited till the missus started. Then our Jim said summat under his breath. The kiddies giggled.

'I won't 'ave that dirty talk in *my* house!' said the missus, and gave him a clout. 'And don't speak wi your mouth full!'

Jim was the one who caught it most—not like our Cyril, *he* was the cleverest o' the lads and her favourite. It was Jim who caught pneumonia, it was Jim who fell in the cut. A fella from Cox's timber yard went over and fished him out; only his little coat saved him. The others started telling about things our Jim had done at school.

'I'm *ashamed* of you,' the missus would say, 'and I'm ashamed of *you* for reportin it.'

They said: 'Is it true? Is our Else comin home?'

'Yes!' said the missus.

The Vicar went to the school on Monday mornings. The kiddies said: 'Whenever e comes an we stand up e allus looks at me!' He was a big man, with a terrible face, dark and glaring. 'E's *'ere!*'

'Yes,' I thought, a-fingering that stone, 'I reckon I've found im.'

There was hymns and prayers. Then he'd seek me out: 'I didn't see you in church, yesterday, Hewins!'

Yes, while he was a-praying I was carrying the coal for the church, chopping sticks!

'I'd prefer you *not* to chop sticks on the Sabbath, Hewins.'

We'd been laying the fires for Monday morning! The very fire he was warming his arse against! There was no reasoning with the Vicar. The flames crackled and jumped and he tried to fix me with his eyes. I knowed what was on his mind. He'd a-liked to have *catched* me!

*

It started like this. I was in the pub one night—the 'Green Dragon'. It was handy for the school, just opposite. I tried the Old Veteran's song:

> Just wheel my chair to the window,
> And wide the casement fling,
> For I want to see the folks
> As they go to greet our King—

'Give us your hat, George!' somebody cried. They was putting pennies and twopences in! The landlord didn't mind. He said: 'You get what you can off em. They *wants* to give you summat.' One bloke bought me a pint!

'I'll never hold my head up again!' said the missus when she heard about it. She didn't go with me to the pub no more. But she took the money.

I had a lot o' songs: I'd picked them up from the old chaps at Cal's, sitting round the table of an evening. 'Ring down the curtain!' I sang when I went in, 'I can't sing tonight!'

They shouted: 'You bain't a-comin out till you 'ave!'

I got to be popular! First one landlord and then another un would send to the school: 'We got a charabang party come—can George pop down for a couple of hours and sing to em?' I dressed myself up as a farm boy, with an old hat on, a kerchief round my neck. I got an old smock, a dirty old smock, and a monk's tail out the hedge in my teeth and I went singing in the pubs. *The Pig with Five Legs* was a good one to get them going:

> I come from the country,
> My name is B. Giles.
> I've travelled one hundred
> An twenty odd miles.
> For a soft sort o' farmin chap I've been took,
> But I tell you I bain't
> Such a fool as I look!

It ends up—

> I beat you this time mister,
> What do you say?
> For you can't get five hams
> Off one pig every day.
> Ri too ra li too ra li too ra li ay.

I got all my beer free—*and* I was paid!

I was singing in the 'Dragon' one night when two gyppos came in, selling paper flowers, mother and daughter. Strange flowers they was, blue, yella, scarlet, like caterpillars' nests a-shaking and a-wriggling, all colours of the rainbow. These two women was weary,

bone weary, you could see it. They was dragging themselves around.
They'd got their truck up the yard, with tents on.

I said: 'You breakin camp?'

The mother said: 'Ah. The farmer's turned us out—we didn't do
enough work.' She'd lost her bloke in the war.

I said: 'Where you sleepin tonight then?'

They said: 'Under the hedge.'

'Well,' I said 'if you likes'—it was the school holidays—'you can
'ave a *room* to sleep in.'

They followed me to the school.

'Only don't touch nothin.'

They had a lurcher dog and it barked. 'And keep *im* quiet!'

I put them two little camp beds down. You should a-seen their
faces! When I saw them off in the morning I gave them a bob.
They thanked me very much, then they went on the move somewhere, towards Alcester.

And so it happened that a couple o' bags o' peas appeared in the
school porch. Later I found plums and apples and mysterious bags
o' taters, by the door. They made it up—in kind. Word got around.
In the summer months the gyppos and the roadsters would come
and seek me out, at the school.

I should have got the sack if *they'd* a-knowed, but I'd got to be
too crafty for them. Where did the roadsters go in winter? Where
do the flies go? I heard tell that some of them went to the circuses,
we used to have a lot o' circuses about then, they looked after the
animals and that. Some turned up for mangel chopping, but most
of them—only the wind knows.

*

Still the Vicar couldn't catch me. Then one Sat'day morning, 'bout
one o'clock, who should I happen to meet on the corner of Arden
Street but Sergeant Sanders—well, he was plain Sanders now. He
said: 'Let's hope!'

I said: 'What is it?' He'd slipped summat into my hand. 'Oh no,'
I said, 'I don't take bettin slips!'

He said: 'Don't talk so daft! Now,' he says, and he touched my pocket, 'there's five of our policemen's bets in there! I'll meet you 'ere every Sat'day—or in the week if there's summat on, I'll come to the school.'

And so he did. Then one day when I went to the coal of a dinner time, to make the fires up, he dropped a note in my hand. 'Read it!' he says, 'afore you gets further. I'll walk on.'

It had got on it 'DON'T COME DOWN TODAY THEYS WAITIN!'

And so I started taking bets for this bookie. He was a Brummie. He had a stand at Brummagem and one at the racecourse at Stratford. It was a battle o' wits. Two coppers come one Sat'day and sat on the boys' lavatory. They'd got permission off the Vicar. There was a passage at the back of the houses behind the school: they reckoned to tell the chaps goin backwards and forwards with their bets by their *feet*. But where these two coppers made their mistake was *smoking*: it went through the grating. An old woman came out of her house and shook her table cloth and she shouted, top of her voice: 'You run out o' fags yet?'

They got off the plank then! I thanked her. She said: 'I knowed it wouldn't be you a-sat on the plank a-smokin.'

'No,' I said, 'there was two of em. They was watchin me.'

After that Sanders said I'd better bring a little parcel o' washing to the 'Red Horse'. But the landlord at the 'Red Horse' he says: 'You takes that same parcel o' washin back with you as you brings in! Look George, you'll get me licence took off me if you ain't careful!' He was a nice chap, so I packed it in. Asides, I'd seen the Headmaster come into the bar, start asking questions. I thought I wouldn't stretch my luck. So long as I did the work and weren't caught the Vicar couldn't touch me! I was *paid* by the Warwickshire Education Committee!

It was the Education Committee decided they wanted some new out-buildings at the school. Who should come to measure up and see what he could put the price in for but Teddy Kennard. He seen me, he was going away—and I stood in front of him.

I said: 'You've got to 'ave it now! A lay preacher! I went an fought in the war to protect you an you stopped my money like that! You 'ad the cheek after close on seven year to say "I'm full up for labourers!" ' I said: 'Call yourself a *gentleman*!'

He kept moving backwards. He said: 'You bad lad!'

I was forty!

I said: 'I know what I'd *like* to do—put a bullet through you.'

A young apprentice came with the builders who got the job. I starts talking to him. He was keen to make a go of bricking. He'd been too young for the war.

I said: 'Would you like my tools?'

I sold them to him, cheap: my hammer, my lump hammer and chisel. 'Well,' I said to myself, 'that's that.'

*

All the old soldiers went on parade when the Prince o' Wales come to Stratford in '23. He came round with the Mayor; he came up to me, held his hand out, shook hands. Already he'd got that miserable, weird look, King George had it too—not like King Teddy, *he* was different!

'Is your pension alright?'

I said: 'Yes, Your Majesty.' What was the point in saying '*No*'?

He never shook hands with the Headmaster. When we gets back to the school the Headmaster says—his name was Crutchley, he'd been a Sergeant Major: 'Come on, afore you washes your hands—shake mine!' He gave me half-a-crown, to shake hands with him!

In the coal-house I laughed! Let them *all* come! I thought: Sullivan would a-made some money out o' this! Sullivan was an Irishman I'd got pally with: he'd been to gaol a time or two. He found me out when he first came to Stratford. I got on well with the Irish. He was a very slick-tongued chap, Sullivan. He went about, free as a bird—but *crafty*! He minded me of Ram, who used to put up at Cal's, peapicking time. Where'd he ended up? I wondered. Funny thing, his name was Sullivan and all.

Well, down Park Road strolls Sullivan one day: 'You got ten bob?'

'What's it for?'

'Well,' he says, 'I got the chance of a damned good van. I got in wi a farmer—*and* 'is wife!' He winked. 'E's got a sawmill and I'm a-goin to cut blocks up an sell em. I need a partner, George.'

'Well,' I says, 'that sounds like a good plan. When shall I see you?'

'Friday,' he says. 'See me in the 'Mulberry Tree' when they open, Friday night.'

I slipped him a bob but the missus was watching from a window. 'Oo's that?'

'A chap oo borrows a bob off us from time to time. E's found an *article* for me,' I said, to take her mind off the shilling. 'It's in the coalhouse at the school.'

She was waving her fist at Sullivan. 'Don't you come to my house again or I'll 'ave the police on you!'

He never did! I reckon he was frit of the missus.

'What article?'

'A pianna.'

She was struck dumb. Then she said: 'Oh George! Oh George, you'll 'ave us in the workhus yet!'

'Don't talk so foolish!' I said. 'I've got to be too crafty for em. Come on, take my arm, we'll go up to the school and 'ave a look!'

'Well,' she said, 'a pianna!'

'You know that chap oo plays at the "Dragon"? E says e'll give our Mary lessons.'

She laughed. '*Im*? E's allus drunk!'

But I could see she was over the moon about it.

It was the night of the Runaway Mop. We was walking round the stalls when it happened. We was by this stall when all at once the missus cries '*Oh!*' and down comes her corsets. She'd got a special set o' corsets to try and keep her rupture in. The laces had bust. Some women stood round her while she picked them up. She went blood red. I rolled them up and shoved them in my waistcoat, put my jacket on.

'I could *die*,' she said.

'Let's go to the "Mulberry" first and 'ave a drink,' I said. 'What you goin to 'ave?'

She had a stout; I kept looking round.

'What the hell d'you keep lookin at that door for?'

The landlord gave me the nod. 'If you're waitin for Sullivan you'll be waitin a long time. The coppers caught im, pinchin a van.'

My heart was thumping! I was part of it, really. I was as bad as him! Was it the start of a life o' crime? I never thought—I opened my jacket—and out fell the corsets! They all stared. One bloke said: 'Where're you goin to change then, missus?'

'I'll smack *you* across the mouth!' she said.

''Ere you are!' I says, waving them about afore it got to scrapping. 'Anybody can 'ave a pound if they'll put em on!'

She got me outside—quick! She didn't know whether to laugh or cry. 'You bloody fool! What did you do *that* for?'

She'd had enough of the Mop. So we walked along Waterside. Cal's was all changed, all but the passage. That was still the same stone flags—you could see where the roadsters had worn them away, like water, with their feet—and the red brick walls. 'See that knife mark!' I said. We walked up past the Theatre, past the Wash where the pleasure boats was moored, and the Vicar's wall. My heart had stopped a-thumping. We stood on the mill bridge listening to the weir.

'Oh!' said Emma. Her locket had broke. It broke and fell in. It weren't her day. 'Oh!'

She was upset. Apart from her wedding ring and the sleepers in her ears it was the only jewellery she had. There was a photo of Harry inside.

It was dark, the water was rushing.

'Don't fret,' I said, 'I'll be back in the morning to look for it.'

And I was. I couldn't see it. I kept shifting from one part o' the bridge to another.

''Ere we stood—no! 'ere!'

The water was still rushing. It minded me of when I was a little lad at Cal's. I used to go every Sunday morning, down to the lock, that first lock, and I'd get some lovely watercress. I'd get a great big handkerchief full. The neighbours would say, 'Bring us a bit if there is any, lad.' I gave half of it to Cal, and the rest I made into big bunches, penny a bunch. All the water running free over it—it was beautiful watercress.

''E'll make 'is fortune!' they said to Cal, shaking their heads and laughing. Cal looked pleased.

But I never did. I could make folks laugh but I never could make money.

I stood on the bridge a-looking and a-thinking. A woman came by and she said: 'What was your thoughts?'

'That,' I said, 'would be tellin.'

AFTERWORD

34. Waterside, 1932: the second official visit of the Prince of Wales to Stratford-upon-Avon

The occasion was the opening of a new theatre. The old Shakespeare Memorial Theatre, brain-child of Charles Flower, with its 'turrets striped like sticks o' Mop rock' and the Grand Tower from which Joshua Farr had so impressed the neighbours, where George and Emma had found, albeit briefly, work they loved, had been destroyed by fire some six years before. More enduring, though subtly changed (like another, more illustrious birthplace in Stratford) was Cal Cook's cottage. It can be seen rising behind the trees and above the Prince's head, at the corner of Sheep Street.

Second from the left in the line of ex-servicemen stands George. In somewhat ill-fitting finery, probably borrowed for the occasion, he is strikingly smaller and more frail than those flanking him. Only the splendid (silver-topped?) stick seems to anchor him to the ground. 'I was such a little minute a puff o' wind would a-blowed me away.' Has the Prince spotted him? Will he get another half-a-crown handshake? We can only speculate, for he never told us. He lived on, incredibly, for nearly fifty years after this photograph was taken. The Great War had been for him, and for thousands upon thousands of others, rich as well as poor, a watershed. There was no returning to the past. In any case, for all he enjoyed relating his story to us, George undoubtedly preferred the present. Despite the ever lengthening odds, and some bad blows to come, compounded by his disability and his need for drink, two bitter souvenirs from the trenches, he retained his zest for life. And like the best storytellers, he had an abiding interest in people, in their foibles and their inflexions. He was, as he said admiringly of an employer whom he respected, 'a laughing man'.

When, in December 1977, well-meaning strangers moved in and 'for his own good' uprooted him, he ceased to find anything to laugh about. He turned his face to the wall and quietly died—of a sudden surfeit of welfare. His life, if not much else, had belonged to *him*. He made the decision to end what had begun so tenuously nearly a century before.

George had no idea of the extraordinariness for us of the tale he had unfolded. His was an innocent testimony. The last recording was made some three weeks before his death; from then on we used a note book and our memory. There was no chronological sequence. It was a tale lovingly pieced together afterwards like one of those ubiquitous peg rugs: scraps of fustian here, a flash of scarlet uniform, the remnants of a much pawned suit.

His six surviving children, aged themselves and poor by the definitions of the new Welfare State, laid him in an unmarked paupers' grave in Stratford cemetery. He joined his wife Emma, their daughter Jess, who had died young and whose name, in a moment of guilt and grief, he had had tatooed along his arm, and—the gravedigger told us—'Minnie Waller from the workhus, aged nineteen'. Where had she come from? Where was she going? No one can say. The unknown pauper girl seemed in a mysterious and moving way to take George's story back to its first stirrings, in 1878. All ends are beginnings.

Mary, After the Queen

Memories of a
Working Girl

FOREWORD

by Paul Thompson

Stratford-upon-Avon today exudes a scented, luxuriant past: from the theatre waterfront through to the ample trees around the stone-spiralled parish church, a sustained image of manicured half-timbering, well-kempt gardens and cream teas. It is as if the town wanted itself thought of as conceived immaculate, and handed down unimpaired through time, rather than as a place made, maintained and reshaped through human effort and pain. Shakespeare of course knew better. That is why, as you read, first in *The Dillen* and then *Mary, After the Queen*, the story of five generations of the Hewins family of Stratford, you have a sense of one of Shakespeare's subplots come alive: the heroes and heroines now the housewives and whores, craftsmen, labourers and gravediggers, whom before we had no more than fleetingly glimpsed. It feels like the rediscovery of a common heritage, a past lost, yet also fascinatingly familiar.

The thread which holds both books together is the life of George Hewins, born a hundred years ago. In *The Dillen* the voice is his, in *Mary* his daughter's; and the subtle differences in language and tone between the two are indications of the sensitivity and care with which both of their stories have been recorded and put together by Angela Hewins. With George, we are captured by the storyteller's image and turn of word; with Mary, much more by an open honesty. But they recognizedly belong to each other.

George begins his story among the rivermen at the wharf, Victorian Stratford's commercial underbelly. Born of a failed abortion and deserted by his mother as an infant, he was brought up by his great-aunt in her common lodging house, in the company of down-and-outs, casuals and prostitutes. Apprenticed to a local builder through her determination, he fell for early marriage and failed to serve his full time. Once married, as his children increased relentlessly his life became an unending struggle for work, turned to bitterness through his savage mutilation in the First World War.

Mary's memories begin after the war, when her crippled father was the Church School caretaker. 'I can't remember anything about school much, 'cept cleaning it.' Her world was the council estate and the new factories at the edge of the town, which the history-seekers pass, but fail to see, on their way in. She re-creates it vividly: on the one hand, the rows between her parents, and the appalling pain which both suffered from ill-health; on the other the loyalty which emerges, for example, when her sister is dying of tuber-culosis, or in sometimes rougher ways when she gets into trouble herself. For Mary falls in turn, giving to old George his final role as doting grandfather of the next generation's orphan child. 'He lifted him so gently: like a chick . . . I thought: E thinks of the ole man as 'is Dad . . . They were inseparable. That did used to upset me, but there was nothing I could do about it.'

If a 'lovechild' to the family, the infant Hewins was made a good deal less welcome by the keeper of Stratford's conscience. 'Good news! There's a babby been born!', old George told the Vicar proudly. 'So I 'ear,' said the Vicar, 'and I wants it *out*, this day, this minute, Hewins! *And* er! Else your job goes, and the house!' Only the doctor's pleadings saved them.

George's best stories were woven around incidents, and other people. Mary can have a comparable pungency—I think of her comment on her deserting boyfriend, 'It was like trying to keep a fox'—but it is, above all, her insights into her own feelings that make her memories remarkable. She conveys in a tellingly simple way what it was to be an adolescent girl on a small-town council estate in the Thirties: the chaffing at the factory, the fun of dressing up and going out, the power of physical attraction, the agony of feeling her own body awkward. Still more unusual is her account of how she first rejected her own baby—'for days after he was born I hadn't wanted to look at him'—but eventually gave in to her mother's pressure to feed him, and was won to him. 'I didn't want to, I didn't want to love him. But as soon as he was there, at my breast, soon as I'd felt his little hands and his little mouth, I thought: E's mine! E's all mine!'

Love, pain, fun, death are the stuff of great drama just because they are also the common experience of ordinary lives. Once you have learnt to listen—whether, like Angela Hewins, as an oral historian; or as a therapist; or from sheer interest—you can find fascination in *any* person's life. But if the intrinsic interest is shared, the way of telling is not. *The Dillen* is a masterpiece of spoken autobiography because George Hewins had a rare gift for telling a story. The more straight-forward candour of *Mary, After the Queen* is in itself less unusual. But the two books put together grow to become much more. The closest parallel is perhaps in the work of Oscar Lewis in Mexico, as in *The Children of Sanchez*. Just because *The Dillen* and *Mary* differ in perspective as well as in generation, and because one is by a man and the other is by a woman, they give us, for one English working-class family, a uniquely deep and intimate history.

PREFACE

35. Mary aged fourteen

This is the story of a working girl, the dreams she dreamt and the rivers she had to cross. A story close to my heart for many reasons, like *The Dillen* it is neither novel or biography, but a compilation of spoken memories, from the transcripts of tapes, and from note-books. Nor is it a sequel to the first book, although the subjects are related. Called Mary 'after the Queen', she was George Hewins's youngest child, the baby born as he went off to war: one of those ends that was also a beginning.

The circumstances of recording Mary's story were different. She was much younger and more mobile than George; we talked out of doors as well as in, and consequently a tape recorder and micro-phone were not always as practicable as they had been in the old man's cottage. George was a story-teller, in the ancient tradition; Mary, on the other hand, liked a 'good chat' with whoever happened to drop by. I realized early on that I would never have a monopoly on her attention. There was considerable social interaction during interviews or chats, sometimes vociferous, and drawing from communal, family memory, which had not been the case with *The Dillen*:

'Ey d'you remember our Else and the *violin recital*?'
Much laughter and badinage.

Sometimes, especially when later days were being recalled, another, younger voice intervened, adding *his* memories:

'That was the night the Americans came ... You *must* remember ... The noise of the horns ...'
'The noise of the horns woke me!'

Like a whiff of scent in the air—lilac? lime trees?—that no one can quite put a name to, the resulting tale is dreamlike yet firmly bound to earth, innocent and coarse, figured and unfinished. Therein, for me, lies the beauty of spoken recollection. Also, because I cared for *The Dillen* too, there was the fascination of seeing familiar characters moving in a different drama, of hearing them speak with different tongues. Only the backcloth seemed the same: Stratford-upon-Avon. But even that, on closer examination, had changed.

Industrial development came late to some parts of middle England. Not many years after the end of the First World War, when Mary's story begins, a report* was published by Stratford-upon-Avon Preservation Committee on the future of the market town 'on which fortune has settled an incomparable distinction', and in particular on proposals for new factories within the borough. These would assuredly be manned 'by immigration'. Existing townsfolk were not suffering undue stress because of the lack of factory employment; indeed, 'if an occasional youth discovers a mechanical bent, it is no great hardship to him to migrate to a neighbouring

* *Stratford-upon-Avon: Report on Future Development, 1923. Prepared at the instance of the Stratford-upon-Avon Preservation Committee; published by permission of Stratford-upon-Avon Corporation*

town'. As for more comfortably established citizens who might be tempted by the prospect of financial profit, they were warned that this would be offset by a rise in rates and in population, which would necessitate 'housing schemes, schools, and a rapid expansion of all the usual municipal services'.

There was really little doubt how the town's establishment, heavy with shopkeepers and estate agents and retired professionals, would feel about such expansion. Nor does it come as much of a surprise to find that in Stratford between the wars social barriers were as strong as ever. Mass education had yet to make much impact on the lower working class. Indeed, Mary's school (in which, ironically, so much of her life was to be spent) seemed to have changed very little since her father's day, in the 1880s. 'Grammar school boys' were beings from another planet. A girl's position in this society could be placed exactly: her clothes, her diet, her home address, what she did in her leisure time, all these things gave her away. Above all, after thirteen, it was where she worked.

Amongst Mary's teenage contemporaries in the 1930s, to be a shop assistant was, apart from marriage, the ultimate career goal, achieved only by a select and envied few. There was one ray of hope in this attitude: by the time she found herself on the labour market, at the very bottom of her list and everyone else's was domestic service. An elder sister had already rejected 'service' in favour of factory work, where 'you knows when you's a-goin to start an when you's a-goin to finish. And you gets your money on Friday night.'*

The Stratford accent, with undertones of the receding country-side, was another give-away. But there was a directness, an earthi-ness of manner, about this new class of working girls, a certain cockiness, that was slightly alarming. Notwithstanding the reports of preservation committees and the Shakespeare lobby and the ratepayers' lobby, new factories *had* come to Stratford, and these girls, who a generation earlier might have been skivvies in private households, isolated and vulnerable, helped to keep industry going. During the Second World War they *did* keep it going, although in 1945 the authorities were swift to hint at a time limit to their new-found freedoms. Of the canning factory where Mary worked

* The Dillen, *p. 214.*

as mechanic's mate, a local newspaper wrote: 'By the end of the hostilities with Germany, the firm [Stratford-on-Avon Produce Canners Ltd] had dispatched the magnificent total of 40 million cans of fruit, vegetables, soups and jams to our fighting forces . . . Much credit is due to the work of the women and girls who took the places of men called to military service.'*

In the factories they found for the first time a sort of collective voice, albeit the possibility of formal organization never seems to have occurred to Mary, for one. She does not mention trade unions, possibly because although working conditions were poor, sometimes down-right dangerous, pay was comparatively good. The collective voice manifested itself rather in comradeliness (new to the women's work-place, if not to the community at large), in a lack of deference, and in 'having a good laugh' at the boss on every possible occasion. There was also, notably during the war, the chance of job satisfaction.

Now and then, outside work situations, the business-owning and professional class which controlled the town's government met the lower working class socially. As Mary observed (in direct contrast to an ecstatic account of a garden party for brewery workers at 'The Hill' in the local press), such meetings were not always 'a success': a reminder that viewpoint is all-important. Occasionally, marriage broke through the barriers. But on the whole, working girls with over-ambitious social aspirations, or even with dim yearnings fanned by the cinema (especially the American cinema) for *some-thing*, were, like Mary, doomed to meet their come-uppance. If 'the worst' happened, some families rallied round. In others, espe-cially where the parents had social aspirations too, the shame was overwhelming. The luckless daughter was sent away, or declared to be 'morally defective' and committed to a local asylum, her child to adoption. Some of these girls, now old women, institutionalized and dull of speech, are still being discovered by vigilant social workers, or in one case by a long-grieving son: a living testimony to social attitudes in the 1930s and 1940s.

Mary, I am glad to say, tells a different tale. Compassion and love did triumph, sometimes, in spite of society. So for those who like happy endings, there is one; for those who like to wonder . . . well,

* Stratford-on-Avon Herald, *25 May 1945*

who is to say what happiness is? It took courage for her to tell what must in part be a tribute to some of the people she met along the way. Most of these I have left with their real names; a few still living have been given pseudonyms, to protect their anonymity. On first mention, but not thereafter, this is indicated in the text. No claim is made for the tale as social history, although as a record of feelings and attitudes rather than historical events there may be something of interest to the historian. Spoken recollection has flaws as well as richnesses. I offer no apology for what is no more and no less than any of us might do without the aid of reference books or original documents, or with very little formal education, and I hope that others will be encouraged to pick up their tape recorders (or even pencils) before it is too late, and preserve some of the treasure that lies within every family.

A. H

36. The boy with red hair, aged fourteen

Friday's dream
Saturday told
Will come true
Though ever so old

Old Warwickshire
saying

Though I am old with wandering
Through hollow lands and hilly lands,
I will find out where she has gone,
And kiss her lips and take her hands;
And walk among long dappled grass,
And pluck till time and times are done
The silver apples of the moon,
The golden apples of the sun.

W. B. Yeats

37. Emma ('our Mother') outside 20 Park Road,
Stratford-upon-Avon, c.1919

✥ CHAPTER ONE ✥

When I shut my eyes I can see us all sat round the fire at number 20 Park Road, laughing. Mostly we was rowing at our house, but I do remember even our Mother laughed, that night. I was sat by her feet, and Dad was there, another wonder, and Jess and Flo—she hadn't gone into service then—and our Else and Ede and Cyril and Jim, even George—he was on leave from the Flying Corps—everybody. The pig was on the hearth.

Where he'd come from I don't know. There he was, in the best place of all, wrapped in an old khaki coat—it was Dad's old greatcoat, I 'spect, from the army—and there he *wasn't*!

'E's vanished!'

'Stuck!'

'Oh God!'

'Mam e's stuck up sleeve!'

'Don't sit there gawpin—go an get the scissors!'

Our Else was helpless with laughing, so was Ede. In the end, as usual, Jess went.

Dad chuckled: 'It minds me of the time . . .'

We knew we was in for a story. Then 'Phew!' went the little pig as Jess cut him out. He fell back, onto the coat, righted himself and went 'Phew!' again.

'Did I ever tell you,' said Dad, 'when *I* was small, ow I walked to Warwick an back once for a dillen pig, just like this little fella?'

*

That was the last time we were all together, *family*. So many things happened. I was the youngest, four years old, and Park Road was the size of my world: two rows of council houses, council cottages they were called then, with long backs full of cabbages and pigs and fowl—and kiddies! The road didn't lead anywhere, it just petered out into a field and a steep bank and a railway.

It was a busy line, a lot of trains went by. We had them all night as well, shunting and doing. You could hear them in your sleep. Clanging in the sidings, pushing up that hill from Stratford towards Brum, push and puff, one engine at the back, one on the front: push 'n' puff, push 'n' puff. If the wind was right you could hear a train coming miles away, and the whistle! Oh the excitement when you heard that whistle!

When a troop train came through we all turned out! You never seen so many kiddies! Swarming down those passages, running for the field. Most families up Park Road had eight or ten; a lot had other folks' families lodging with them, young marrieds, and they

38. Else (in cook's hat) and Jess (front) with friend in Red Horse yard, Stratford-upon-Avon, *c.*1920

had kiddies too. I was good at running but sometimes I was slowed down cos our Else had suddenly got the idea of *taking* me to see the trains. It was nice at first, I liked the fuss; then it started to annoy me.

She was my eldest sister, seventeen. She worked at the Red Horse so she thought she was something, and very bossy. Why she wanted to be wading through the bottom field with us kiddies—it was always flooded, that field—Heaven knows. But our family was noted for being unpredictable.

There was plenty of time to get to the bottom of the embankment, even with our Else in tow: the trains couldn't go fast, *they* had to slow down and all. From Park Road into the town they were slowing down. We could see the driver and his fireman, see the red hot glow, feel it! And the soldiers! They hung from the windows and they shouted and waved, and out of the sky came hurtling corned beef tins, quite big uns, medium size, you had to watch your head—and biscuits. Praps they'd got fed up with them. At any rate, rolling down the bank they came, lovely corned beef and biscuits, and hundreds of kiddies fighting for them, me included.

'Come on Else!' I cried.

I didn't linger; you grabbed what you could. I was small, but I was quite aggressive. I'd come back with a tin, maybe, if I was lucky, and I always got some biscuits. They were big square uns, hard, ever so hard, just like dog biscuits. Looked like one and all, that colour.

'Ugh,' said Else.

'I gotta *tin*!'

I could picture our Mother's face. But then I saw our Else was in a bad mood, you know, whipping the heads off the flowers, scowling.

'Us'll wait for next un,' she said.

I couldn't believe it! 'I gotta *tin*!'

All the kiddies were rushing home. I knowed there wouldn't be another troop train that day; there never was.

'Come on Else!'

'You can bloomin well wait 'ere with me,' she said, 'you selfish little bugger.'

She was in a flaming mood.

*

If you'd asked me who was the most important person in Stratford I'd a-said: '*Mrs Windsor!*' They lived further up the road than us, the Windsors, and she was the only one with a mangle. She used to mangle our clothes for us—no charge! I often took our mangling up to her, and the school towels. Dad was caretaker at the Church school, and every Friday we had to wash all the towels, fifty or so of them, and the dusters. She was a very good woman, Mrs Windsor; even though she looked like a gypsy, and that was my big dread, gypsies, I liked her very much.

We went to her for everything. 'Cup o' sugar, Missus Windsor?' 'Bit o' tea, Missus Windsor?' Even for home-made wine: you took your own rhubarb. But most of all we went to her for *money*. You could always be sure she'd have some. What she did was insure her kiddies—Beryl 'n' Norman 'n' Ernie 'n' Sid 'n' Freddie, he was called Flash, 'n' Ivy 'n' Lol 'n' Myrtle—had insurances on them for so many years. She had so much in, see, had so much out, and *we* borrowed off her, for a penny or twopence.

'Mam says: "Can we 'ave two bob, Missus Windsor, just till er gets er wages?"'

She writ it all down on the wall, who owed her, and how much was left to pay: 'GARDINER' 'HEWINS'.

There was a Mr Windsor. He was very handsome, well, I used to think so, with a little moustache, but sort of insignificant besides her. He was always falling off his bike. He'd get on again, keep falling off; lean on it, push it. It was impossible for him to *ride* it. I used to wonder why it was he could never stay on his bike. Years later, after the Abdication, they became the Duke and Duchess of Park Road.

Myrtle, their youngest, had a club foot; Flash had a cock eye. That was unlucky—unlucky for me. When I started school he threw stones at me, every day. I don't know why he frit me so—praps there's always got to be another kiddie you're scared of, at that age—he was little, littler'n me, fat. Anyway, he showered these stones at me as I came from school, and I was frit to death! By the canal, up the Brum Road, there's a dip and a gate and there *he'd* be, laying in wait. 'Flash' we called him, Flash Windsor, and that's what he was: *sly*. He'd be waiting for me, every day. Now I think: why ever didn't I tell our Jim? But when you're small, when you're a kiddie, it's a different world. Like Park Road—look at it now!

Mrs Windsor was the most important; our Mother was the most beautiful. And once—I think . . . Well, it was the worst row we'd ever had in our house. I felt, you know, really afraid, sick, much worse'n Flash Windsor chucking stones.

She never had a 'best friend'. She didn't like folks popping in and out, much, she said it was asking for trouble. So she didn't have any special acquaintances, only the Sweets on Brum Road. Now it happened that Hilda Sweet got married and she went to Leicester. Our Mother got quite friendly with hers.

She said: 'Hilda's invited me for weekend.'

'Ey?'

'I'm a-goin to Leicester for weekend and I've got my ticket.' The echo said: 'Just you try 'n' stop me!'

'You sure you ain't got summat else 'n' all,' said Dad, 'like a fancy man?'

He shouted, there was a big row, but she went. She went and left us all behind. I can still remember the fear: it was worse'n when Ede lost me at the Mop. I thought: She ain't comin back!

Sunday afternoon, Dad took me to the LMS station. He'd been wounded in the war, Dad, he was a cripple; he had to go with a stick, so it was a slow trip. He didn't get a pension, well, he'd took the lump sum. Sometimes when they were rowing our Mother would say bitterly: '*Lump sum*! The bloody army must be laughin its bloody head off!' and he'd shout back: 'Oo spent it, I'd like to know?'

I'd seen his wound once, when she was bathing him. He came home covered in coal dust, and chalk, and she bathed him by the fire. When she was bathing him, or me, or anybody, our Mother always kept the others out, but one day I rushed in and I *saw*. Horrible. He was covered in scars, and one side of him, low down, where there should a-been flesh, there was—nothing. You could see the bone! I'd guessed it would be horrible, like the butcher's shop. I'd seen his washing in the bucket, all blood and stuff, every day his clothes were put in to soak, but till you've really *seen* . . . How could our Mother bear to touch him? And every day, well it seemed like every day to me, he was drunk.

This Sunday afternoon, I will say that, he'd stayed sober. We watched every train come in, every last passenger go. By now I was in the grip of terror—and who knows what was going on in Dad's head? He kept asking the chap at the station about trains from Leicester, over and over again. Then—it seemed like the very last train—out she got. Oh the relief!

He started shouting: 'You *bin* with somebody!'

She hugged me to death, nearly. The feel of her! That lovely safe smell of Cologne! She had a lot of Cologne for her heads. Dad and her seemed quite pleased to see each other, even though he was shouting and raving and that. I couldn't make it out. I'd never seen him hit her once, and she never hit him. She was a big woman, our Mother, bigger'n him, a powerful big woman, she could a-done, cos when she was roused she had a temper and a half. She could shift a copper on her own, though she wasn't as strong as she'd used to be. 'You should a-seen me then,' she said. At the station she just shouted back: 'You're an ole pot, you is! A-callin me black!' and 'Oh shut up!' That's all she said.

Later she showed us a photograph she'd had took at Leicester. She looked just like she did when she got out the train—Flo sent that hat, from London, she'd gone to work for Jews—beautiful. I never did know where the necklace came from, or where it went. She never wore it, after. It was like a little new moon. I'd gaze and gaze at that photograph and wonder. Maybe Dad did the same. Did she do it to teach him a lesson? Whatever the truth of it, she never went again.

*

39. Emma, early
1920s: taken at
Leicester during
her first (and only)
escape from home

That trip to Leicester seemed to start it off. 'Flo's gone to London, Mam went to *Leicester!*' That was the chant. 'Why can't *I*?' Not to her face, of course, just clucks and grumbles, like the start of a fight in the hen run. Oh God, I thought, another big row. Only words, here and there, then, suddenly . . . Else did it first. Half a mile up the road, that's all, but it was a start. She took a living-in job, at Bishopton. It was even nearer the railway than Park Road; the trains ran through the kitchen, practically. When I went up to see her I thought: Praps she'll be satisfied now!

Our Jim said: 'Did you see a motorbike in the bushes at Bishopton? An *engine-driver* on a *motorbike*?'

Flo was in London, as I said. And Ede fell for the drummer in the town band.

I woke up one morning and my guardians were gone. You'd a-thought it would have made a very big difference to my life, at home, everywhere, but it didn't! Else and Ede kept coming back; they might as well still a-lived at our house. In and out, in and out, asking our Mother's advice, bossing me about, gossiping. And there was still four in our bed. That was three too many, as far as I was concerned.

↜ CHAPTER TWO ↝

'Sides to middle!' our Mother would say. That meant another sheet was going home; the sides had to be put together, joined up. So it was '*Sides to middle!*' My heart sank when I heard those three words. You had to lay on a ridge, then. Our George always had a bedroom on his own. There was Jim and Cyril at the top of our bed, and who was at the bottom with me? It must have been Jess. Well, even the *prospect* of George going opened up a new horizon.

This is how it happened. He fell in love.

'I'd like you all to meet—Miss De Bonelli!'

We stared. Her dress was covered with millions of tiny beads, all sparkling beads and tinsel. I thought she was lovely. But when they'd gone, our Else was there and she giggled and she said: 'Er's from Fossett's, *I* reckon!'

Fossett's Circus came every year to Stratford; they lodged at the Green Dragon.

You could see our Mother was a bit upset. It was so unexpected. George never stepped out of line, he always toed it. She was even more upset next week when they turned up carrying a violin!

'Miss De Bonelli can play. Er's goin to teach me ow to do it—upstairs.'

Up they went, and from our George's bedroom, from the ceiling, came this awful noise: *Eeeh! Eeeh!*

Dad said, 'Oo's learnin *oo?*' Our Mother was dumbstruck. Well, she'd always given George preferential treatment; he'd always done what he liked. He was the eldest, out of the Flying Corps, apprenticed to a Stratford printer. George had to have a room to himself; George had to have a back leg on Sundays. Being the youngest I had the head. Imagine, a rabbit's head, the little tongue in still! I ate it. 'Course I did. They say that's how I came to have the gift of the gab, eating all those little tongues; I don't know.

The result was, our George had always been one to himself,

thought he was a cut above the rest of us. He was *glovey*, wore kid gloves, a proper toff. He was the toffiest chap on Park Road. The Windsors used to call '*Glovey!*' after him, but he was alright to me.

Sat'day dinner time, one o'clock, I always went up the Brum Road to meet him, and always he'd got a penny or a ha'penny for me. You could buy a lot for a penny: kali suckers, sherbet. I liked anything in the sweet line.

His pal laughed and said: ' 'Ere she comes!'

But Sat'day night! I paid for it then! We all had to sit there while Marg performed—that was her other name, *Margery*. She seemed nice. It was just that violin—she couldn't do a blooming note right—and her clothes! I thought her clothes were lovely, but the others didn't half pull her to bits, 'specially Else and Ede:

'Did you *see*?'

'Oo didn't?'

'I thought I'd *die*!'

Even our Mother joined in: 'That wench should be on top a Christmas tree.'

George said: 'Miss De Bonelli's goin to give you a *selection*.'

Marg started up. *Eeeh*! *Eeeh*! And our Else starts laughing. She started up her sleeve but she couldn't stop. I felt a giggle coming. I nearly wet my knickers trying to hold it in, and I was glad I did cos George gave Else such a slap across the face.

When they'd gone, Dad—he'd kept quiet, he'd never said a word—he said: 'Er name's *Bonehill*. And er comes from——.' It was one of the villages. You could have knocked us all down with a feather.

'Ow do you know?'

'Oh I know,' he said.

But he went on calling her Miss De Bonelli, even if we never, after that. When he wanted, Dad could be a perfect gentleman. He'd just chuckle afterwards, to himself.

*

When the tallyman came for his money—we used to have all our shoes off him—our Mother said: ' 'Ide! 'Ide under the table!'

She locked the door.

Somebody'd say, 'E's comin!' or: 'I's seen im, Brum Road!'

We always knew when the tallyman was coming, or the insurance. That was only sixpence a week, Fridays, a matter of sixpence, but our Mother was borrowing, all the time! Sixpence was a lot to her. Under the table we went: everybody, our Mother 'n' Dad too if they were in the kitchen, cos we had a back way, people could get round the back. If the insurance caught her, he caught her sometimes, she'd say: 'Well I don't know what you's a-moanin about—it ain't a debt!'

She told him off, as if it was his fault she couldn't pay! He started stammering: 'Alright then missus, we'll leave it till next week.'

Then there was the school attendance officer. Jim never went to school much, he went running round Wells' back. There was a good passage there, see, between the houses. He hid round there while our Mother told the lies. She had to do that. He wasn't well, she used to say, things like that.

We had to keep a watch out for all sorts of people, according to the day.

But once a month, the last day of every month, Dad got paid! He took us for a treat: me and our Cyril and my best friend Sis Wells. The Wells lived opposite—they were eleven—and Sis Wells was my best friend throughout our lives. Dad always took us to the fish 'n' chip shop on Rother Street!

They had benches and a wooden table, well, not a proper table, a trestle. You could see the Fountain through the window. Eating out—we loved that! We sat there and the chips spat and crackled in the fat, they *talked*!

'We'll soon be done!'

The smell! We sat there slavering, you know, like three Jack Russells round a rabbit hole. I think Dad got his entertainment watching *us*! They served the chips to you, on a plate. Salt and vinegar . . . ready . . . set . . . *go*!

Sis said: 'Our Bomber's got a horse for 'is cart!' He had a fruit and veg round.

I said: 'Our Jess's got a tiny little babby!'

Dad looked! Then he laughed and said: 'That's right!'

Oh the taste of those chips!

Every night when she got into bed I used to stare at Jess. Her belly was swelled, huge, like a pumpkin. It grew and grew. I knowed she was going to have a baby, she'd told me, but I thought it would burst out. In some ways I was quite innocent. I used to lie in bed waiting for the *pop*!

'I missed it!' I said. It was my one big regret.

Dad seemed upset.

''Ave some pop, you three,' he said, ''Ave a blow out. 'Ere—'ave some pop!'

And he bought us a whole bottle between us! That's how Jess's baby came to be mixed up in my mind with lemonade.

Our Mother chose the names. She said, ''E's goin to be called after the Prince o' Wales.'

We called him Bert. He looked so unhappy.

*

You'll notice I haven't mentioned my education. The fact is, I can't remember anything about school much, 'cept cleaning it. I'd been helping to clean it since I was a little girl, four or five years old; we *all* had, cos as I said, Dad was a cripple and our Mother—well, she was a big woman, lovely looking, but she was weighed down by the biggest rupture you've ever seen. So by the time I was thirteen I knew every nook and cranny of that school, every gas mantle, every rat hole, every ledge where the bloody dust gathered. Oh the coal dust and the chalk! It's a wonder it hadn't killed us all.

I wasn't good at anything else—'cept outside games. I couldn't write proper, add up. I don't think I was dim, I just thought: There must be better things to do'n this! You could see the teachers thought the same. Some of them, like Miss Farmer, had been there years; they'd grown old and fat so they *hit* you, never moved from their chair, just called you up to the front and gave you a swipe across the head. And the young one! We used to be praps at netball in the front yard, and Miss Salt the young teacher, she always wore a very short gym slip. Up and up she jumped, up and up; she loved jumping! She didn't pay much attention to us, cos by this time a big crowd had gathered on the pavement: chaps going by to the station, the boys from the Commercial school on their way to games. There were whistles and shouts. We never realized it was Miss Salt's limbs, and her lovely attire. *Then* we thought it was us, in our navy blue knickers. But really it was Miss Salt, jumping and jumping; she was the great attraction.

The Vicar came round regular. We all stood up for him, all at once; the classrooms were partitioned with glass, you could see through the whole school. He walked through—if you didn't curtsey you got a swipe off the teacher, after—and then we were allowed to sit down. I used to think: 'Why's *e* come?' and 'What's it all for?' For example, I weren't too bad at needlework, but you never *made* anything. All you did was stitches, different sorts of fancy stitches, and then you had to unpick them and do some more, with the same bit o' stuff. Naturally, it got black as your hat. Then there was *Empire Day*. They planned weeks in advance for that. The teacher said: 'Hewins—Jamaican Banana!' My friend Betty who married Joe Shakespeare was a Tasmanian Apple. Sis? She was lucky; she went to the Board school.

Our mothers did their best: we all had something on our heads, like Christmas crackers. You can imagine some of the boys! Their faces! I had a shift with '*BANANA*' on it, made out of wrapping paper; Betty had cardboard. When the great day came we paraded in the front yard. I was dying of embarrassment. Somebody whispered I'd got '*BANANA*' spelled wrong; I hadn't o' course, but I believed them. We was marched around, then one by one we stood on a platform with a Union Jack draped across, and streamers.

I had to say: 'I'm a Jamaican banana.' I felt like one and all. For once I prayed the boys from the Commercial school wouldn't come by. If anyone giggled they got a swipe. Miss Farmer hit very hard. She leant over the piano stool and she hit you as you marched past. She'd got it off to a fine art.

Once, I remember, I'd done a sum wrong, so I put a cross. That wouldn't a-been so bad if I'd left it, but I put this cross hard on the paper, ever so hard, spoilt the page. 'You spoilt the page!' she shouted. I got a swipe over the head for that. 'You spoilt your

40. Hockey team, Church of England School, Stratford-upon-Avon, late 1920s: Mary second row, far right, in a smart turn-out that says much for her mother's ingenuity (the tie was knitted).

book!' That was exaggerating, but you couldn't argue with the teachers, you couldn't even reason with them. So you can imagine how I was longing and longing for Christmas, when I was fourteen.

*

For the last and the thousandth time Miss Farmer went *Ping*! ' 'Ere's your note!' And we all sang 'God Save the King'. Then she said: 'Today we 'ave to wish Mary Hewins well in er new career.'

Career! Two of the girls were smirking; they'd got their names down at J. C. Smith's the Draper's. Oh they thought they were something, those two girls. Later, some of the others went to Woolworth's; Woolworth's was coming to Stratford—'*EVERY*-

THING IN ITS PLACE NOTHING OVER SIXPENCE!'—and when it did, all the girls who were clever, but not clever enough for Smith's, they went there for interview. It was hard to get in; well, the ones they picked were a better class'n me. I wouldn't a-stood a chance.

I wasn't dressed like them in those days: we'd got more fleas'n clothes in our house!

I'd wake Jess up: 'Ey Jess! There's a flea in bed!'

We lit a candle, tried to catch it. Once you know there's a flea, you can't stop. If it gets you first it'll mark you so's everybody knows. They could tell at school if you'd got fleas: the marks were all round your blooming neck. Mostly they bite on your neck. The girl behind you . . . oh God.

My looks were alright, but you'd got to be—well, a bit posher. J.C. Smith's could take their pick. And Woolworth's, when they opened. Dora went, and Madge—she was a teacher, after—and the Bromley girls. The Bromleys lived at 'Glencoe', in Arden Street, by the school, one of those big houses. They took in lodgers. Madge's Dad was only a baker but they were a bit superior. Woolworth's seemed to go for that type of girl.

I told myself I wouldn't a-liked it, anyway. As for service, well, that had been suggested! One of the teachers said: 'I think you might be suited to domestic service, Hewins.' Little did she know I'd already done enough service at home to last me a lifetime—*and* at school! Who dusted the classrooms? Washed the partitions down? Who did she think cleared up after her? As the others left home, George and Else and Ede and Flo and Jim—one after another to get married they'd left home and were gone—there was only me and Jess left to do the school at night. Jess was a little 'put on', but she'd never been strong. Most of it fell on me.

No, I thought, you can stuff service.

It boiled down to the brewery. The brewery was the only place, really, for girls like us. But there was a list! There was even a waiting list for the *brewery*, you had to have your name put down! Sis was accepted. Her Dad wasn't 'church', he was the only one on Park Road who voted Labour, so you can imagine how he got laughed at! And he sent Sis to the Board school. The result was she'd had a better education 'n me. She was accepted, and I wasn't! The brewery turned me down. It was a nasty shock.

Sis said: 'Never mind, Mary, it'll come up,' meaning my name, 'bound to.'

I remember I thought: They think I'm not good enough.

*

There was nothing for it but the Alum. I went to the Aluminium Factory on Brum Road and they said: 'Yes, you can start.'

I was buffing up the pans and kettles and things, with a duster, shining them up when they came from the polishers. You got filthy—*black*! It got on your hands, on your face. And you went home filthy; there weren't no washroom. You had to walk home looking like that—one o'clock on Sat'days, in broad daylight! I used always to be glancing at my face in the bottom of the kettles, to check.

'Oh God, it's on for the day now!' or if it was clean, if I'd escaped: 'Am I prettier'n er? What does *e* think of me?'

There was quite a reflection, you see, and as the chaps went by, well, you wanted to look nice. You could see yourself in the saucepans too, but not so well. One boy I fancied, his name was Harry, he was from Warwick. They used to bring them to the Alum in charas, men and women, from all over. They couldn't get enough from Stratford—not like the brewery, no strangers got in *there*. Well, all the girls at the Alum were set to cut one another out over Harry! But I was the one who got friendly with him! I used to gaze and gaze in the bottom of the kettle and think: If my clothes ain't much my *face* is alright!

But I pined for the brewery. Sis was there, all my friends, Jess and our Jim. Early every morning the brewery hooter went, you could hear it all over Stratford, and I used to feel so out of it. I was terribly jealous of Sis, though I never let on. We were still best friends. And at fourteen, with the world in front of you ... I didn't stay down for long!

⋘ CHAPTER THREE ⋙

One day I said to Sis or Sis said to me: 'Let's get fancy garters!'

So we did. They were lovely, ruched ribbon and elastic, with a bell. Mine was bright green; that was my colour then. You could have two bells, but Sis said two was overdoing it. We put them on in the toilet up our yard, so's our mothers wouldn't suspect—well, once you'd got them on, you can imagine, it was jingle, jingle, jingle—and we set off for town.

There was nothing else to do, nothing else you could afford to do! We thought we were the sexiest things in Stratford: dresses up at the front, a dip in the back so's the garter showed when you moved, just a bit, burnt cork on our eyebrows, a dab of powder, high heels! I was in agony most of the time, what with the shoes and the binder. I had to wear it, to flatten me. I was slim, I'd got slim hips, but oh God! My bust! Your figure had to be *straight*, you see, and my bust had grown that big. Sis was lucky, but all our family was big busted; we took after our Mother, I 'spect. I used to think: 'If only I hadn't got this bloody bust I'd get er chaps!' Sis used to get better chaps'n me; well, I used to think so. She seemed to get the pick. She'd get the best one, what *I* thought was the best one!

We walked anyhow till we got to the Fountain; we almost ran, cos we knowed we'd got to be back before nine, before it got dark, cos there weren't no lamps much, up Park Road. When we got to the Fountain we slowed up, we started walking proper: down along Wood Street, Bridge Street, down along the 'croft. That's where we made for—the *Bancroft*!

There were wooden steps there, then, with a little bridge, where the wharf was. We went *up* the steps: watch-each-step-mind-your-heels-don't-catch-keep-your-head-up! You try doing that! Walk-along-like-Lady Muck-and-*down*-the-other-side.

'They're *'ere*!' said Sis.

There they were, right as the mail: Eddie 'n' Jack in their brown blazers and cream flannel trousers.

'What oh,' said Eddie.

'What oh,' said Jack.

They used to dress alike, we thought they were brothers for ages. They came from country, 'specially for it, every Sat'day. Well, we put the brakes on then, we went really slow, I can tell you—they was attractive chaps—had a bit of a chat. That's all we did: *talk*. Then we went on, towards the Tram. That was our walk: down as far as the old Tramway then back again, with them watching— we hoped! Well, you could feel it, if you'd made an impression; and then of course we pretended we couldn't care less.

My trouble was, I always made the biggest impression when I wasn't trying. Sure as fate, there was Dick, and his friend Eric. Eric was a great tall chap and Dick was little and dark. He didn't wait for you, Dick, he *lurked*. He wasn't a tramp, but nearly; he worked on the fields and he always wore a long raincoat and a funny cap. He loved me from afar.

'Oh heck!' I said.

But I was pleased to see him, really, cos he walked from Clifford, every Sat'day, to bring me a bar of chocolate. He was that shy, Dick, looked all sawney at me, held the chocolate out at arm's length, a half pound bar! Cadbury's Milk!

'Frightened you'll bite,' Sis said.

All of a sudden, he *flung* it at me! I took it—and we ran! I thought: It is wrapped up!

We didn't stop till we got half way up Sheep Street. We weren't half puffing and panting.

Sis said: 'You goin?'

'Where?'

'Puntin wi them two.'

Yes! It was what you might call a *break through*. Jack and Eddie had asked us to meet them next Sat'day to go punting on the river!

*

Just my luck, I got Eddie. He was the quiet one; well, he always left the talking to Jack, butter wouldn't melt in his mouth. I thought: This is goin to be bloomin boring. They were alright *together*, if you know what I mean, but seeing them separate . . . Praps they thought the same. I'd got my new green suede shoes on.

Well, Sis and Jack set off down river towards the Theatre, and that's when I got my first surprise. Eddie pushed off *up* river, towards the bathing place.

'Ain't we followin them?'

'Two's company.' He winked at me.

'What's wrong with your eye? You got a fly in it or summat?' I ignored all the hints.

When we got to Bird's Corner he drew into the bank and said: 'This is it! The end of the line!' Wink wink.

He pulled in and jumped out and left me to manage best I could. He was a real gentleman.

'You jokin?' I could see he wasn't.

He said: 'You don't think I'm goin back there and 'ave to pay for this bleedin boat do you?'

Well! I *called* him! It didn't do much good. He went up by those private houses, but I was too proud to follow. I set off across the fields. Squelch, squelch! It was thick mud. My shoes! You should have seen them; they were ruined. I thought: What'll I *do*? Our Mother'll 'ave a fit if she finds out where I've been! It was only the second time on.

Fortunately, that very day Dad found a pound note in the pub. You see, every morning after the school he cleaned the Green Dragon opposite, swept it up, did the toilet. I wheedled ten bob out of him and I went to Brum and bought another pair of shoes, exactly the same. You'd a-thought it would have taught me a lesson: beauty is only skin deep. It didn't, o' course!

❧ CHAPTER FOUR ❧

I'd been at the Alum six months. Then one day, I shall never forget it because of all that happened since—you could say on that day the wheels were set in motion and there was no turning back—Sis came running to the factory door. I can see her now, in her clogs, and everybody's astonishment.

'*Mary!*' she shouted. Even at fifteen she'd got a big mouth, Sis had. 'Mary yer name's up!'

You might wonder why I was so excited about starting at the brewery. I was soon wondering myself. It weren't light work, not like the Alum. There was broken glass all over the place. I was a washer, at the bottling end. That's where the women were. I had to wash the bottles when they came back from the pubs, smell them, guess what some dirty bugger had put in them. You'd be surprised—paraffin, piss, all sorts—*ugh*! You nearly heaved, every time. It was terrible. You had to smell each bottle; you could be smelling all day at the back of the washing machine. It made you feel sick; sometimes I *was*.

I noticed Kate always had to wash the stoppers. That was pretty heavy work; buckets of stoppers are heavy to keep carrying. Poor Kate, she always had to do that. Jack Timms the foreman decided; he decided everything. I suppose he thought cos Kate was big 'n' strong . . . She had a fatter sister who was on the washing too; she had to wash the bottles as long as I can remember. That was a rotten job, washing the bottles, wet and horrible.

I was moved a bit higher up: I was on the bottling machine. You put the bottles on and you changed every half hour; another girl stood by you and took the bottles off and put the stoppers in. That was the worst job of all, tightening the stoppers, cos sometimes the bottle broke and then your hand would go. You had a strap on your hand, a big thick strap with an iron thing in the middle with

268

spikes. It had got to grip that stopper. But if something went wrong . . . *Aaagh!*

And then the bottles went round and you sat down and labelled. The next girl put them in cases, and so on. We changed round every half hour. We didn't have a break, but if the washers didn't keep up with us we *had* to have a bit of a rest, we had to shut the machine off then!

Phew!

It was different at the brewery, and not just the work—a lot o' the chaps was *drunk!* I'd seen men drunk often enough, well, Dad was drunk Sunday dinner time regular, but at the brewery they was always drunk! It shook me at first. They were allowed so much a day, see, the men were, and they could pinch as much as they wanted, drink it on the spot, dip a bucket in. They said they had to sample it! They were never sober. You should a-seen them rolling home breakfast time: drunk in charge of push bikes, a lot of them.

I was earning fourteen and six a week, and I had to give our Mother twelve. That left half-a-crown. We went roller skating at the Hippodrome; in the summer we went dancing in the Bancroft Gardens, to the Town Band. Well—'dancing'! We thought we could, but we couldn't, really. Kate was the dancer. As I said, she was fat, so she danced with her sister—but she was a brilliant dancer! We just sort of scuffled around, waltzes, that sort o' thing—but Kate! She was light as a bird. Sis and me practised the Charleston on Park Road, when we got home. We'd try it, show off, in the street. But Kate was the dancer. You wouldn't a-thought it possible, would you?

With our spending money we bought face powder and high heeled shoes, Woodbines. It was Sis taught me to smoke. We shut ourselves in the toilet. She said: 'You want to try one!' I did. I wonder if smoking killed her? You paid twopence for a packet of Woodbines, but generally I pinched Cyril's. He smoked a lot, sent Bert down to the shop for them. I'd waylay him and take one out.

Cyril got so annoyed! 'Do they only sell fags in bloody *nines*, now?'

He weren't like Jim—Jim was generous, he'd give you half of
what he had and that was never very much—our Cyril ranted and
raved.

So picture my surprise, my *face*, when he said: 'Ow should you
like some new clothes? For brewery trip?'

I thought: 'Bugger me!'

He said: 'Well I can't 'ave my sister disgracin us.'

He gave me *two pound*!

'Don't go askin for no more,' he said, 'cos you won't get it.'

*

Sis and me had been planning our outfit for months, what we'd
wear, down to the last detail. We sat on the railings at the end of
our road, scrunching apples and discussing it. That was our entertainment, after work: chatting, watching the traffic—charabancs, a
car, lots o' bikes . . .

'Look at *im*!' said Sis.

He was cycling along the Brum Road. Every day five o'clock
sharp he cycled past in his blazer and his tie and his posh cap, and
every day from the railings there we watched him. He never
looked, but he knew we was watching alright. You could *tell*. He
used to turn colour a bit, blush, push down on those pedals to get
past us, fast, faster and faster.

'Ya ya grammar school boy!'

It was windy cos leaves from the apple trees kept falling in our
hair and he was struggling so with his bike. That bike! Oh he had
a lovely bike—and bright cheeks from the weather. And just at that
minute—his cap blowed off! We jumped down and ran out and
grabbed it! We threw it over the railings into Schofield's orchard.

'That's got rid of im!' said Sis.

'Did you see 'is *'air*?'

' 'Is *what*?'

We laughed! But his hair! It was the colour of autumn; it was
dark red, gold. I thought he was like nobody I'd ever seen: beautiful.

'Sis—e can't go *no*where without 'is cap!'

'That's the idea!'

I said, it came out, I hadn't meant to say it but it just came out:
'E's different.'

'Stuck up you mean.'

'Where's e live? I wonder where e's goin?'

Sis said: 'Give me a proper chap, any day.'

I thought: If she means that Dougie . . . But I kept it to myself.
Sis was my friend, but I was always frightened of her mouth.

'Talkin of red—what 'bout *hats*?' she said.

That got me laughing again.

In the end we decided on bright orange. 'Course I'd been
thinking all along I wouldn't be able to afford it! The Wells had
more money'n us—well, they always seemed richer. One of her
brothers, Harry, he worked in the Sale Yard, picked up fruit and
veg on the side; another un, Bomber Wells, went out with his cart,
redistributed it. Folks on Park Road used to have to buy stuff off
him; though in our case I don't know that we ever paid for it, cos
our Mother never paid anybody much. She wasn't what you'd call
good with money.

When there was a rummage sale our Mother always came back
with fancy cushions. She didn't need them; well, you can't do
anything *with* them, can you? She got as many fancy cushions as
she could; Mrs Wells got nice woollies and that. 'Course, none of
them paid, they just said: 'I'll see if it fits,' or 'if this colour goes,'
and passed it to the back. That was it! They'd got it!

Mrs Wells went to Mitchell's and got them to save her cakes,
regular, the ones that had gone stale. She planned in advance; our
Mother never did. She was more—*on the spur of the moment*. The
Wells always seemed to have those lovely doughnuts and cream
horns and things on the table. When I went over there Mrs Wells
used to give me one.

' 'Elp yourself Mary love.'

I thought that was wonderful! *We* never had any cake!

Sis was as thrilled as me 'bout Cyril's unexpected present.

'We can match now! Like we planned!'

I said: 'We'll go to Smith's!'

So we did. We went to J. C. Smith's on the High Street. You

should-a-seen the amazed looks those snooty girls gave us! We was paying cash—none of your 'on appro'! We bought orange hats, like we'd said, orange felt hats with a little bow at the back—we took our time, you bet we did!—and grey coats, exactly the same. The shoes—well, Sis didn't have them quite as high as me—we got them from Brum, we went there special.

We was all set for Blackpool!

*

Blackpool! That word has a mysterious ring, hasn't it! '*Black*-pool!' The brewery always seemed to go there; every year our Ede and our Jess or Jim would be talking about Blackpool and the next trip or the trip they'd just been on. In our living room we had a wot-not, and there were easy a hundred little Goss china ornaments that the others had brought back with them from brewery trips. 'BLACKPOOL' or 'A PRESENT FROM BLACKPOOL'. They took some dusting!

I remember Ede saying once: 'I'm goin to break some o' these buggers. I'm fed up wi dustin em.'

She did. She used to break one or two, gradually, to get rid of them. Then our Mother caught her, gave her such a sock o' the earhole. But she went on doing it. That was Ede—not deterred. How many times had I lifted up those little ornaments—boots 'n' shoes, dogs 'n' urns, you name it, we'd got it—read the letters out aloud: '*BLACK*-POOL!' One was bigger than the rest: a china shell. You were s'pposed, when you put it to your ear, you were s'pposed to hear something. When I was a baby, then when I was a child, Else and Ede used to say: 'It's magic! It's the *sea* you can hear, the sea at *Black*-pool!'

Now I was grown, and I was going there for myself! It was the big treat. Every year the Flowers who owned the brewery had a 'do' at 'The Hill', like a garden party. They invited the workers up there: little sandwiches and that, a band, walk about the gardens. Sis and me went once, out of curiosity, but it wasn't what you'd call a *success*. We didn't like to be watched, see, we didn't feel comfortable. The *trip*—that *was* a treat!

We went by train, took all our own beer, loaded it up at the

41. Sis, Mary and
'chaperone' Doll
on a brewery trip
to Weston-super-
Mare, 1930s: not
the photograph
referred to by
Mary, which, tanta-
lizingly, has
vanished

station. It was a special train; every year they had it. Now that's a
funny thing, I can remember the train but I can't remember anything at all about Blackpool! Only a photograph: there was me and
Sis and Doll Harben who was keeping an eye on us, walking along
the Prom. I don't know what happened to it. The wind was
blowing. That's all we did there, walk along the Prom; we didn't
see the illuminations, or the funfair, or the sea—it was the *train*!

A lot of the chaps and wenches had been drinking before we got
back to it—they were paralytic! But once aboard, nobody worried
you then! It was our very own train! Sis and me walked along the
corridors, up and down, up and down, you could say we *walked*
back to Stratford! Doll had lost interest in chaperoning.

'Ey, when did Doll disappear?'

'Miles an miles ago,' said Sis.

We shrieked! We thought we were very sophisticated. If we spotted somebody we liked, somebody who was reasonably sober, we went in. I didn't drink, nor did Harold Fogg.* He was a nice chap and in the end I went and sat with him. The din! You could hardly hear yourself think!

'You goin out with anyone special?' he said.

*

The older women didn't half tease me, Monday! They pulled my leg 'bout Harold. He phoned up.

'Your *chap's* on the line Mary!'

It was a blower thing; you called down for more beer. ''Ullo!' I shouted. I loved using it.

Harold was in the cellars, but you could see he wasn't going to *stay* there. He didn't lark about, Harold, like a lot of them did, he didn't drink. He was a nice quiet sort o' chap, read books and that. He didn't have a Dad, and his mother was quite old, nearer sixty 'n fifty. He had three sisters. They all worked at the brewery; they were very friendly, they were nice to me. They lived at the 'Eighteens' at Wilmcote: a row of eighteen little stone cottages. I used to catch the train and go there for tea, Sunday. Then Harold got a motorbike and he used to pick me up on it, take me over there.

It was lovely! So peaceful—no rows, not like our house. After tea we went for walks, long walks on the Wilmcote moors. There were moors at Wilmcote, it was all gorse and rough land at the back of the Eighteens.

Our Mother trusted Harold, cos he was so nice; she never worried about me. She'd say: 'That lad's too nice for you, Mary Hewins!' I think that was why she was never strict with me, because she trusted him. She knew there was nothing to be strict *about*.

* *Pseudonym*

﹌ CHAPTER FIVE ﹌

Every Sunday night at our house we had card parties, for pennies and ha'pennies. Cyril organized them. All the young chaps came, and Dad kept a look out for the police. He'd be creeping upstairs, creep back, back'ards and for'ards, back'ards and for'ards, till our Mother shouted at him to stop, it was getting on her nerves.

I used to sit about and watch, look at one hand, then another. Jim slid one up his sleeve. You had to keep quiet... Arch Sweet was there, and Tom Holtom, Harry Wells and Fred Wells, Archie Smart, our Jim o' course and Brock Brookes, he was Jim's friend, a nice chap. He gave me two bob once. You know what two bob's like when you're fifteen! I don't know why he gave it to me—praps he'd had a big win.

' 'Ere y'are Mary—Mary Mary Quite Contrary!'

That's what they called me sometimes.

Anyway, I hid those two bob all over the place. I hid them under the oil cloth—we had oil cloth on our living room floor—nearly to the middle I got, you should a-seen me scrabbling away! I kept moving those two bob about, to be one step ahead of our Mother.

I thought: She won't find em 'ere!

You see, she'd never got any money. By Tuesday she was borrowing. She used to have Cyril's; Tuesdays she'd ask him if she could have her wages, what weren't due again till *Friday*! She'd be quite frightened to ask him—and *I* used to dread it! It was so regular! He ranted and raved, our Cyril, he grumbled so: 'What you *done* with it?' But the money was always there, in the end he always let her have it.

And Jim! He popped round on his bike dinner time and she said: 'Can I 'ave a couple o' bob?' He was married—he'd got married young, nineteen—but she asked him! She knew she could ask Jim and he wouldn't show off. He was the *giver*—and he was married, he'd got kiddies! Oh, our Jim, he used to let her do it. She knowed

275

she could have anything she asked for, there. I felt so sorry for him, sometimes.

Always she was well in front of her wages; she could never catch up. 'Could I 'ave some money, Cyril, off me wages?' That's how it started; that was the warning sign. Or she sent me up to Mrs Windsor. Quick as I could without it being obvious, I went to my coat. I'd moved my two bob to the pocket of my top coat. My heart sank. She'd found it: there was nothing there! You never got it back.

Then Flo came to stay. She brought Ern—he was a Cockney, praps she'd met him when he came to do the gas, I don't know, Flo was very secretive, and their baby Teddy and Ern's brother Fred. He was only a young lad, ten or eleven, but so hungry!

'That lad could eat a horse!' our Mother said.

I thought: ''E very nearly *as*!'

I always dreaded them coming, so did Jess, though she never said anything, not like me. Jess was so quiet, 'put on'. I think that's what got on Dad's nerves. She took it all laying down, and her voice when she did speak was so low you'd a-thought she was apologizing for *having* a mouth.

'Speak up!' Dad shouted. 'Why don't you speak up?'

Straight from the brewery she went with me to clean the school, then half past six we came home and did the housework. I hung back a bit, got out of as much as I could. I was a little devil in those days. It was slabs in our kitchen; Jess scrubbed them when she got in, that was her first job, every night. Flo and Ern and Fred had been out somewhere, visiting. In they came, and the pram.

Jess said: 'Oh I've only just done that, Flo!'

Only a murmur, but just her luck, Dad heard! 'Bring it in!' he shouted, '*right* in! Don't take no notice of *er*!'

Jess was nearly in tears. The state of that floor, what with their muddy shoes, and the pram! They were all unfair to her: Flo, Dad, everybody. I was. Poor Jess! She brought out the worst in people; she never meant to, but she did. She was always the odd one out. She had a nice face, Jess, nice features and hair; only thing was, she'd got a mottled skin, as if she'd had smallpox. It spoilt her. She must have had smallpox as a child. It didn't seem fair.

She was the one who had *accidents*. You know, she went to the Mop, it was Sat'day night, packed o' course. You had to queue up for rides on the Big Horses and *then* they didn't stop proper at the end, to save time. Everybody was acting about but it was Jess who lost her balance when she tried to get off. The horse's head, its ears, came up and caught her here, on the breast.

We brought her home covered in bruises, sobbing. You never seen such a sight.

'They're *ruined*!' she said, over and over again, meaning her tits. Well, they were. Our Mother gave her some stout, made her drink it, cos she didn't like the taste.

'It'll fade, Jess,' I said, 'give it time.'

The funny thing was, she was a lot older'n me, but you always wanted to protect her, even if you did take advantage. Like when Flo and Ern and Fred came in with the pram I thought: So long as *I* don't 'ave to do that bloomin floor, now. Poor Jess!

*

Every summer they came like the swallows for their summer holidays: it was a good roost! Where did they sleep? I don't ever remember them sleeping—I only remember them *eating*! We'd got to feed them, and go to the shops to strap the food. Mostly it was me had to do it. It was a little shop in Brum Road, the strap shop, end of that terrace. I used to be frightened of going in. It was a horrible feeling, cos I *knowed* our Mother wouldn't pay. I was trembling, wondering what the man would say.

'Mam says, "Can we 'ave it..."'

He looked a bit desperate and all. Oh, if only the floor could a-swallowed me up!

'Er says, "Only for this week Mister Hirons."'

'You ain't paid for the week *before*!'

In the end he let us have it. Well, it was his living, I suppose, if you can call it that. Then I had to go somewhere else, for the next week or two.

One day towards the end of their holiday Flo said: 'I could do wi a bit o' money, to go back to London with.'

Jess and me looked at each other!

'I'll go peapickin—with our Mary.'

Peapicking weren't too bad, better than potato picking. That was hard! I'd been potato picking once with Ede. She went regular; she had to, to make her money up, her Tom didn't have much of a job. In bad weather he was out o' work. And our Else, she went once and all, I remember, cos her legs swelled up like an elephant's. Potato picking was terrible. They fetched you in an open lorry. Our Ede had to come and help me do my drift. I couldn't pick them up quick enough, see; the tractor seemed to go so fast. They'd do it for spite, some of those drivers. Oh it was dreadful, back-breaking. Ede helped me to pick up, else I'd a-been too far behind.

Peapicking was easier, you could go at your own pace, put stones in the bottom of the sack. I couldn't say 'No' to our Flo. We walked up to the farm. The foreman was giving out the sacks and bawling:

'If you don't pick you don't earn!'

We knowed him well.

'Ullo,' he said, 'ow's Buckingham Palace?'

Flo pretended she hadn't heard.

'Ey that were a scrap and a 'alf your Jim was in Sat'day night, weren't it?'

The first thing I seen in the field was *gypsies*: lots of them! There was no turning back.

I said to Flo: 'Us'll go up far end.'

But when we came to have our peas weighed—a shilling a pot, 'bout that—it seemed the foreman had let one of these gypsies have a *pram* and she hadn't paid for it. He stopped her money. Ooh! That's when it started—in the barn. It was ugly. I can see this gypsy woman now, with plaits, twisted up like ram's horns.

She stood back and she laid a curse on him: 'Mark my words Mister, you'll be dead and in your coffin afore twelve months is out!'

He laughed! He just laughed. He said he'd got his money: he didn't care! But our Flo panicked! She ran! I had to run with her, over the fields. A storm was brewing. We dropped all the peas we'd pinched. I was more cross with Flo than frit—that surprised me. It was such a tradition in our family that I was scared of gypsies. It started to rain and then our Flo thought it might lighten. 'Ooh!'

'Come on Flo, let's shelter!' It was pouring.

She started counting. 'It'll *thunder* now!' She was terrified. 'Y' *see*!'

Stratford was below us, and the river. You could see the Parish Church and the river, like a scar, silvery white, fading. It was all fading, turning invisible, gone.

We ran across the fields in the blinding rain and we came home. It weren't till we was stripping by the fire I cried: 'Bloody 'ell! I never picked me money up!'

'I did,' said Flo.

Ern went back to London in advance. But that didn't make much difference; three could eat as much as four. When it was her turn to go our Flo started to cry. She was always one to cry when she went back. She cried and cried. All I could think of was: No more strap!

Our Mother said: 'You gotta go back to your 'usband!'

'Yes.' I said. It just came out.

Flo turned on me: 'What's it gotta do wi you?' She said: 'I know! Our Mary can go!'

There was me, hanging out the flags, and there was Flo in floods of tears! That was the unfairest thing of all, cos although she was so pretty, she was prettier'n any of us, with dark hair that waved on its own, big blue eyes, she was the cleverest too, our Flo.

⋘ CHAPTER SIX ⋙

You know how you can get fancies? Your nose is too short or too long; if only you had hands like that, or longer lashes, something impossible. I hated my hair. It was dead straight, black; besides, bobs were out. Sis had lovely hair, wavy and fair, like Mary Pickford. They called me Anna May Wong—she was a Chinese film star— *Wonger* for short. 'SHE LURES MEN TO THEIR DEATH!' Permanent waves had just come in. I thought: '*That's* summat that ain't impossible!'

I saved up and I went to Inglis's on Henley Street and had a *perm*!

Well, it went all fluffy! Fluffy weren't so bad, but then it went frizzy! I looked such a sight!

I wailed: 'I look like a golliwog, Mam!'

Our Mother was picking through my hair; she always did it every morning, before I went to the brewery. I could tell what she was thinking: I *told you so*!

'It's 'orrible! I'm a freak! What's Sis goin to say?'

I knew Harold would say: 'You look lovely,' even if I'd got no teeth in. But Sis! I dreaded her opinion.

You had to check your hair every day, working at the brewery, cos some of them were so scruffy. There was one woman there, Agnes, she was definitely lousy. You could see them. When she combed her hair I always thought: Oh God! Can they jump? If she flirts one with that comb...If she was in the messroom, and I'd gone down to change into my clogs, if she was in the toilet, even if I was bursting I'd come out, quick.

All of a sudden our Mother shouts: '*Nits!*' She said: 'And you've been to the bloody hairdresser 'n' all! They must 'ave seen em!'

Oh no! I thought: She'll never get em out! It was so curly! I'll be late!

She had a job—scratch, scratch scratch with a black toothcomb—

but she did it! She got every one out, she got the last nasty little bloodsucking nit out, cracked its back with her nail.

'When you're at brewery,' she said, low—I thought she was going to say 'Watch out for that Agnes,' but she said: 'D'ye notice Jess?'

'*Notice* er?'

'What er's like? Ow er *is*?'

'I dunno, Mam.'

I never gave our Jess a thought; I'd got better things to do.

'Ede says er's a-coughin.'

Well, Jess did cough. I thought: What's she gettin at? Jess used to annoy me cos when I smoked, sometimes I smoked in bed—'course, I slept with her—and she used to cry and tell our Mother the smoke got down her. I thought: She's been goin on again 'bout me smokin!

'Oh never mind,' said our Mother. 'Now you watch out for that Agnes—'

*

Jess had a trunk she kept her prizes in. She went to a lot of whist drives at the Hippodrome and she was always winning. That was the one thing she was lucky at. I loved to go through this chest with her, look at them: a complete set of cutlery, a mantel clock, beautiful stuff. One night she came back with a box that big.

'What you got, Jess?'

She was excited, pale—well, she always was—but this day she looked really happy.

'It's a *lemonade set*!'

I'd never heard of one of those. It was beautiful: a jug and six green glasses, magical, each one different but the same.

'They're hand made' she said, 'see the bubbles.'

'They're *lovely*, Jess.'

There were tiny bubbles in the glass. When you held one up to the light it was like the river, you know, if you put your head under, swimming.

'Won't e be pleased!'

'Oo?'

'Frank.'

'Oh *im*.'

She was building up her bottom drawer. Well, she was going out with Frank Pollitt;* she'd went with him a long time. I didn't like him, but you couldn't tell Jess. She was nicer'n any of us, she never saw the dark side o'folks.

Then she had this terrible row with Dad—or *he* had one with her. She never argued back. She just bit her lip and bowed her head and that seemed to make him more infuriated—or started coughing. She couldn't get her breath; she coughed and coughed and coughed. And she'd stopped eating.

At first it just seemed to irritate Dad, but when she got thinner and thinner then he got angry, 'specially Sunday dinner time when he came back from the pub, half past one, two o'clock.

'Eat it!' He was up the pole: not rolling drunk, just argumentative.

'I *can't!*' said Jess.

'I'll show you if you can or can't.' And he chucked her dinner up the fire! Sometimes he chucked his and all—the whole table! *I* was alright, well I'd always ate mine—*fast*—before he got back.

The more Jess didn't eat or argue or do anything the more wild it made him.

'Where you goin?'

'I'm meetin Frank.'

'Not that bleedin Frank Pollitt?'

Our Mother used to come between them, and o' course I always stuck up for her, cos I was on her side, always. I couldn't abide Dad, 'specially when he was drunk.

'Let er go, George!'

'She oughta see a *doctor*. That's oo she should be seein.'

'She 'as.' That shook Dad. ''E says it's a touch o' bronchitis.'

'*Bronchitis!*' Dad cussed and raved. He thumped on the table and shouted at Jess: 'Do you *want* to die?'

Well, this day there was an argument and a half. Jess snook out, but Dad wouldn't let up; even after she'd gone he was carrying on about how she should eat and where was her spirit and fancy taking up with a bastard like Frank Pollitt.

Our Mother never tried to stop him when he got into one of his

* *Pseudonym*

282

rages. She just let him go on. He never hit her, or tried to; he
never hit any of us. *She* used to do the hitting! Hit you round the
head, she did, but not Dad—never. That was one thing about him,
he never did that. No, it was *words*—terrible. He was a real devil
with *words*, Dad. As for our Mother, she never cried, she just got
in a flaming temper.

It was all the time, the rows in our house, practically all the time.
This day—well, it was night cos the row had been going on since
dinner time, on and off—Cyril joined in, and then it was three
against one.

Suddenly Dad shouts: '*Out!*'

We stared.

'Both o' you! *Get out!*'

I realized he meant me and Cyril! We were so astonished—we
did! We got outside; it was dark, we didn't know where to go. The
only person we could think of was our Jim. We thought: That's
where we'll go!

It was a hell of a walk to Wilmcote. I'll never forget it: all that
way! It was August, lucky for us, not too cold, but I had high heels
on. I was more dead 'n alive by the time we got there, past
midnight. Jim and his wife lived in the Number Tens; the Eighteens
where the Foggs lived was up the road. If Harold could see me
now! We started throwing stones to knock Jim up.

His head poked out. 'What the hell?'

When we told him he said: 'I'll come back with you—now! Sort
the ole bugger out!'

'I can't, Jim! I can't walk back in these!'

Jim was wild. He was going to fight our Dad, he said. We'd be
better off without him; we were better off when he was away in
the war. I 'spect we was, but I couldn't remember.

'Pity e ever came back! Mam found a letter, y'know, from a
woman.'

I did know, cos Else had told me.

'It made er cry.'

That shocked me; I'd never seen her cry.

'She's 'ad a rotten life, our Mother.'

He seemed to have forgot 'bout Cyril and me—and Jess.

*

After that night, you can imagine, Jess panicked. Well she'd been the cause of it, really. She thought Dad would throw *her* out. She started to pack all her prizes up. In the rush she broke two of the glasses. She wasn't half upset, crying and sobbing. 'The jug's cracked 'n' all!'

'Never mind,' I said, 'they was too delicate, really.'

'It's spoilt,' she said, 'the set's spoilt!'

'What you doin it for, Jess? All this packin? Where'll you *go*?'

It was bad enough her coughing all night and going on about me smoking, and tossing and turning—but *sobbing*!

She made me promise not to tell Dad, or Cyril, or Bert.

'I'm sendin em to Frank,' she said, 'for safe keepin. There's a railway wagon comin round in the mornin. Don't you breathe a word our Mary, *promise*!'

She made me swear I wouldn't tell.

I thought, No chap's worth this, and 'specially *im*. But I kept my thoughts private.

*

I was proved right. As soon as he knew, Frank Pollitt, soon as he knew she'd got it, he gave her up. And he kept all those lovely things: all except the four green glasses, cos the set was spoilt so she hadn't put them in. She was broken-hearted. She'd been going with him three years, but he never came round again, when he heard she'd got TB.

She left the brewery. She did the school for a bit longer—all that dust!—but in the end she didn't go outside any more. Then the day came when she didn't come downstairs; she stayed abed. Her back was all hunched, her bones sticking out of her skin.

I heard the doctor say: 'It's the best solution, Mrs Hewins . . . oo wears them shoes?' He'd spotted my shoes by the bed!

'My youngest.'

'Tell er she'll be a cripple afore she's thirty.'

Our Mother said, low, cos Jess was there, I had to strain my ears: 'She ain't a-goin!'

'If she don't t'other un'll get it, bound to, sleepin with er—everybody—the boy—'

I think that's what made our Mother agree for Jess to go to Hertford Hill. Bert had never been fit, well, ever since a babby he'd been sickly. He had a cough, always had a dry cough. But about this time he started, you know, to blossom. I remember seeing him riding Bomber's horse back to the field and getting quite a shock: he was laughing, little rosy cheeks. Jess was dying and he was starting to bloom. A flower on a rubbish heap, that's what life is like.

⚜ CHAPTER SEVEN ⚜

There were no letters from Hertford Hill. We all knew that was a bad sign.

'Floods or no floods,' said our Mother, 'I'm a-goin.'

'You won't get through, river's right up,' said Dad, 'water's this deep, bottom of town! Swan's Nest's marooned!'

'What's swans' nests got to do with it?' You could see her mind was made up.

I said: 'Harold'll take me Sat'day, Mam, on 'is motorbike. E can try back way.'

Nothing we could say would budge her. She stuck her hatpin through her hat. It was only an ordinary little movement, I seen her doing it every day of my life, but even now, remembering, it stabs my heart. She put her coat on, then her hat, with a hatpin—without looking. There was a whiff of Cologne. It was like reaching for a gun, the way that hat went on and the pin went in, a similar sort of movement. You knew she meant business.

Watching her, I was a kiddie again; she was big, and I was small. She never walked very fast. We'd get outside and her hand reached down—a precise movement. When her hand came down you didn't hesitate: your hand was there, waiting for hers. It was a firm grip. You felt confident she would get anything she wanted, from the shops, the market, anywhere. When she said she'd get through the floods you didn't argue.

Hours later she came back, soaked to the skin, drenched.

'Bloody bus driver!'

That's all she'd say. She poked the coal till I thought: God, er's goin to set chimney on fire! I could see Dad thinking the same. But it was more than his life was worth to douse it; he daren't, with her in that sort o' mood. 'Bloody man!'

'I'll get Harold to take me tonight,' I said.

42. King Edward VII Memorial Chest Hospital, Hertford Hill, near Warwick

So I went. Harold took me to the bottom of the hill and waited. E's a nice chap! I thought. 'Too nice for *you*, Mary Hewins!' the echo said, 'too nice!' It was the worst springtime in living memory, so you can picture the weather, and getting dark and all. When I got past the trees a terrible sight met my eyes: the shadows of hundreds of little huts, on the hill, some with lights flickering, most of them black and *dead* looking. I told myself: Just don't think 'bout it! I kept climbing and climbing. It was like a dream—a nightmare.

'Er'll be at the top,' they'd said at the gate, 'in cowsheds.'

That's what they'd called them.

I was climbing all the time. I was past being frit. Harold had said he'd come with me, but I knowed our Jess. She wouldn't a-wanted anyone 'cept us. I found her, God knows how. It *was* a hut, right at the very top, and all open. They'd each got a little wooden hut, 'bout the size of a garden shed. There was no door, no glass in the windows; the wind and the rain blowed through.

'Oh Jess,' I said. You could see why she hadn't writ; she was too weak for anything. She didn't even want to talk. I looked at her and I thought: She's got no life. She was skin 'n' bones, she just lay there.

There was a plate of cold taters on the side, with a number on it—number fourteen—and some gravy. You could see she hadn't touched it. I felt I'd got to try to feed her. If she eats summat, that might save her! All of a sudden I thought: That's why Dad used to get in such a rage! I tried her with a bit of apple. I'd brought a bag of apples, saved from the autumn. We scrumped them from Schofield's orchard: keepers, with a bitter skin. I never knew their name. They weren't much cop now, cidery, wizened, but I thought maybe the smell of them . . . It was no good. She was pleased to see me, I could tell from her eyes, her eyes was open, all the time, but she wouldn't eat. She didn't even cough. There was a pot to spit in: that had number fourteen on it too. I went on peeling apples, the whole bloody lot, one after the other. Number fourteen—what did that mean? Well, it was the only thing I could think of to *do*, trying to feed her, and talk. I talked and talked and talked, about what was going on at home, and our Mother and Dad. She always wanted to be *family*, Jess, not like me; she clung to the family.

I began. I said: 'There was a big row at our 'ouse, Monday mornin. A real scream 'n' shout.'

That got her smiling, well, the shadow of a smile. *That* was just like home!

'You know ow I lets Mam or you answer the door?'

I always did, in case it was gypsies. You see, when I was little our Mother would say: 'If you don't do what you're told the gypsies'll 'ave you. They brought you, they'll take you back!' All of them used to say I was brought by the gypsies, I don't know why. Maybe it was on account of my hair—as I said, it was black, straight as pump water—I don't know. 'If you don't be'ave, our Mary, gypsies can 'ave you back!'

Well, Sunday night there was a hammering on our door and I said to myself: 'It's Arch 'n' Norman come for cards!' I never *thought*! I opened the door—and there stood the ugliest and blackest woman you ever seen! Like a tramp, with an old shawl over her head—horrible. I wanted to say: 'Bugger off!' but she'd struck me dumb, just the *sight* of her.

'I come for George.'

'Oo is it?'

I never answered our Mother; I couldn't! That brought her to the door. Even she was took aback.

'What d'ye want?'

There was summat mysterious 'bout that cock-eyed Irish woman; for a start, she hadn't got a basket, nor kiddies. 'I come for George, missus.' She was quite polite. 'I tried the Dragon but e ain't there.'

You should a-seen the look our Mother gave her! 'E ain't 'ere neither. What d'ye want?' She wouldn't let her over the step. 'Never let em over the step' was her motto.

'I've summat for im.' She brought out a little package. It looked like a half-crown, wrapped in a mucky bit o' brown paper. Our Mother took it, quick, she almost snatched it! Well, generally it was the other way round: our Dad giving money away!

'I'll see e gets it.' She said to me: 'Go'n cut a slice off that puddin in the kitchen. *I'll stop 'ere.*'

I cut a big slice, bigger'n I meant to, I was that nervous. There goes my dinner tomorrow, I thought—well, the best bit of it.

'The Lord bless you, missus,' said the cock-eyed Irish woman.

Our Mother slammed that door! She put the bolt across! She wasn't half in a temper.

'Not that er don't owe it us!' she said, ''alf County Cork owes us money! It's 'avin to take it!' and: 'I wonder where the bugger is?'

I watched the woman from our window. When she got down the road a few yards—do you know what she done? She throwed that pudding away! As far as it would go. It landed in the Wells's front garden.

'Well,' our Mother was saying, '*well*!'

It wasn't money, after all, it was a silver badge. I saw: 'FOR SERVICES RENDERED'.

'Well,' I said—Jess was still listening, her eyes never left me, 'our Dad wasn't 'alf upset!'

For a start, he got locked out. I had to creep downstairs and let him in. And then the badge: that seemed to upset him. But missing that cock-eyed Irish woman upset him most of all. Next morning he was still on about it: 'Did she 'ave one blue eye and one *brown*, our Mary?'

'I dunno.' I wished he'd shut up; it would only get our Mother going.

'Which way did she go, our Mary?'

'I dunno.' It was true; I never seen.

'Brummagem way? Was she headin to'ards Brummagem?'

'She was headin to'ards Devil's country by the looks on er,' said our Mother. 'I never seen a more evil looking personage, in all my born days. 'Cept your Gran, o'course.'

Then they rowed! You can imagine! His Gran had brought him up, you see. They were still rowing when the brewery hooter went. That was me off, like Cinderella, only glad to be out of it! I didn't leave a slipper behind! No fear! I dreaded coming home, but when I did—there was our Mother polishing up that silver badge, as sweet as pie. 'It'll come in for the *next* time your Dad meets the Prince! If we can keep im sober!'

I looked at Jess. I thought: I can't stop now! I said: 'You heard 'bout the Prince o' Wales openin the new Theatre,* didn't you?'

I gave her a running account of everything that had happened in our family, every little thing. And when I went, I felt I was helping to kill her, going. But I was glad to get out. I can't describe it; it was like being *with* death. I had to escape! When I got out I ran down that hill—it was pitch black—high heels and all. I couldn't get away fast enough. When I fell down all I thought was: I'm still alive!

*

So I wasn't surprised when our Mother said about the guinea-pigs.

The river was down. She'd went on the bus to Hertford Hill, well to Warwick, they would only take you as far as Warwick. She'd walked miles and miles along that road to Hertford Hill. The buses never went up there—no fear!

---

* *The new Shakespeare Memorial Theatre was opened on 23 April 1932.*

'I seen em,' she said, 'like furry rats.' She'd been on about the guinea-pigs ever since she got back. She couldn't get them out of her mind. They was on mine and all now! And Dad's! 'Like furry rats,' she said, 'only fatter.'

'I'm off,' said Dad.

I thought: I don't blame you!

'They shown me. They said: "We inject em from the patients. This is er un. We inject from the patients and if one of em dies . . ." '

She didn't say Jess's guinea-pig had died; she didn't have to. But what she said next did surprise me: 'She's comin 'ome.'

She had our George's old room. Bert and Cyril came out, slept with me. She had to have a room on her own. Poor Jess, even at home she had to be alone. As for Bert, well he wasn't upset; he didn't know what was happening. Jess had never had much to do with him, really; she'd been at work all the time. Our Mother had brought him up. He didn't understand. He was only nine.

I never sat with her; our Mother wouldn't let me.

'You gotta go to work in the mornin,' she said.

I think she was frit I might catch it. Mostly she sat with her, and Jim's wife, and Dad.

On the seventh day she said: 'Fetch Vicar, George, don't argue,' and to me: 'Get er good nightgown out,' and: 'It was the Big Horses at the Mop. I knows it was the Big Horses.'

I didn't say anything. Our Ede reckoned it was the brewery killed her. In the early days they'd had to stand in water, up to here, and no daylight. But our Mother wouldn't have that. She didn't want to hear, so I didn't say anything. I tried to sew a button on. My fingers were trembling. I remember I couldn't thread the needle.

Dad was with her when she died. I can see him now, when she died, cos I ran in, I heard this *sound*. He'd pulled the pillow from under her head; he was hurling it against the floor. He bashed it on the floor. You never seen such a mess! Feathers everywhere. It was snowing feathers. Jess just lay there, silent, dead, but out of his throat was coming this horrible sound, like a wild creature being throttled.

Four men pulled the bier from Park Road. We walked behind.

All the neighbours were out. Mrs Wells, she was in her front, she shouted: 'It's no bloody good *now*, George, you should a-looked after er when she was alive!'

Sis came with me; she was crying ever so.

Flo wrote from London: 'I want to remember my sister as she was.'

Our Mother said: 'Flo's too upset to come.'

I could picture Jess smiling, you know, how we used to share a smile over Flo, just the shadow of one, but a smile. Oh Jess! I thought, I'm going to miss you.

We followed her all the way from Park Road to the church, and from the church to the cemetery.

Our Mother said, 'Ow funny,' she said, 'there's Sis—' Sis Crowe was Jess's only friend, she'd died twelve months before. I think a chap had chucked her up and it broke her heart.

'And ole Mister Beard off the road—'

She knew where they all were, under the grass.

'And er.'

A stranger came round; we were examined, everybody. And the bedding was burnt, in the garden: her mattress, the sheets, her clothes, everything. Poor Jess, there wasn't a trace of her left, 'cept those four green glasses—and Bert. She was so quiet, she was the best of us all. She'd never had any life.

'I can't abide this house,' said Dad.

For once, there was no argument.

❧ CHAPTER EIGHT ❧

That's why the school house seemed so magical. When Dad came home and said: 'School house is vacant. The new headmistress don't want to live there', we didn't think much about it. What was the point? But when he said: 'There's a chance for *us*! If I gets round Vicar there's a chance!' and 'Ow about it?' it seemed as if, you know, we'd each had a wish and it had been granted. 'We'll 'ave to go to Communion, Sunday,' Dad said. He'd got a plan. 'Course, he asked our Mother first, everybody did that. She said 'yes' or 'no'. But there was no need, hardly. Her face! The *school house*!

43. The School House, Alcester Road, Stratford-upon-Avon (1983)

She chucked everything out. The wot-not went, the fancy cushions from the rummage, the photo of Dad in his Volunteer's uniform, all the Theatre ladies hanging along the wall with their signatures, signed to her, signed specially to her because she'd used to dress them. '*To Emma, with love*', '*Dearest Emma from Violet Farebrother*'. All those beautiful things went crashing into the bin, one after the other, all gone 'cept the china shell. That survived, somehow—I remember seeing it later—and Dad's certificate. When I was little I used to lay there and read it and read it: '1917—*Discharged*—George Henry Hewins—Royal Warwickshire Regiment—*Honourably* Discharged—1917.' Somebody had signed it for him: '*George*'. I rescued that. I rolled the certificate up and I kept it. God knows why.

'It's a new start!' she said. She was whipped up with excitement. Her eyes shone. Her hair started to come back: she'd lost it in great handfuls, after Jess died. Rip-rip, bang-bang, smash-smash. Dad let her get on with it. Well, it would a-been like trying to stop a March wind. We all have our own ways of grieving.

'Just look at that larder! Fancy!'

It was a lovely larder, ever so big, with shelves all round, red tiles on the floor.

'Like larder at "Shakespeare",' she said.

She couldn't get over it.

'And a cellar! Just think what us'll be able to keep down there!'

I thought: 'Alf the brewery, if I knows our——

'*Look!*'

We went from room to room and she was flushed with happiness. Then we went outside. There was a high wall round the back garden so's nobody could see us; the playground was over the wall. One side was dirt, and a few flowers.

'We can keep hens, still,' she said. 'That's where I'll 'ave the hen run.'

For her the school house was a dream come true. It stood on its own, beside the school, separate yet *part* of it, with stone-faced windows, some with diamonds. There was a porch and a front door with four arch shaped panes—like a church! Wonderful! She kept going in and out of that door, in and out.

'Well,' she said, '*well!*' and 'This porch'll come up lovely with sand!'

Dad never said what put the new headmistress off. But he always kept a bottle on the front window sill, with '*RAT POISON*' on it, in big letters.

You'd a-thought *I'd* have been in seventh heaven too. At last I'd got our Mother to myself—with the Dragon just opposite Dad was out permanently and our Cyril had got just as bad—that's what I'd always wanted. But it wasn't enough. I was restless. I loved her, but you can't explain feelings. They're like the river; you can feel it pulling you always, pulling you away from the bathing place, pulling you where you don't want to go, where you know it's dangerous.

*

'This young gentleman's startin today and I'll be obliged if one of you older uns ud show im the ropes.'

'It'll be a *pleasure*, Mister Court!' All the women laughed.

I pitied the young lads, starting. You see, they didn't know what was in store for them. It was like lambs to the slaughter. When a

44. 'The bottling end', Flowers Brewery, Stratford-upon-Avon, late 1930s

new lad started at the bottling end, the women—the older women—would be waiting... They'd have a laugh, get him on the floor—well, you can picture it—get a bottle of Guinness or a Number One Strong Ale, that was a long narrow bottle, shook it up a bit. It was *potent*, not the bottle, the ale, and it started to fizz and he'd shout '*Ow!*'

I used to dread it. I kept out of it if I could, went outside to the heap or down to the messroom.

'Come on, Sis. Let's tek this lot to heap.' This day I hadn't realized there was a new one starting. There he was, before I could escape.

It was *him*! The boy on the bicycle! I couldn't believe it! What was he doing at the brewery? There was no mistaking!

'Ey Ginger!' one of the women shouted. 'You ginger *all over*?'

'There's only one way to find out!'

He *wasn't* ginger; he was auburn. His hair was like dark copper. Well—he stood there and he grinned! He grinned and he gave them such a look—not nasty, but... it shut them up.

I thought: Oh God, e's goin to pay for this, later! I had the wild idea of warning him. What was he doing at the brewery? He must be in the office! But he wasn't! He was only unloading the wagons when the empties came in, he was only doing a labouring job. What was a grammar school boy doing *labouring*? I thought: E's goin to be for it!

Lucky for him there was a commotion that morning, took their minds off everything else. Sis fell in the glass heap.

I went to the hospital to see her. She wasn't half in a mess, covered with bits o' glass. We used to have to take crates o' glass bottles that had broke to the heap, you see; two of us had to carry them. It was like a slag heap, like they have at pit heads: just a great big sparkling heap of glass. They'd got nowhere else to put it; nobody wanted broken glass. Well, I was dreaming, Sis tripped and fell right in! There was bits o' glass splinters everywhere, all over her hands and her legs and her back. She was in tears still.

'They 'ad to pick em out wi tweezers! They ain't done *yet*! Look!'

'S'not on your face, Sis. That's one good thing,' I said. 'Ey, you know that lad oo started today? Do you remember im?'

She didn't.

'On 'is bike! The boy on the bicycle!'

She didn't remember! I was glad, somehow.

'I seen im once at Wilmcote. I reckon e lives near Wilmcote.'

I'd seen his bike when I'd been out walking with Harold, propped against a wall. It was so distinctive—like him. Poor Sis! I was more interested in solving the mystery than sympathizing with her, and she wouldn't a-gone to the heap in the first place if it hadn't been for me.

*

Next day in the messroom—I had to take beer down there for a couple of the women—I was straining my ears. They never mentioned him. They were still debating whether Sis's beauty had been spoilt forever—*hopin*, I thought. One of them, she only had one eye; a bottle had bust and took the other out. She used to start on Guinness before breakfast; six o'clock she was usually drunk, by breakfast she was up the pole. Jack Timms the foreman was on to those who drank. The women weren't allowed beer, not like the men, so they got one of us young ones as didn't drink to take bottles down to the messroom.

'I've gotta go to toilet again, Mister Timms!'

One of the Mattock* girls kept a couple back in her knickers, went out with them at night and her elastic broke—half way down Windsor Street! In the middle of the pavement!

I was just going back up the steps when I heard a woman say: 'Did you see? Ow that ginger lad looked at Sal yesterday?'

'Took the wind out er sails!'

'You know oo e *is*?'

'Poor lad!'

'You'll console im I s'ppose?'

They laughed.

I daren't stop no longer. I'd had to get somebody to take my place. Besides, the foreman knew everything that went on, and Gargy Court the manager, he had an office right up in the ceiling

* *Pseudonym*

so's he could get a bird's eye view. He watched you pull your stockings up. When you went downstairs he timed you. He didn't dock it, but he'd call Jack Timms and get him to tell you off if you stopped a long time.

*

When Sis was better, her and her chap and me and Harold went to the pictures, in the good seats. We lashed out; well, Harold paid. Sis said after: 'Did you see that lovely brooch?'

'Ey?'

'That lovely brooch er was wearin. You know, in the farewell scene.'

I hadn't. Sis laughed. 'What was you two doin?'

We hadn't been doing *any*thing. And I'd got a blooming awful headache. I felt my head was going to drop off. Another few steps, I thought, and it will. I didn't tell Harold—I couldn't a-stood the fuss—nor Sis. But when I got home I told our Mother.

'You'd best go to doctor,' she said.

So I did. I went to the surgery on Rother Street.

'Please I've got bad headaches!'

I was frit to death; I'd never been to a doctor before! I didn't know what to say, what you were supposed to *do*. So imagine my face when Dr Pembrey smiled and said: 'We'll go down the cellar.'

He lifted a trapdoor in the floor and I thought: It must be a dream! It can't be happening! There were plenty of people waiting—I could a-screamed and been rescued—but I was too frit! I saw stone steps, going down.

'Follow me,' he said.

Now if there's one thing I can't abide it's a cellar. I never could share our Mother's pleasure in the cellar at the school. They are dreadful places.

'Come on,' he said, ''s alright.'

How I managed it I do not know. It was pitch black. We'd only gone a few steps and he said: '*Stop!*'

He shone a torch into my eyes.

'Hrumphhh!'

I thought: E's goin to murder me!

'It's very bad,' he said, 'did nobody ever test your eyes at *school*? Ow've you managed?'

I was struck dumb. He sounded so angry! I thought he was blaming *me*. But my brain was racing. That's why I couldn't follow the film proper! *Any* film! Or thread needles. Or read, or tell the time! That's why I'd always gone by colours more'n faces, how somebody smelt, sounded, the touch of things more'n the look. I couldn't *see*!

''Ave you any money?' he said. His voice was quite kind. 'You'll need 'bout two pound.'

Our Mother said: 'Us'll get it.'

Two pounds was Dad's weekly wages. I knowed Mrs Windsor wouldn't have that sort o' money to lend, nor our Cyril, nor anybody at short notice. Well, to cut a long story short, everybody clubbed in, our Jim and all.

'Ask no questions!' he said.

That was one thing about our family, they would help you if they could, no strings attached.

I got the two pound and I went to the optician's. He was an old man—well, I'll tell you straight, he was a dirty old man. He took me into a little dark room, he was awful. When I went for my fitting—'It's your fittin, innit?' leer-leer—he touched me like this. Ugh! I was glad to get out—glad till I remembered what I'd paid those two pounds for: *glasses*!

I didn't want to wear them, I didn't want to *see* myself. I avoided looking in the shop windows. I didn't like them a bit. 'Course, Harold said they suited me! How could glasses *suit* you? Everybody stared at work. Well, not many people like us wore glasses then, it was toffs did, mostly: I was the only girl in the brewery with them. Horrifying things.

'Ooh!' they said, 'Mary's got glasses!' and: 'Ow does it feel to 'ave four eyes, Mary?'

I thought: That's it! I've 'ad it now!

But I was determined to keep them on; that was my stubborn nature. Through that glass—it's hard to describe—the world was a different place, so bright, shining. I could see the tiles on the school roof and the bell, I could even see a bird on top of our chimney stack and know before it started squawking that it was an old crow, watching our Mother's chicks most likely, and the lime trees, and every single leaf and the sun turning the clouds . . . a shining, shining world.

CHAPTER NINE

I'd been laying elaborate plans how I could get to talk to him. Once I got those blooming glasses I thought: That's it! So picture my surprise when he comes up to me at work one day, cool as a cucumber, and says: 'Shall I give im a message?'

I was that took aback I was quite rude. 'Oo?'

'Harold o' course.'

'Oh.'

He knew I went out with Harold! He must a-seen me at Wilmcote, visiting the Foggs. Just my luck. He didn't say no more, well, he probably thought I was gormless the way I looked at him, stared. He went back to humping the crates. Once or twice after that in a quiet voice he asked about Harold; he had a quiet, deep sort of voice, but cheeky. Trouble was, I wanted him to be more'n just cheeky. I wanted him to mind, to be jealous . . . I'd go red with my own thoughts.

'Penny for em,' said Harold. He put something into my hand. 'It's a present,' he said, 'for the nicest girl in the world.'

I should a-said: 'And you're the nicest boy!' That was true! But I was too choked up. It's hard to explain, but even Harold *breathing* was an irritation to me. I could a-screamed. I opened the box and there was a wrist watch! None of us had wrist watches. It was lovely, with a square face, silvery coloured.

'It's the latest style.'

I knew. I'd seen them up the town. Sis and me had hung over them in the jeweller's window. It had cost a lot of money.

'It's not a cheap un.'

'Oo wants to know ow much it bloody cost?'

'I only thought—'

I heard myself say: 'It's 'orrible. I can't abear *silver*. Nor square watches. Nor oblong ones.'

Harold looked shocked, you know, as if he'd picked up a ferret by mistake.

'' 'Ere,' I said, 'I don't wannit.' I thought: I'm doin you a favour, Harold Fogg. You're better off wi'out me.

He didn't argue. Who could blame him? He had his pride. Off he went, across the 'croft, squaring his shoulders up. I wished he'd a-said: 'You little bitch!' I wished he'd a-said something nasty. I thought of his old mother and his sisters waiting at home for him—'Did she like it, Harry?'—and for a moment there I weakened. I felt sorry, ashamed. But his future wasn't mine. It's something you know. We've all got our own star to follow.

*

He was my star; well he changed my life, you could definitely say *that*! When he said: 'You comin to the Mop tomorrer night?' I said 'Yes!' And I sang inside.

Collins's *Dragons*—that was the star attraction! They'd got the music, the organ! They were lovely; each dragon had red velvet seats. You ran your hand over it—soft, soft!—like thick moss, plush. Everyone was drunk, even I'd had a port and brandy. The dragons were magical. You chose one and you sat in it, you felt you were sailing through the clouds. They were my favourite. Every now and then they switched the lights off, the main lights, and it was *dark*! Everyone screamed! Round and round the dragons went, round and round, music blaring away and our skirts flew up.

He said, 'I shall 'ave to get off.'

Funny, but it was when he admitted . . . There was a feeling inside of me—happiness? I don't know. It was more ex*cite*ment. Tonight! Tonight! Some chaps you'll keep messing about for years . . .

A man was shouting: 'Tonight! The *Wall of Death*!'

We watched from the top.

'We're mad!' I said, 'ain't we mad payin to watch this?'

You could see he was fascinated. He felt it too now! The ex*cite*ment! They went faster and faster, those chaps on motorbikes, round and round they went—they'd rev up—faster and faster and faster. They got to the top, smothered in oil and stuff. I touched one of them—and jumped back! All the girls did it—'*Oooh!*' We thought that was wonderful.

When I cried out he catched hold of my arm. He was laughing at me.

'S'alright,' he said, 's'alright!'

'It's terrible,' I said. 'Ey, 'ave you ever *seen* a death on this thing?'

'No,' he said, 'I never.' He laughed!

'It's bloody marvellous ow they do it, though.'

'Let's go back to Cross Keys.'

'No,' I said, 'I can't stand chaps oo drink.'

'Nor me roundabouts.'

So we walked through Old Town. Most of the lights was off—it was late!—by the Parish Church there and over the bridge, till we'd left the Mop behind, and the music and the screams.

CHAPTER TEN

I snook out the bottling end and walked along the bridge, just to
see him. Lots of times I did it. There was a wooden bridge, way
up, like in the sky, over the Golden City. I used to walk along it,
trying to catch his eye. If the foreman caught me I'd say:

'I got a message for our Jim!'

Every so often they cleaned the vats out, and all the chaps they'd
strip down to the waist, well down to their underpants; some didn't
wear nothing, just a strip o' cloth and canvas shoes. They went
down the ladders and they cleaned the vats out with a sort of
pumice stone. You could see the froth on the beer of those that
were still full. Deep they were, deep as a house, and you know
how beer stains! It was filthy work, hard, but as it came up, the
copper, the whole place started to shine gold, you never seen

45. 'The Golden City', Flowers Brewery, Stratford-upon-Avon

anything so beautiful—and the chaps! They turned to gold, with the reflection.

I'd make him look up. The others laughed; I didn't care. He could stand on his own with them. He was well developed for his age, muscular, you'd never a-thought he weren't one of them. He worked alongside the other chaps, he could work as hard as our Jim or anybody. I used to think: He's mine! A golden prince in a golden city.

I must have been mad.

*

I hardly noticed Sis get married. We had a row; it was over a chap—it was over *him*. Well, she used to tease me 'bout him, say she'd been out with him, that sort o' thing. Then one day, on the spur of the moment almost, she got married! 'Course, we weren't speaking so I didn't get an invitation. It served me right; I'd started it. She married Syd, and afterwards she went to live at Coventry.

I've often wondered since: if Sis hadn't gone . . . She was my best friend; she was never frit of saying what she thought, and maybe . . . You never realize how you value something till you lose it, you know, like being careless with a necklace, and then you think: Oh if only I'd took good care of it! After the beads have scattered.

Missing Sis get married was very ironical cos I'd always loved a wedding; we both had. We'd never had one in our family, a good wedding: our George and Marg went to Leamington, on bikes, Flo did it in London and Jim went to the registry. Folks'd look in the photographer's window and say: 'Oo's she?' or: 'What's them two doin?' I got on everybody's photo. There I was on the shot of the bride and groom coming down the path, or with the relations by the gate. I didn't do it on purpose, it was just we couldn't keep away if we heard the bells, and we liked to get a good look.

We'd planned ours and all! We opened the *Herald* and it said: 'The bride, Miss Mary Hewins,' or 'Miss Emily Wells . . . wore a dress of parchment satin and carried a bouquet of red roses with a sprig of myrtle. The bridesmaids, Miss So 'n' So, cousin of the bride, and Miss Da de Da, friend of the bride, wore floral georgette and carried posies of sweet peas. The bridegroom's gift to the bride was a string of cultured pearls . . .'

Well, not long after Sis had gone, one of the girls at the brewery sent me an *invitation*! Lily wasn't a friend to go out with, more refined, she didn't swear or anything like Sis 'n' me; Hilda Mattock was her very best friend. She always appeared one above us. She had the nicest jobs at the brewery, you know, where it wasn't *dirty*, like putting the tops on the bottles—pleated, a little red cap, then you put a rubber ring round. That was a nice job. I 'spect Jack Timms . . . Anyway, Lily invited me to her wedding, so I went.

The reception was in the hut up Clopton Road. Afterwards *he* came to meet me. 'Course he hadn't been invited; he was different, wasn't one of us. They all said he was stuck up, and he drank too much and what could I see in him? *They'd* gone off him completely!

I ignored it. I thought: They're jealous.

He'd been drinking. This night up Clopton Road he was drunk as a lord.

I said: 'Poor Fred, e always wanted Lily. E wanted to marry er really. I think e'll 'ave Hilda now,' just to take my mind off it. He was being sick by the palings.

'*Why*?' I said, 'why do you *do* it?'

The sound of it sloshing out, the retching! I stood and watched him being sick all over the palings there—I'd got my new Marina dress on for Lily's wedding—and the pavement. The stink! Princess Marina had just come on the scene. It was a very pretty blue-green, Marina green they called it.

Oh God! I thought, I can't bear it!

There was a cape, with frills round, at the top, just a small one. It reminded me of Dad. And others.

I asked him: 'Why do you *do* it?' I said, 'You'll never catch up with them, no matter how hard you try.'

I shouldn't a-said that, probably. It was red rag to a bull. But I could see no sense in it, I didn't know what was driving him. *Some*thing was.

Why did I stop with him? It must have been his looks. It gets you, it gets you into trouble, it leads you into God knows where.

There's nothing else, I thought, only his looks! He's wild, terrible wild. To have Councillor Smith tell him he was a disgrace! Yes, that's what he'd said! He told me, laughing.

'You *are!*' I said.

But I loved him. There's no accounting for it; I'm not asking anyone else to understand. Why should they? He was one on his own, he was unique.

Then the most amazing thing happened: our Mother had a win on the Pools! Not much—but it was like thousands to us! Four aways she got it on. Oh God! It was like Heaven! 'Course, she spent it straight away, practically. She bought a suite for the front room, a lovely dinner service from Lambert's the posh china shop, yellows with an orange stripe, and a little pedigree dog that died.

Dad said: 'I told you so.'

He didn't believe in buying dogs. You didn't buy kiddies, did you? They came. There were plenty of dogs about Stratford looking for a good home.

'Yes,' she said, 'that's what's worrying me.' She said to me: 'You can 'ave a party! A *twenty-first!*'

I got in a flap, then!

'I ain't twenty-one, Mam!'

I wasn't, but I'd always dreamt of a twenty-first.

'You want one don't you?'

She was determined I was going to have it.

'Yes.'

So I had a party in our dining room, well, the front room. It was the first time we'd ever used it, to eat in or anything; we used the living room always. There was this very nice suite, and a sideboard our Else had got off one of her ladies, some carpet the old head-mistress had left. Our Mother's new service was on display; we never used that either—no fear!

The guests arrived. They weren't *my* friends, 'cept *him*, they were Cyril's! It was more an extension of the card sharp parties: our Cyril and all his pals as used to come and play cards, Arch Sweet, Brock Brookes and Jim, they all came over from the pub. So you can imagine, they were three parts.

She'd bought a Hornby trainset for Bert, and guess what our Mother bought me? A new pianna, with bronze candle holders! That was typical—I couldn't play a note! And a cake. Now we had a nice settee in that front room, part of the suite, never sat on as a rule, but you know how they are, young chaps. They sat on it, put their feet on it, and then one of them put a cigarette down it. She came in, with the cake. It was a big un! They put it in the fender, it was so big, that cake, lowered it down, and all those candles, flickering.

'Come on Mary! Blow em out an let's 'ave a bit!'

I nearly fell in the fender trying to blow those bloody candles out. Dad was chuckling. Our Mother seemed not to mind about the settee; she was puffing away at a fag herself! I couldn't believe my eyes.

'Don't mind if I do!'

They were all laughing and joking; one of them tried to play the pianna and Dad sang a song about a Jolly Coon on his Honeymoon.

Then somebody shouted: '*Fire!*'

I thought it was something to do with the candles; I was feeling a bit woozy.

> 'The porters in a mob they grab
> 'Is luggage from the 'ansom cab...'

I thought: What a funny smell!

It was the settee! It was on fire!

Jim came to the rescue, just in time, and Brock Brookes. They carried it into the front garden. Another minute and the house would a-burnt down—and the school!

'This is the last party I'll 'ave,' said our Mother, 'the first and the last.' But she couldn't help laughing. 'Ow d'you like it?' she said, meaning the cake. She was fond of him, she liked him coming round; that was surprising cos she wasn't one for open house, it was only our Cyril's pals got past her as a rule.

'It's lovely ta, Missus Hewins.' He grinned. Oh, he could turn on the charm unexpectedly; when you weren't expecting it you were stabbed here, in the guts.

'Hmm,' she said, 'well you stick to cake!'

She thought he drank too much; well, he did. Working at the brewery, what could you expect? It's a wonder *I* wasn't a drunk and all, cos us girls, we had to *suck* the Guinness, suck it off! We had to bottle the Guinness by hand. The chaps pinched it out the hogs-head—it came from Ireland in barrels—siphoned it out with a tube, on the sly. But us girls had to sit with a sack over our legs in *front* of the blooming barrel, with six copper tubes, and suck and suck. You know how a little pig sucks its mother? We had to pull the bloody stout off like that: six copper tubes, six copper tits. When it got to the top of the bottle ... you shut it off, *quick*! Otherwise you was swilled.

The smell wouldn't go away; you had to wash and wash. When I thought about the brewery sometimes I shivered. There's got to be something else, *some*thing! I wanted to ask him why *he* worked there. He needn't a-done. If you've been to grammar school you can work *any*where. I wished I could a-talked to him about it, but how can you describe feelings? We didn't talk much.

He said: 'Cheer up! Cross Keys tommorrer night?'
I said 'Yes.'
And I cried inside with wanting, even though I sensed he was growing away from me.

A funny thing, the settee was still burning inside when I went out next morning, smouldering.

CHAPTER ELEVEN

I heard two girls talking and one of them said: 'Try gin 'n' quinine.'

So I thought I would. I hadn't told our Mother, she didn't know then. I sat upstairs; I was doing it on my own, trying. The quinine was a white powder; you got it from the chemist's, for toothache. Our Cyril—he was in the same room, and Bert, cos there was only two bedrooms at the school house, our Mother and Dad was in the other one—he said: 'What's up with our Mary, Mam?'

'I dunno.'

'What's er drinkin like that for?'

You could tell he was shocked. I thought: The times I've laid in bed with my hands over my ears while *you* was bein sick in this po, Cyril Hewins!

'Er's *drunk*, Mam!'

I was. I was drunk for three days, sick drunk; just my luck. I never touched a drop since. I thought: I'll go to the doctor. I felt so ill. I'd only been to the doctor once before. There were two brothers at the surgery; I prayed I'd get the one who'd done my eyes, cos I knew him. Fate was against me all the way: it was the other one!

'What's wrong with you?'

I panicked. He was so young, sort of pompous. How could I tell him? I said: 'I've got bad headaches.'

He gave me a check-up. All the time I was thinking: Is e goin to guess? I wished I'd never come. He looked mystified. Oh, if only it was the other one! *E'd* a-guessed! He'd guessed 'bout my eyes.

'That all you got Miss Hewins?'

'Yes,' I said.

So he told me to go and buy some pills for my head. He was right really, I did need my head seen to—for not speaking the truth.

I sat by the fire watching our Mother peeling apples. It was

Christmas, plum pudding time. I never seen anybody peel apples like our Mother. The skin was off, and the core out—before you could blink! She got the cores out, complete, with a little bone. She had a little hollow marrow bone, that's what she used for coring apples. Well, the sight of that peel curling about on the floor and on her lap . . . I had to go out.

When I came back she said: 'You'd better *tell* im.'

Our Mother was a remarkable person. That's all she said. She didn't carry on at me; she didn't fuss. She went on peeling the apples. All she said was: 'You'd better tell im.'

*

So I did. And soon as I told him . . . I wished I hadn't! He didn't say anything. He just looked at me and went quiet. He was shocked. Then he didn't call at the house so much; it started to drop off. How did *I* feel? I'll tell you. I turned to ice inside with the dread of not seeing him and the dread of seeing him changed towards me. I'd read the signs; I knew he'd been waiting for an excuse, I knew better'n he knew himself. I couldn't keep him, that was all. It was like trying to keep a fox. Bert had, once. He'd caught a fox cub up the railway, made a pen; it was a marvel how he looked after it, loved it. But that fox scraped and scraped and scraped till it had made a hole big enough to escape. That's all it wanted to do: escape.

Our Mother said: 'What's up?'

'It's 'is mother. Er's against it.'

'Huh!'

'Er says we ain't good enough, Mam. We ain't respectable. Well, that's what er says: I'm a scruff!' I said: 'I'm *not*, Mam!' I was miraculously clean, always. That was what hurt so, when he said, 'My mother says you're a scruff.'

'You're better 'n *any* o' *them*!' Our Mother was pink with anger. 'I could tell you a thing or two 'bout *er*. Oighty toity cow.'

'I know,' I said, 'e told me.'

He hadn't. It was our Jim's wife, she came from Wilmcote and she'd told me his Dad was an old toff who'd got an *important* job in Brum—and another wife there and all, she reckoned. He'd hid his secret family away in that tumbledown cottage—well, it looked tumbledown to me, all trees and creepers, at the bottom of a little lane—and every day they must a-lived in dread that somebody'd find out. 'Course, they all knowed 'bout it in Wilmcote; as Jim's wife said, you can't keep secrets in a place that size, even if you can in Brum.

When *he* was eight, he was their only kiddie, they'd sent him to the Grammar School, at Stratford, *paid!*

'Oh 'is Dad was proud of im,' she said, 'you could tell. And e loved *er*. She was striking lookin, ever so *elegant*.'

'*Er!*'

'Well she was then. It was very *romantic*,' Jim's wife said. 'Then one day the old man didn't get off the train... She left the village, went to live in that Theatre cottage on Waterside. She lives for *im* now...'

My heart turned over.

'E's a *love child*, and Mother's love,' Jim's wife reckoned, 'is a terrible load.'

I asked our Mother: 'D'you think e did it just to shock *er*? I mean, go out with me?'

'If e did,' she said, 'e '*as* done it in a dish, 'asn't e?' She was quite upset; she'd liked him. 'Give im time. E's a nice lad, deep down. E'll come round.'

There she was wrong! I knew better. She wasn't always right. She never knew 'bout *him*. I didn't understand him, well, nobody did, but I knew him. I knew more about him than she did—or anybody. I knew in my heart that he wanted to escape. I just kept praying nobody would find out, 'specially our Jim.

Jim's wife said: 'I won't tell im, don't worry.' She knowed what would happen if she did. She said, 'I've got an address in Brum. But I think it's too late.'

I went to the Parish Church. I didn't go in, it weren't that sort o' church. I just walked round and round the outside, praying. I wondered about the river, 'course I did. But I was too afraid.

*

The foreman at the brewery was a man called Jack Timms. He lived on Park Road and he didn't like me. Well, I was a bit flighty, you know, I used to answer him. When I was little I'd used to call after him. He was a bloke who held grudges, stored them up; a discontented man. He liked to think he was all powerful. At the bottling end he might a-been, but down Park Road...

He'd say: 'You can go on washin machine today, Hewins!'

I didn't like it; I tossed my head. 'I ain't a-goin on washer!'

There was an argument then! 'I'll bloody *make* you!'

He'd put me on smelling the bottles—you can imagine—smelling the bottles when they came back from the pubs. He knew it made me heave. Or looking for mothers. *Mothers*? We used to call them that. They lurked in the bottom of bottles, looked alive, like slimy slugs. Jack Timms had it in for me.

One day me and Beat Crowe and Kate took some beer down to the messroom. Now that was a funny thing: Kate was so fat I never suspected *she* was expecting and all! Yes, Kate worked right up to having it, all that time, washing the stoppers, and nobody knew anything about it. But me! I was fated! Jack Timms had a glint in his eye. I should a-guessed when he said: 'Go down and fetch em up, will yer?'

That was the trap! He never spoke polite to you, normally. He used to tell us to fetch the older ones up cos they went down to the messroom to have a smoke—and a drink!

'Go 'n' fetch em up,' he said, 'they bin long enough down there!'

We took a bottle each, in our hands, never thought, you did it automatic.

He caught me on the stairs. 'What you doin wi that?'

'I dunno.'

He said: 'I shall 'ave to report you.'

I got the sack. I didn't get it for stealing, I got the sack cos I wouldn't let on why I was taking beer down to the messroom. All I'd say was I took it down there; I wouldn't say what it was for.

Gargy Court the manager left Jack Timms to do it. He wouldn't a-missed it for the world, anyway!

'You know you ain't s'pposed to drink on the job?'

He smiled. He *knew* I didn't! Talk about ironical! I didn't drink beer, and I got the sack for drinking! All the others drank like fishes, all the older uns; before breakfast some of them was drinking!

Kate and Beat got out of it. How? Praps they put the blame on me. Praps he cast a blind eye. They'd got a lot of relations working at the brewery; he couldn't afford to upset them all, could he? I told Beat. I laughed and said: 'You two oughta 'ad the sack 'n' all, Beat! Same as me!' It was mysterious to me how they got out of it.

But I didn't argue with Jack Timms. I thought: it's an *opening*, really. It saved giving my notice in. I'd have had to a-left, the babby would a-started to show—think how he'd a-crowed over that! And I couldn't a-got no dole, then.

*

The dole office was in Brum Road, a little shed by the canal. There was queues of folks! Men, women, old uns, young uns, all sorts. I didn't want them to take me, but I didn't want them to know *why*. They kept sending me away for jobs—the roughest ones they could find—cleaning jobs, cleaning public houses. I couldn't escape from bloody beer! But I was getting to be crafty. When I got there I'd say, 'I never done this sort o' work, mister!' or: 'I come from brewery, missus,' hinted, see. I made out I was too rough for their rotten job.

'Oh,' they said, 'well I don't think you're quite suitable.'

But then the dole office sent me to the Horse and Jockey. Out came the usual story. She was a nice woman.

'Ow old are you duck?'

I looked at the floor, all sawdust, worse'n the school: gob, beer, the lot—horrible.

'Ah, it could do wi a good go,' she said, 'nobody's bin on it since Sat'day.'

'Could I use your toilet missus?'

It was worse in there! I didn't care; I felt I was dying. The worst of it was, I couldn't get the bile out: retch, retch, retch, but nothing came up. Nerves, praps. When I got back, I told her, quick:

'I got sack from brewery!'

Well, I had to say it to get out of the job, I was desperate to get out of it.

'I won't be no good to you.'

'You sit down duck,' she said.

Oh God! I thought, I've overdone it! Er's goin to take me on out o' kindness! Er's took a fancy to me!

Sure enough, she patted my arm. But to my surprise she said: 'I'm goin to tell em you's *most* unsuitable. Now where's your paper?'

I felt myself going red. How'd she guessed? You couldn't *see*. I was about six months, but I'd been starving myself, practically, to keep thin. I used to get a sheet, rip up an old sheet, bind it round myself, tight. And I had a short coat, trimmed with fur—well, rabbit.

'You take care of yourself. And the babby.'

I could have died! She signed the paper and I thanked her and rushed out.

You see, if I'd refused a job I wouldn't a-got any dole. It wasn't much, but I did get some, I got a bit o' dole. I was still working at the school, o' course, but I didn't get paid for that.

He still called at the school house: not very often, now and then. It was as if he couldn't stay away *al*together. He liked the family, I think—there was always a lot of comings and goings at our house—our Mother. He liked to come and sit in the larder, while she was working. What they talked about I do not know; not me, cos he made her laugh.

'E's a case, that lad,' she'd say, 'worse'n your Dad.' When I *looked*, she said: 'You didn't know im afore the war. E was different then.'

Sometimes he seemed so—*comfortable*—I started to wonder: Praps she's right! Praps he is coming round!

We'd all reckoned without Jim.

Dad told us how it happened. He was picking up the glasses in the Dragon when who should stroll in, Dad said, bold as brass, but our Mary's chap. That's what he called him: 'our Mary's chap', or 'Ginger Nut'.

> 'Ginger Nut
> Fell in the cut . . .'

Our Mother would shake her head and laugh and go grave and say: 'Ah. E'll come a cropper. I've seen it afore. It's 'is *hair*.' She said: ' 'Is fancy words won't protect im.'

What fancy words? I wondered. He never talked to me, hardly.

Well, bold as brass into the Dragon, into the dragon's mouth he strolled, and 'course there was our Jim, looking for trouble.

Jim shouts: 'You go over the road 'n' see my sister! You go 'n' see my sister—*now*!'

It was as if we was his personal property! He was the same with everybody. He was determined to win you back for King and family; trouble was, he didn't ask you first if you *wanted* to be rescued. Years before he'd tried to frighten off our Else's Tom.

316

They'd had a terrible fight on the railway bank, stopped all the trains, cos Tom was an engine driver and Jim was so provoking he'd had to stop his train and get out.

He was all bluster, our Jim, when he'd been boozing, but it never seemed to affect his strength. He was good looking and he was very strong. You always felt proud to have a brother like Jim.

'Go on!'

'I'll go when I'm ready.'

'You what?'

'I'll go when I'm ready.' He didn't say he'd *never* go, Dad said, he just said: 'I'll go when I'm ready.' That haunted me, after, that '*when I'm ready.*'

Jim saw red. 'Outside!' he shouted.

'Alright.'

And he went outside with our Jim.

As I said, he was well made, but our Jim was a man, and fighting mad. He loved a fight; I think it was that more'n hate, or protecting me. It was the opportunity to have a scrap. He might even a-*liked* him, really! That's Jim.

He beat him up. He beat him up outside the Dragon there, in the yard, from the yard onto the pavement, from the pavement into the middle of the main road. It stopped all the traffic.

He fought back, Dad said, but you couldn't help feeling he'd been half *expecting* it, from the start. His money went spinning wild over the road—pennies 'n' sixpences 'n' shillings. Blood spurted everywhere. His clothes was ripped. Nobody called the police; nobody cared for him, really. He wasn't one of us. They stood and watched and when our Jim had done his worst somebody picked him up and they took him to his mother's house, on Waterside.

*

The next night Jim said: 'I done it Mam! The bugger never turned up for work! E got the thrashin of 'is life!'

Just like a cat dropping a mangled body on the step for her to say 'Oh very good! What a clever pussy cat!' our Jim said: 'I done it Mam!'

Dad said: 'E did! E takes after your Harry 'n' no mistake.'

317

Harry Bayliss our Mother's only brother was a legend in our family. He was s'pposed to have knocked out the bloke in the booth at the Mop—in *one*! He was killed in the war through not having his helmet on.

'E was the strongest man I ever seen, Harry Bayliss,' Dad used to tell us, when we were kiddies, 'but e forgot to put 'is 'elmet on. Once, that did it. Only once.'

I thought: I hope you're all bloody satisfied! I went down to Waterside, I nearly winded myself getting there. I leaned against one of the trees, watching his mother's house, hoping, praying, you know, for a sign of life.

People went by to the Theatre. I waited till it was quite dark. The Theatre had started ages ago. He'd told me she worked at the Box Office. It wasn't true, but I didn't know. I thought: She's bound to come out! I don't know what I was planning to do, or say. I didn't care! I'd lost all my fear of her. I thought: She's bound to come out soon! But she didn't. The Theatre looked dead, how it does when a play's on. There was no smoke from the house— nothing. It was all as dead as a doornail.

He'd gone. I knew he'd gone. Oh how pleased she'd be, how she would enjoy saying: 'I told you—scruffs!' I walked up and down Waterside and I thought my heart would break.

A week after, Jim said: 'The bugger's sent for 'is cards, from away! I done it Mam! E's *gone*!'

*

Both our rooms at the school house, the living-room and the front room, had painted tiles round the fireplace. I used to sit and say to myself, oh for hours: 'Spring, Summer, Autumn, Winter . . .' There were four lovely ladies, with bonnets on. When it was Spring there were flowers; when it was Winter there she was, still only in a dress but huddled up a little. Spring, Summer, Autumn, Winter, Spring, *Summer*—Oh God! *June*. That's when it was due.

Then it came to me in a flash, and I wondered why I hadn't thought of it before. I said aloud: 'That ud be the answer, Mam!'

'Wot?'

'Adoption.'

'Answer for oo?'

I could see she didn't approve, but she said: 'You must please yourself.'

There was a girl I knew who'd had one adopted. She gave me an address, and I wrote. I was determined. They sent me papers and things—complicated!—I couldn't understand the *words*! But I kept thinking: It'll ruin my life, else. There was no-one to ask. Vicar? We kept away from him, never used to let him come near, let him see us. Doctor? I'd told him a lie. I didn't know *any*body educated. I was on my own.

Well, nearly. There was a knock on the door. I saw a shape; through the panes I saw a big black shape—tall! It was a chap! My heart missed a beat. I went without thinking—that's the story of my life—and there stood a tramp.

'Could I 'ave some water please, ma'am?'

He was a real old tramp, from the workhouse, with cans, billy cans, and a sack. They were a common sight still in Stratford. I told him to wait there, fetched the kettle.

'I'm sorry,' he said, 'was you expectin somebody else?'

He wore the filthiest old coat you ever seen; his hat looked as if it had been rolled in cowshit. But his ribbons! He had a row of ribbons, all colours of the rainbow, and his voice was, you know, like running water.

'It's a marvellous and terrible world,' he said, 'to be bringin a little child into. Beg your pardon, you ain't got nothin stronger 'ave you?'

'It won't 'ave a Dad.'

I don't know what made me tell *him*!

His face changed. 'That could be an advantage ma'am,' he said. 'Didn't do some well-known folks much 'arm. Think about it.'

'I 'ave done.'

After that he called fairly regular. He had a round, most of them did: Warwick, Stratford, Alcester. Once he turned up with an old woman. It was the old workhouse round; they'd got into the habit, I 'spect, couldn't stop. He was quite harmless, took an interest in me, God knows why. I only gave him water, never let him further'n the porch.

319

He talked in poetry. 'I learned em by heart,' he said, 'so I don't need no book. "The silver apples of the moon, the golden apples of the sun." Keep em 'ere!' he said. 'It's summat they can't tek off you.'

Then one day he didn't come; I never saw him again.

It was a Friday night. I had to move the desks every Friday night, when the kiddies had gone. They were big iron desks, well, iron feet with solid wood tops, terrible double desks: two sat in them. I had to drag them to the front of the classroom, put wet sawdust down and sweep the floor. Dad helped, did what he could. It was boards, that floor, dreadful, sometimes a kiddie had been sick, and all the time I was thinking: There's the polishin, an those bloody glass partitions to clean an dust, an the winder sills.

I was tired as hell. I remember Dad saying: 'Yer Mam's worse. She should 'ave the operation,' but all I could think was: There's more'n fifty of them towels to wash, an the dusters, an you'll be buggerin off any minute now! He'd do his share, Dad, I'll say that, help with the desks when I asked. But then he'd be edging off, towards the Dragon.

'She likes it 'ere.'

I thought: What's all this in aid of?

'She loves it in the school house, she's happy 'ere. Well,' he said, 'I'll be off then, duty calls. I'm promised tonight.'

It was true! Our Mother did love it! She loved to see the people going by to the station, all the comings and goings. I was glad somebody did! I gave one of those desks a shove . . . and that was it!

'Oh my God!' I said. It was the surprise more'n anything—water gushing. I shouted aloud. I was on my own; nobody could hear me. Our Mother was in the school house and Cyril sleeping. He was on shifts, at the flour mill. Water was gushing down my legs onto the floor, and I knew then what it was, I sensed it. I kept saying: 'Oh my God.' I got out of the school somehow. It was a terrible feeling, not being in charge of your body. There was something else—some*body* else—trying to get out! Horrible!

Our Mother must a-*known*: she was coming down the stairs. When she seen me holding myself she said: 'You better lie down.'

Then she shouted for our Cyril, she knocked him up! 'Fetch Ede. Tell er water's broke,' she said, '*quick!*' Her calling to Cyril like that really put the wind up me. If she was getting him out o' bed, our Cyril, it was serious!

And that's how he was born: in the school house, after I'd been moving the desks, before I'd filled in those blooming adoption papers. You could say he beat me to it. The pains weren't bad, well, he was so small. The doctor was saying—Cyril'd had to fetch doctor 'n' all in the end, I had to have stiches—he was saying: 'She ain't bin eatin! Why ain't she bin eatin?' And: 'It'll be touch 'n' go. She's a very foolish girl, she's bin holdin erself in.'

It was the same doctor! I thought: Does e remember? What'll e *think*?

'Look!' said Ede. She lifted the babby up and showed him me, all blood and yolk. 'E's got no finger nails, the little duck! E's come out the egg too soon!' He had! Six weeks too soon! 'But 'is 'air's lovely! Fancy! Look at 'is 'air!'

Mother and Dad looked at each other. I knew what they were thinking. Nobody in our family had hair like that.

I wanted to die.

Monday morning as usual the Vicar came. He came to the school, there was always hymns and prayers, then he sent for Dad who said: 'Good news! There's a babby been born!'

'So I 'ear,' said the Vicar, 'and I wants it *out*, this day, this minute, Hewins! *And* er! Else your job goes, and the house!'

Dad dropped his shovel. He *had* to, he said, or it would a-come down over the Vicar's head. And he went to break the news to our Mother. I heard them talking, in the larder.

Our Mother starts shouting: 'She ain't a-goin!'

'Don't worry, our Mary,' said Ede, 'I'll 'ave you.'

Well, I was a-sobbing, I was frit, you can imagine. Jess had died; why couldn't I?

Ede had her ear pressed to the door. 'Dad's gone for Doctor!'

I didn't see how that was going to help. I was thinking: 'She's got a houseful already! She took in everybody in our family who hadn't got a roof. There was always somebody at our Ede's, not just one at a time neither, and she had plenty of her own. It was only a tiny council house. God, I thought, I don't want to go up there. But Dad managed it, somehow; he fetched the doctor back. There weren't half a kerfuffle.

The doctor was excited and all. His voice was raised: 'The room's clean. She's got help. Where's the objection?'

Our Mother told him.

He said: 'I'll see 'bout this! That girl's not to be moved! It'll kill em both. *Christians*!' he said.

I never heard no more about it. I don't know whether Doctor Pembrey saw the Vicar, but I think he must a-done. I never heard a word about us having to go, after.

*

That's why we went to Shottery to have him christened. The Vicar wouldn't do it—well, we didn't ask him. We knew he'd say 'no'.

Dad said, 'We won't give im the *satisfaction*.'

So we went to Shottery, after work. I stopped by the stile; I wouldn't go farther, to the church, I was too ashamed.

'I'll wait 'ere,' I said.

Tom Dyke carried him and the others followed; he was too quick for them, whistling away. Our Ede's Tom was a happy chap. He hadn't got a bean but he was the happiest chap I knowed.

I thought: That could be a good sign.

Tom first, then Else who was going to be godmother, and Dad.

'What's '*is* Dad doin?' I wondered. What's e doin now? But I kept my thoughts to myself.

Coming back over the fields they were in the same order, only Else had the babby.

'Ooo!' she said, 'ain't it 'ot?' and: 'E ain't 'alf 'eavy! 'Ere, you can 'ave im now.'

It was hot that evening, hot August. Else held a buttercup under his chin:

'E's goin to be rich!' she said.

They all laughed. That buttercup had took some finding! Even I had to laugh. But I couldn't help thinking 'bout *him*—and Sis.

What does she think of me? I wondered. I dreaded her mouth. I dreaded what she'd say. She was married, she'd had a fella alright, seen a man in all his glory. It seemed a long time since *I* had. Yes, I'll confess it, I was aching in my heart for him, I would a-done anything to see him, hear his voice, feel him, anything. I knowed it was wrong, wicked, but you can't help *feelings*.

I was in a daze; there were so many feelings spinning round in my head. Oh and it was hot! We seemed to be walking on the sky, and the grass and the trees growing downwards. There was a spell on everything that summer's night.

When we got home our Jim was there and he said to our Mother: 'I'm goin to kill im. Next time I catches im I'll kill im.'

'Where's e buggered off to?' she said. But she meant Dad. 'I've made the tea! They ain't gone to Dragon—'ave they?'

He had! And Tom! By the look on our Else's face she'd a-been there and all—if she'd dared!

As I said, Else stood godmother, Tom Dyke was his godfather. We called him Brian. I don't know why, it just came to me. I broke the royal tradition. At the registry I'd asked for *Bryan*, but the woman there looked down her nose and said:

'That's not ow you spell it. It's B-R-I-A-N.'

Being an early child he looked, you know, *old*, but his hair! He had red gold hair, it caught in the sun. Nobody ever said, aloud, but he was the spit image.

Ede and Else was whispering: 'S'weird, innit?'

'No mistakin.'

'Poor little duck.'

I was frit to death nobody would love him, except me.

I hadn't wanted to. For days after he was born I hadn't even wanted to look at him. I wouldn't touch him. The resemblance! I couldn't bear it.

Our Mother said: 'E's sickin up tinned stuff. E's gettin no nourishment. If e don't get proper nourishment soon, e'll *die*.'

'Let im!' I thought.

They never weighed him when he was born. She wouldn't let them, said he was too tiny, it was tempting fate, bad luck. There was quite a battle with a nurse who came.

'You gotta 'ave im weighed, missus! E's *premature.*'

'E's our babby, not your'n. It's a free country ain't it?' But she kept hounding *me*! 'You'll 'ave to feed im!'

'I can't Mam, I can't!'

The *idea* made me heave!

She said: 'You'll 'ave to. You'll 'ave to try.'

So I did. I didn't want to, I didn't want to love him. But as soon as he was there, at my breast, soon as I'd felt his little hands and his little mouth, I thought: E's mine! E's all mine!

It was the most wonderful feeling I'd ever had. I used to sit out in the yard there, in the sun, nursing him for hours and hours. It was the school holiday, the kiddies had gone. There was only the sound of the hens chuck-chucking. Oh it was the last long hot peaceful summer.

There was a family conference in our larder. Well, it was more our Mother making up her mind and telling us. She used to do her baking in the larder. It was like a small room, with big wide whitewood shelves and a whitewood table where she could work. That was all she did now, really, the baking—she was in so much pain—I did the rest of the housework and the school. The others came and helped when they could.

We all squashed in. Her hands! She had big hands but she was light as a feather with pastry. Oh her pies! Her puddings! She was a miraculous cook, our Mother, she could make a pudding out of nothing! She never weighed *any*thing; there were no scales in our house. And something else! She could skin a rabbit in one piece, with the head on, so's we got full price at Warburton's! Break the legs, roll the skin back: it came off perfect, like a glove.

Our Mother was in command in that larder. She never let me *touch*. The result was, I never did know how to bake proper, I was never handy 'bout the house, only the cleaning, the rough stuff. She never let me *near*! Only to finish the bowl off with my finger, or lick the custard pan. Now I was grown, with a kiddie of my own, but it was just the same.

''Ere y'are!'

That's how she saw us all: as kiddies.

Everybody was there, 'cept George, and Flo of course, she was in London. I thought: Oh God! Our Flo's comin down to Stratford for safety! That's what it was about: the *war*. Our Mother said there'd be one; she could read the signs. Well, we'd had a letter come round asking if we'd got any spare sheets. Spare sheets! That was a laugh. We made nappies out of the old uns.

I dreaded it: the thought of asking for strap, and Flo taking our bed, and Flo's two lads with appetites like billy goats champ-

champ-champ through everything: 'Mam's told us to eat as much as we can!'

Our Mother said: 'You'll 'ave to 'ave im up.'

They were all looking at *me*!

'No!'

'It's the only way—'

'Kate never!'

Kate had hers 'bout the same time as Brian, at her sister's. It had been a surprise to everybody, her sister and all.

Ede said: 'If you don't, they'll say you been with Mop men—'

'Bein a Whit un.'

'You gotta do it.'

'No!' I said. I couldn't bear the thought of going to court.

Our Mother said: 'If you don't, there's no knowing what folks'll say.'

'You gotta go out *some*time!'

'For 'is sake!'

'*Mam's!*'

''Elp with the money!'

I wouldn't go out. After he was born I never went out the school for months; well, I was too ashamed. I thought people would be talking about me.

'I *can't!*'

'You should 'ave *some*thing,' our Mother said, 'then folks'll know you ain't a tramp. If you take im to court it'll show you ain't a tramp. That's settled then.'

I thought: They'll never find him.

It was my only hope.

*

He wouldn't look.

The solicitor did. He took one look at Brian, said quick: 'Bring the child to court, *in case*.' He meant in case he denied it. So Dad waited outside with him, in the passage at the Town Hall. He was good as gold. But he didn't want to see him, he didn't want to see his own child, he wouldn't look at him.

Right! I thought, I won't look at *you*!

I just looked at this woman on the bench, this Justice of the Peace. I kept my eyes fixed on her and I gave evidence. I kept telling myself: It shows I know oo 'is father is. If I'd just a-let it go . . . The funny thing was, I wasn't frit, I was blazing! The newspapers was there, writing it all down, what I said, the private private things, so's people could crow over it and say, 'Shockin!' or 'She was headin for a fall!' I'd always been so smartly dressed, you see, it annoyed them.

Let them! I thought, let them say! I wouldn't look at him; I was blazing with anger.

He didn't deny it. He just said: 'I'm very young, Sir.'

It was seven-and-six.

He never paid, half the time.

I had to go to the town clerk's office, in Sheep Street.

''As e paid?'

'No!' they said, with a smirk on their faces, those girls at Lunn's. I had to go there for it; he sent the money to Tom Lowth, at Lunn's. I went every month. Tom Lowth was a gentleman, but they were snooty girls; they looked down their noses at you. I had to say: 'Mary Hewins. 'Ave I got any money?'

They could hardly be bothered to look in the book.

'No!'

They didn't want to know, they looked through you like, and then they'd shove you out. That broke me down where the Magistrates and the papers hadn't. Once I came home in tears, I was feeling so depressed, and Dad said: 'I'll go.'

After that he went a lot for it, with the pram—he never minded what people said—and fetched my money. He always seemed to be more successful than me.

When we did get some—oh that was a field day! We could buy something: food, mostly. Seven-and-six a week! There was never more'n two pound something waiting at Lunn's, but it was better'n nothing! It did show he'd got a father, didn't it? My milk had dried up. That was no great surprise, well I was so thin! So he had to have cow's milk, from a little dairy on Greenhill Street. A Mrs Davies kept it; she had a green apron and a nice rosy face. One day our Ede rushes round:

'Ey, that little girl at "Thatch"—er's sick! Mortal! They say Mother Davies's sellin *consumptive milk!*'

It worried me to death. She'd been born the same week as Brian, that little girl. Her Mam and Dad ran the Thatched Tavern. Well, she died, and you can see her statue in the cemetery: an angel. When I go by I always think of those days. I dreaded TB. Her name was Beck; she was eight months old. But Brian lived.

*

He hadn't paid for a long time, so we had to have him up again. He said he'd broke his leg; he came with his leg bound up, dragging it. He always was a bit of an actor. I looked the other way. If I look, I thought, if I catch his eye, I might weaken.

He said: 'I can't work!'

Even his voice, quiet and deep . . . I had to sit down, have some water.

The Magistrate said to him: ' 'Ave you eaten today?'

'Yes.'

'Well your babby's gotta eat 'n' all.'

It didn't make any difference.

He'd left Stratford, for good. Some said he'd gone Stroud way, over the Cotswolds: his mother had relations there. Some said he'd been called up. He'd took to the road, joined a theatre company. Praps it was true; praps he did break his leg.

I wonder.

*

When the air raid siren sounded I ran upstairs for Brian, grabbed him. I said: 'We'll 'ave to get to shelter Mam!' It was up by the workhouse, they'd got air raid shelters up there. I forgot about the gasmasks. I wasn't half in a panic. Our Mother said: 'You're better off 'ere. You stay 'ere,' and: 'You ain't takin *im.*'

'I thought it meant you'd gotta run 'n' get in the shelter?'

'Never mind what it *means,*' said our Mother, 'you stay 'ere. It'll be alright.'

I believed her! Well, you didn't argue with our Mother. I stayed, but I was in such a panic. I panicked when that siren sounded; I

panicked when it stopped. I panicked when the 'All Clear' went.
'*All Clear!*' Your stomach went with it, like the chairoplanes at the
Mop. But she was right: it never sounded again.

That was all we had of the war, till one night when I got home
our Mother said: 'I'm just goin out for some chips.'

She didn't do much cooking now. The pain had got so bad she
couldn't bother, even for Cyril. Our Cyril's hot supper was coming
from the chip shop. That was a bad sign.

She got to the front door—and she was thrown back!

'God,' she said, 'that shook me!'

There was a noise like old sheets being ripped up. Coventry
was on.

Next morning they started coming into the hospital or just
walking to Stratford, for safety.

'It's *gone*,' Dad said, 'the whole bloomin city, blasted off the face
of the earth! A chap told me.' He was very upset. He said, 'I'll go
to buggery!'

I held on to Brian, tighter and tighter.

'Ey praps they won't bomb 'ere cos of *Shakespeare!*'

'There's Alum.'

'That munitions place our Else works at!'

'S' only a shed!'

'Jerry wouldn't waste 'is shells.'

I thought, sudden: They shouldn't a-put im down the well! It's
a punishment.

Dad said what I was thinking: 'Why should e bother 'bout
Shakespeare?'

When we didn't? You see, some of the young chaps had found
a big crate on the sidings, ever so heavy. They thought it was
whisky. When they got it opened—lo and behold—it was *Shakespeare!* Hundreds of complete Shakespeares.

Dad laughed when he heard about it. He said: ' "Good Attendance" prizes!'

What he meant by that I do not know.

They were so disappointed. They put him down the brewery
well, and there he is, to this day.

Bert said: 'I've put in for Navy! I've been to the recruitin office only they wants to see me birth certificate, Mam.'

'Huh.'

'I'm old enough! They said I can be a boy sailor!'

A funny look came over our Mother's face. She said: 'Alright then, please yourself.'

'Wot?' Dad hit the roof, nearly.

'You 'eard im. E's old enough.'

'E'll be *exempt* where e is! You said it yourself. "Our Bert'll be exempt!" '

'Well,' she said, 'I've changed my mind. If e wants to be a boy sailor e can bloody well be one.'

Next morning she gave him his birth certificate, in an envelope. Bert rushed off. It was always his great ambition, to go to sea; nobody ever knew why. You couldn't be much further from it 'n Stratford. Dad reckoned it was on account of a trip he'd took him on once, to Weston.

'You never seen a kiddie so en*joy* himself as our Bert, that day at Weston!'

I knew what he meant. Bert's happy days stuck in your mind.

Half an hour later he was back. 'I hate you!' he cried, and he burst into tears. Bert idolized our Mother, so it was a shock when he said: 'I *hate* you! I'll hate you for ever!'

She flushed, bit her lip.

I didn't find out for weeks, when Bert had got over it; he did, of course. But for weeks he wouldn't speak to her. It seems she'd writ a letter, put it in with the certificate.

'Why did she do it?' Bert said. '*Why?*'

He was under age, the letter said, she was his guardian, and she would never give her permission for him to go to be a boy sailor, and if they took him . . . just let them try . . .

'Oh,' said Bert, 'the shame! I'll never be able to hold my head up in the street again! *Every*body'll know!'

'Don't be so daft,' I said, though I was a fine one to talk.

CHAPTER FIFTEEN

They'd all took to Brian. To think I'd worried whether anybody would!

'Can I take Brian out?'

'I'll 'ave our Brian today, Mam!'

You know how some kiddies are? Always laughing, sort of blessed? As if they've been kissed by a good fairy? That was Brian when he was a babby. It was a marvel how they'd *all* took to him, and they'd got kiddies of their own, even Marg, and she wasn't really family. That caused a bit of jealousy.

Else said: 'I wouldn't leave im up there, our Mary!'

'She's only bein kind!'

She was; Marg was very kind. She was a bit, you know, airy fairy, but she came regular to do our washing. Dad did the nappies—I could never face doing that, or changing him—and Marg did the rest.

Else said: 'I'll take Gwendoline'—that was her little girl, she was seven—'and 'ave a walk up the Swincotes, just to make *sure*.'

She came back with the pram. 'I told you!' She said: 'I picked im up and e was soakin wet! So I changed im and e put 'is arms round me neck'—she loved him, our Else—'and I said: "Marg, I'm takin our Brian back 'ome."'

Dad lifted him out so's he could put the coal in. He lifted him so gently, like a chick, like this! When we moved to the school house the Vicar said: 'Use the church coal, Hewins, at your discretion.' We *did*! Our Ede went home with a pramful, always, so did Else. Today she looked a bit flushed. I thought: I do 'ope she 'asn't offended Marg! I liked Marg, even if she was in a world of her own.

Else said: 'I've just seen 'is other grandmother!'

We were all ears.

'She tried to look in the pram!'

'Go on!'

'Huh,' said our Mother, 'I 'ope you put the hood up.'

'I did,' said Else, 'and the apron! La-de-da bitch! Lookin as if she owned Stratford! Er face didn't 'alf change when she seen us comin! I said to im: "Your other grandmother ain't goin to see you— ever!"' Else said: 'She might *look* like a lady ...'

Suddenly I got frit, you know, as if a *witch* was after him. I wouldn't let go of him, all evening, and when we went to bed I laid awake for ages feeling his little heart beat on mine, like a butterfly, fluttering, so tiny, so delicate, you couldn't imagine it would survive. 'Course, then it happened: I forgot his bloody milk.

You see, when he woke and started whimpering I'd creep over to the gas ring and warm some milk. It took ages to do. 'Shh!' I'd be whispering, 'shh!' rocking him and whispering 'shh!' cos the big thing was not to wake our Cyril. Little bubbles were gathering round the side of the pan, he was whimpering and I was dead tired and...

I was woke by the milk going 'Whoosh!' spitting and spluttering all over the ring and Brian screaming and Cyril cussing in the room next door and our Mother muttering in her sleep: 'Not again! Can't you ever stay awake while that bloody milk boils? Cyril's on roads ... e's gotta get up 'alf-past...' When Brian was born she and Dad came in with me and Bert, and Cyril went in their room, so's Cyril wouldn't be disturbed. Cyril this and Cyril that! Sometimes I thought the house was run round our Cyril's every desire. I was past crying. You know the smell of burnt milk? I thought: I'll get it off in the mornin. I crept downstairs and fetched some more.

Hours later I crawled back in. It was dreadful, really, the sleeping, cos we had to have the dog in with us as well. Now Dad could never resist a stray dog. The trouble was, *he'd* took to Brian and all! He was an old Labrador; well, Labrador cross, a lovely dog. Only thing was he hadn't got a tail. We called him Blackie. He always came and slept with me and Brian, got in first, with his head on the pillow. I had to climb over him. It was a single bed, pushed against the wall, by the lattice. Oh God!

You can imagine, I was always bleary eyed in the morning. 'Mam, I 'ad a funny dream last night.'

'So did I,' she said. Then I remembered: I'd woke her up! 'I dreamt our Cyril was disturbed. You gotta *think* of Cyril,' she said, 'e's only one earnin!' She didn't count Dad.

'Mam, I dreamt 'is other grandmother snatched the pram and we was all chasin, and things kept falling out, like bottles and sacks o' coal and a great big cheese!'

'A *what*?'

'A great big cheese, like in the Maypole. A whole un. *Round*. We all started chasin that instead of er and when we came back er'd gone. It was empty, the whole of Rother Market was empty. You never seen nothing like it. All the streets of Stratford was empty and I ran up and down, up and down, and I couldn't find a living soul—'

Our Mother said sudden: 'It's Sat'day.'

'Oh no!' Nothing was going right for me!

> Friday's dream
> Sat'day told
> Will come true
> Though ever so old

She'd always told us that, our Mother—and I'd gone and done it!

She said, sharpish: 'Hanging about the house ain't doin you any good.'

I could have told her that!

'You'll 'ave to get work. We could do with the money. Asides,' she said, 'now this bloody war's on ... you got a babby but you ain't *married*. They'll call you up—and Cyril.'

'Oh Mam!'

I didn't want to leave Brian.

'Why did that bloody flour mill 'ave to go 'n' burn down? E was safe, there.' She said, 'They'll 'ave im now e's labourin.'

'You'll think of something Mam!'

She shook her head: 'No.'

That '*no*'! My stomach—you know how it is when you realize, finally, definitely, that your Mam can't protect you, really protect you? *No*body can. Ever?

We were on our own, all of us, even our Cyril, the apple of her eye.

They put him in the Royal Artillery. All I can remember is how he hated his hat. At the station he was still pulling it about. He looked so disgusted.

'Oh you don't 'alf look *handsome*, Cyril!'

'Stop laughin!'

He couldn't do anything with it. 'It's like a bloody paper boat,' he said. 'Fancy goin to war lookin like this!'

He took Brian up and said he'd send him Hitler's balls for breakfast, something like that, and promised our Bert he'd get him a lot of German medals. Not English ones, German medals. That's what Bert wanted, till he could get some himself. He still hankered after the Navy. Cyril was avoiding our Mother's face. We all were. She must have had some thoughts, seeing him in that khaki uniform. And Dad.

'I'll be alright Mam.'

Knowing our Cyril, I could believe that. He'd never 'got on', well, what people call 'gettin on', but he was quiet and crafty. He was a quiet one, not like our Jim, who always let you know he was coming miles away—he'd been turned down, 'unfit for fighting'. What a laugh.

I said: 'Poor ole Hitler!'

Our Mother spread out her arms; she couldn't see for the tears, none of us could.

'Ow'll you manage wi the food, son?'

⊰ CHAPTER SIXTEEN ⊱

I didn't wait for a letter; I volunteered for war work. I was no heroine. I was just terrified they'd send me away if I didn't, make *me* join the army. And like our Mother said, we needed the money. So I volunteered.

They said: 'She can go to the Alum.'

I was back where I started! Square One. Only this time round it weren't pans 'n' kettles: it was aircraft bits, soldering them with a flame. Well, I think it was aircraft bits: you couldn't tell *what* you were making! That made it worse. I hated it; the heat made me ill. And I was still losing weight. Praps they were worried I'd die on them; any road, they said, quick: 'The Canning's just as good.'

I was transferred to the Canning Factory, next door.

What part did I go to? Oh God! I was put on the tables! It was piece work—that was a joke for a start, *peace* work!—so you had to work blooming hard, filling the cans: rhubarb, spinach, carrots, peas, strawberries, plums, whatever was in season. I did that at first. The fruit and veg, the raw stuff, was tipped onto a long table; then you had to scoop it up in your hands and put it in the can and put that on the line. The line took the can to the machines.

The stuff was never washed, though the spinach always seemed to be wet, but sometimes we had to top and tail it on these long tables, or chop it. Oh, chopping made your hands dreadful. I used to think: What's the worst thing—and what's the *best* thing 'bout this—or that? There's generally *some*thing. The best thing about the Canning was the smells: the fruit cooking, and the jam. And when the strawberries was in: oh that was lovely, when the strawberries came in! Mmm. We ate them, pounds 'n' pounds of them!

The worst thing was 'take off'. When the full cans left the machines two girls had to take them off, you know, lift them off and place them round great big containers. And oh it was such back-breaking work, that was! I think that was the worst. The cans were put in these great big containers; they'd got to go and be cooked, see. That was heavy work. I used to get out of it when I could. Well, I was 'in' with Ethel. She looked after the labels. She was very glamorous, Ethel, she went out with the foreman's son, so she got all the best jobs, she never soiled her hands. There was a little office for the labels . . . piles of labels, had to be checked: 'RED PLUMS' and 'YELLOW PLUMS' and 'TATERS'. They handed them out to the labeller; that's all they did in there. Ethel was very good to me. When she had to take sample cans—she did that for the travellers—she asked for me:

'I'll 'ave Mary to 'elp me.'

I got out of 'take off' as much as I could. So imagine my surprise when I got 'promoted'! I went up to the top end at the Canning! Well, I was always early. That impressed them, I s'ppose; they thought I was keen. I used to creep out early so's Brian didn't realize I'd gone. At first he used to get so upset if he found I'd gone. If he'd cried *before* I went I couldn't a-gone, I couldn't a-left him, crying. Sometimes I got there an hour early. That impressed them.

There were two girls on a machine. All the cans came along, see, you had to fill a funnel with lids. There was a girl by me stamping them, stamping what was going to be in the cans, you know, 'PLUMS A1.', and I ran the machine. Well, one day the mechanic came by, his name was Bob, and he saw how my machine was oiled. I kept it perfect, always running, never went hot; the oil was always topped up.

He said: 'I could do with a mate.'

The other girls laughed. *Did* they! But he meant it, he asked for me. And the foreman said: 'Alright, she can go.'

That's how I came to do mechanical work. I loved it! It was something I really liked doing! I had the knack, Bob said so—and it was true. At the brewery, at the school, I'd always felt like a servant, a slave. You just thought: Another bloomin day! or: Roll on 'alf-past four! or: 'Alf-past six! I was always counting the time. I never did that when I started on mechanical work.

Bob was mechanic for the whole factory, a shy chap, quiet; he used to do all the repairs, if a machine stopped. The cans had to be kept going; they had to go round and round and round, you see, in the cooker. He'd come over from Canada, volunteered for the British army when the war started. But he weren't fit or something, too old, so they sent him to Stratford, and that's how he came to be in the Canning up the Brum Road.

I'd never felt good at anything before. Bob would say: 'What do *you* think, Mary?' He took me with him to Evesham to look for a nailing machine. They needed one for the cans; they had to be nailed into crates for the troops. We went to Evesham on the bus,

46. Lunch-break at the 'Canning' during the Second World War (Mary standing, 2nd from right). Some of the girls are eating one of the factory's raw materials—carrots.

had a walk about, a good laugh—lunch paid! Oh we had a lovely day! We chose it—bought it! I did some nailing then: the machine came down and nailed it, all the top, nailed the crate, nailed it beautifully.

Don't get the idea it was all work, no play! I couldn't stay serious all the time, it wasn't in my nature. That's where I was a disappointment to Bob, I think. Every morning after I'd oiled—I told you I got there early, I'd done by eight o'clock, practically—I took my oil can and my rag and went and chatted with the other girls, 'ave-you-'eard-this, 'ave-you-'eard that?

' " *'Ome Guard*" Thomas?'

Everybody laughed. It was Mrs Whickey* the manager's wife. Poor woman, we loved taking her off.

' " *'Ome Guard*?" You're never *'ere*!'

He wasn't.

I was oiling a machine and Whickey's latest girlfriend was on the other side. He hurried down the slope, he couldn't stay away for long.

I said: 'When's it *my* turn, Mister Whickey?'

I was wicked! Fortunately, he was very good-natured. He was alright to me, Whickey; he'd give me cans that was opened to take home for Brian, damaged cans and that.

Well, this morning he comes right up to me, makes a beeline for me, and I thought: You've gone too far this time Mary Hewins! I could never resist being cheeky.

He looks over his glasses at me and he whispers: 'Do you think *Gladys* 'as got over er 'usband?'

'I'll 'ave to investigate, Mister Whickey. S'only six months since e was killed. I'll let you know.'

I thought: Winnie'll be back on 'take off' next week!

Poor Whickey! We all took advantage. And when he did put his foot down he always made a cock-up of it. Like when he sent Rose Grinnell home—for talking! Rose was deaf and dumb, and she got sent home for talking, if ever you could believe it. Well, Rose always wanted to *try* to talk to you, and this day the girl on the table with her felt so sorry she had to stop and listen, or pretend

* *Pseudonym*

339

to listen—so nobody was getting any work done. All the machines stopped. So Whickey sent Rose home for the day.

I laughed. I said to Whickey: 'Fancy sendin a dumb girl 'ome for *talkin*!'

He was like a kiddie in a sweetshop with all those girls and no competition much, cos the young lads got called up, fast, soon as they reached eighteen. It was his sight got him off, I 'spect: he was blind as a bat without his glasses. I know, cos one day he bent over the sugar vat to look at something—and his glasses fell in. It was the syrup for the plums. His glasses fell in and they shrivelled up before my eyes. They were never rescued.

He wasn't half in a panic. He said: 'You'll 'ave to go 'n' get us some more!'

I said: 'Ow about the prescription?'

'Just say "Specs for Mister Whickey." ' He said: ' 'Urry up! I can't see!'

'Ullo!' said the girls when I went along with my oil can and my rag. 'We seen im give you them plums! What you shown im for that?'

'It ain't what I *showed* im . . .'

Then I told them the latest news. When I got to Gladys she'd describe everything that had gone on—'Oo-er!'—every little thing Whickey had done, the night before, and I'd pass *that* on.

'Oo-*er*!'

It was better'n *News of the World*.

And don't think the chaps didn't join in: they were the worst of the lot!

Old Tommy who stoked the boiler said: 'Er's gotta 'nother *parcel*!'

One of the girls, she was very attractive and a bit stuck up, she used to take these mysterious parcels to the incinerator. Nobody knew what was in them.

We *all* had a guess, 'course we did!

As I said, I think Bob was a bit disappointed with me; he couldn't change my nature. But I did love it, working with him. My title was 'mechanic's mate'. '*Bob's mate*,' the girls said. There was no jealousy; we was all together. I got fitted out with a blue boiler

suit, and one of the girls, her young brother, he could *draw*, he
pencilled a picture of me, in my boiler suit, with my oil can. Well,
it weren't a proper picture, it didn't look like me much, he did it
for a bit o' fun. He put it on the wall, above the machines.

The cans for the potatoes had to be lacquered. That's how it
came about that Bob and me invented a lacquering machine—we
made that machine, on our own! I had a pound for my help; Bob
gave me a pound and he had five pound. We found the materials
on the scrap heap, outside. Bob designed it; he was clever, that
chap, made little pieces o' metal. I helped, drilled two holes in each
of them. When we tried it, it *worked*! A big wheel went round and
the lacquer was in the bottom. It was marvellous!

'This is only the start!' said Bob, 'you'll see! Next time we'll
invent summat bigger 'n' better!'

We'd got all sorts of ideas.

*

At nights, when we finished, Ethel and me walked home together.
She lived up the Alcester Road. Dad used to bring Brian to meet
us; they never got very far, only 'bout as far as the hospital gates.

'Your Brian's the spit image,' said Ethel. I knew what she was
getting at, well she was curious, but I wouldn't be drawn. She was
my friend, Ethel was, she was alright to me, but I thought: That's
my own, I'm not sharin it. It was the only thing I never did share
with anybody. Even our Mother. It was a secret room, a room only
I'd got the key for. And inside . . . my secrets, laid out there. I
looked at Brian on his little three wheeler and I thought: E thinks
of the ole man as 'is Dad! They were inseparable. That did used to
upset me, but there was nothing I could do about it.

'There goes Lieutenant Whickey!' cried Ethel, 'on manoeuvres!'

We laughed. We knew where he was off to: he'd got his Home
Guard outfit on! Biking down Arden Street, he didn't half look
comical, what with his specs and his helmet and all his parapher-
nalia.

I nearly said to her: 'I could 'ave got some sugar out this mornin,
when I went to cash 'is cheque!' But I didn't.

Whickey used to send me up the town to cash his cheques; I

could get out of the Canning then without being searched. They picked on so many, see, every night, to search, but Whickey sent me in the daytime.

'I'm just goin to cash Mister Whickey's cheque,' I told the man on the gate, 'and I gotta parcel to post for im.'

I looked at it and I thought: I wonder?

'What's your Brian got in 'is 'and?' said Ethel, when we got close. 'Ullo Mister Hewins!'

She got on alright with Dad. I s'ppose if you didn't have to *live* with him...

'We went to see the animals at Cattle Market and I've bought im a whip,' said Dad, 'it's a good un.'

Not another bloomin whip! I thought.

'Should you like a demonstration, Ethel?'

It cracked! Ethel shrieked.

'It cost seven-and-six,' said Brian.

It was my turn to shriek.

'You're only earnin two pound! You want your brains examinin, you do!'

'E fancied it,' he said. That's all he'd say: he fancied it! It was like water off a duck's back with him. 'And so do I,' he said, and winked at Ethel.

◆❧ CHAPTER SEVENTEEN ❧◆

' 'Ere they come,' said Dad.

The evacuees came to the school to be sorted out. Ever since war was declared they'd been coming, not so many now, but every time still when I seen them my heart missed a beat: little flocks of them, from Brum mostly, trooping from the station. Clothes! Shoes! Chocolate! Little grey jerseys, brand new! When I seen them I thought: I hope there's some Cadbury's *Milk*! There was a lot of Bournville always, with a red label, but Brian didn't like the plain, he liked milk.

Teachers and volunteers helped, and Dad was in charge of the stores. The kiddies were sorted out, kitted out, and people came and collected them: they were all labelled, according. Lucky for us, some of them never turned up. They'd dropped out, I s'ppose, changed their minds, or their Mams had, so there was generally something left over: a nice little coat, a pair of socks, funny trousers down to the knees. It was all new stuff! I can see Brian now, he looked so smart, his gas mask in a little box on his back—he had six, two Mickey Mouses! He was growing and all, what with the chocolate and the sample cans Whickey let me have, and the extra eggs.

There was a good fairy about us; now and then there definitely was. Every night when I got home and before I went to the school I had to make the beds. I got up so early, you see, left the others sleeping, and our Mother hadn't got the strength any more. Well, this night I went upstairs as usual, and I was about to drop down on our bed, just for a minute before I started, just roll down into the valley there still smelling of last night's sleep, when I seen it. An *egg*! In the middle of the pillow—a golden-brown egg.

I picked it up: it was a real egg, warm, perfect. I thought: E's playin a game with me! The next night when I went up—there was another egg! But Brian said 'No!' He hadn't been up! I didn't

343

47. Brian

tell our Mother in case it *was* him. I couldn't a-stood to see her lamming him. Else said she had done, once. He was running round and round the table and it got on our Mother's nerves. Else told me: 'I wanted to 'it *er*!' By the end of the week I'd collected six eggs.

Now as I said, our bed, Brian's and mine, it was a single bed, pushed up against a tiny casement. On the seventh day, Sunday, I kept watch. Lo and behold, late afternoon, up the slate roof comes one of our Mother's hens—she was a Rhode Island Red—so stately, squeezes through the casement. I left it open for airing, well, just enough to let a bit of air in; how she got through I'll never know. She plonked herself down on the pillow—and laid an egg! I could hardly believe my eyes! How proud she was! The clucks! I laughed out loud, clapped my hands.

'Brian! Mam! Come quick! 'Ave a look at this!'

She sat there so regal, looking at us from the pillow.

'*Just in time!*' said our Mother. 'That's why the bugger weren't layin!'

Brian had the eggs. Our Mother looked on them as *extra*, so he was having an egg most days! He was growing; you couldn't tell he was an early child, hardly.

*

New Year's Day at the Canning Bob came up and said something to me. I think it was 'Happy New Year!' I smiled. Well, I was happy. I know I had to leave Brian, but he loved our Mother and Dad; sometimes I thought he got on better with them than he did with me. I was oiling the machine that you put the cans in for the syrup. It was going round. I had to do some jobs with the machines running, see, and the oil can—well, you could get the spout caught if you weren't quick. You'd got to be *quick*. It was a heavy machine. I smiled at Bob. Yes, I was happy! My thumb went in. It was in the cogs.

I might have screamed; I think I did. The only thing I can remember clearly is Bob's face—*white*. I was taken to the nurse at the Alum, but they had to take me to hospital in the end so that just wasted time. The blood! They couldn't stitch it, cos it was so mauled. There was nowhere to stitch!

Three months it took, to try to put my thumb right. There should have been a notice saying: '*Don't touch the machines when they're going.*' There wasn't. I didn't get any compensation. I was paid my wages, but now I think I should a-got something. It's a disfigurement—*look!* And when I went back to the Canning I wasn't with Bob any more.

48. 'We all had to turn out.' Stratford-upon-Avon Produce Canners Ltd, Second World War (Mary sitting, 2nd row, 5th from right)

' 'Ave you 'eard?' said Ethel.

'On that bloody machine?'

It was a sore point with me. When I came back Whickey put me on the potato machine. I think he was annoyed cos I'd been away for so long, and I'd been handy for him. It was dreadful, the potato machine: scalding water splashing over your legs, even through trousers. I have the scars still. He'd got a new girlfriend—independently.

Gladys came crying to me. 'E wants to be near er,' she said. 'E just stands on the slippery slope'—that's what we called it—'pretends to be lookin at us.'

Well, all the tables faced him.

'Straight from *school*!'

'Yes,' I said, 'what a pickle.'

We both knew it was all over, but Gladys kept hoping... I couldn't think of anything to say, to cheer her up.

The new girlfriend had quite a hard job, actually. She had to *bend* all day, put the tins o' taters in the machine Bob 'n' me had made, to lacquer them. Gladys was right. There was prettier, better girls he could have had, the Harrises for example, they came on bikes, they had *green* boiler suits, I don't know why. I had a blue one, a boy's, cos I was so thin, but the Harrises were glamour girls, and Mrs Whickey was ever so pretty. So was Gladys.

There was nothing I could do to help her. She was crying all the time.

'*Er*! What's e want with *er*?'

And I used to pass it all on to Ethel. I was a sneak.

Ethel said: 'Why don't you ask for a move? Get your old job back? I could put a word in. Nobody can do it like you! Bob says so, all the time. You should 'ear what e says 'bout you.'

'No.'

I think it was my pride. I was frightened things wouldn't be the same, that I wouldn't be able to do it, with my hand.

'Any road,' I said, 'what'm I s'pposed to 'ave 'eard?'

'We've gotta 'ave our *photograph* took! Whickey wants a *photograph*—of *er*!'

'Poor Gladys!'

So we all had to turn out, the whole Canning. And there she is still, so meek 'n' mild, and there's us, and there's the Director, he wasn't in the know but it was slowly dawning ... You can see his expression. That young boy, he was called up, after. He went and got killed; his name was Jackie Boyce. Whickey put all the glamour in the front row; that was typical, always one eye on the future. But Ethel was right. This time he'd met his Waterloo.

He got sent to Africa! *Af-ri-ca*! She went with him—to a canning factory in the middle of the jungle. He was the nicest boss I ever had, Whickey, and that's what happened to him.

✿ CHAPTER EIGHTEEN ✿

I told you I would always avoid opening a front door. Our Mother had a lot of warnings: don't pass on the stairs, whatever you do don't cross the knives! If you spill the salt chuck some over your left shoulder, quick. Her favourite one was: Never look at the new moon through glass! She went spare if one of us did that. Dad used to have to go outside, tell her if it was shining.

'Yes,' he said, 'it is.'

Then she said: 'Don't look out the winder, there's a new moon.'

'What about me glasses Mam? When I goes out?'

'Spectacles don't count.'

But opening a door! That was my own private dread. The door to the school house had four arched panes, like four church windows, with frosted glass. Through them you could see shapes in the porch, against the light. I could tell if it was gypsies, they were very distinctive: a big basket, shoulders out to bear the weight, like this, not tall... '*The gypsies'll fetch you!*' But today... my heart turned over. It wasn't gypsies, but there was no mistaking.

I let our Mother go. I sat tight at the bottom of the stairs, with Brian. There was a long passage at the school house, from the front door right to the stairs. We were playing with a ball. We got plenty of rubber balls from the playground; they sailed over the wall, got stuck in our guttering. Bert climbed on the roof for them. I went on playing with the ball, but my heart was thumping too.

'Well,' our Mother was saying, 'I'll leave you two together.'

'Oh Sis,' I said. I had a little cry.

She put her arm round me. She said, 'Don't fret, love. E was a bastard, most of em are.' She laughed. 'Trouble is, e *was* different. You couldn't 'elp likin im.'

'Yes,' I said, 'just my bloody luck.'

349

'D'you *remember* . . . d'you remember ow you did cartwheels, top of our road and e was goin by on is bike and—e was always on 'is own.'

That was true! He was. Sis remembering annoyed me.

'E was always alone,' she said, 'I reckon e just wanted to join in.'

'Well e did do didn't e?'

It's hard to explain, but I was still a bit jealous of Sis.

Later she said, 'I've come back from Coventry for good, Mary. I'm goin to start to en*joy* myself.'

I was shocked; I'd no idea she hadn't been doing! Although she was laughing she was very upset about something, I could tell. All my jealousy went.

'Oh Sis!'

It was such a comfort to know . . . Well, I'd always dreaded Sis, what she was going to say. And here she was! She saw Brian and she never said a word. She just said, 'Don't fret.'

'You never had un then, Sis?'

'No. But I might do now I see what a lovely lad *you* got . . .'

She was kindness itself. We both had a little cry and a laugh.

That wasn't the only knock on the door gave me a turn! The next came six o'clock in the morning! I was the only one up. I was creeping downstairs with a candle . . . and the door starts to open. The front door! Oh my God! I thought, Dad forgot to lock up! I heard a voice: 'It's only *Boll*rus!'

I froze.

'Don't be frightened—I got summat *for* you!'

'Course, I was frit to death. I ran back up the stairs, grabbed Brian. That was my first instinct, always.

It was our Jim's mate, Bollrus Chamberlain, and he wasn't half laughing at me! He'd brought a cheese, big as a full moon, the biggest cheese I'd ever seen—at that time of the morning!

'Jim says, "Ask no questions 'n' you'll be told . . ." '

I was thinking: What our Ede ud do for a piece o' this! She was worse'n a mouse for cheese!

Afterwards I saw him up the town.

He laughed and said, 'It's only *Boll*rus!' He does still, to this day.

I said: 'Yes, you bugger!'

I thought: It broke my dream, that cheese!

'Ey weren't it big! Where d'you find it?'

He just laughed.

We had a bit ourselves. Some went to a hotel. The rest was sold to a farmer from Snitterfield who handled stuff people had found, or couldn't manage.

*

Then I got a parcel. Everything was coming at once, and every time, it wasn't, you know, what I was expecting. I was waiting, hoping, for *some*thing. I couldn't put it behind me, like Sis.

She said, 'The past is past. Don't sit forever on an addled egg, Mary. There's plenty of fresh uns about! Forget it!'

I thought: I can't!

The postman said: 'There's a parcel from India, Mary, and you've gotta pay duty on it.'

I said: 'I don't know anybody in India!'

I didn't, but I had a wild thought...

'Well, you gotta pay if you wants it. Look—MISS MARY HEWINS — SCHOOL HOUSE — ALCESTER ROAD— STRATFORD-ON-AVON—ENGLAND.'

I paid him. I'd come over all queer, looking at that hand. It wasn't our Cyril's; I didn't know it. A little voice said: 'It's *im*! E's in India! E's sent you a present!'

I daren't open it. I put it on the table, sat staring at it. I pictured him in India, fighting the... who *was* they fighting? I got all my courage together and opened it. There were some lovely scarves inside!

'Oh!' I cried, 'Mam! Come an look! Ain't they lovely?'

Silk scarves, all colours of the rainbow!

'See *this*!'

I unfolded it once, twice, three times. It was all colours—mauve, red, brilliant blue—the colours gypsies like, lovely, light as air. You could a-drawn it through a key-hole. But what it *was*—I couldn't make that out. I tried it as a shawl. I put it over my head.

Our Mother said, very firm: 'It's a tablecloth.' You could see she loved it. 'Oo's it from?'

I looked again and found a note. 'WITH KIND REGARDS DONT FORGET ME WILL YOU REMEMBER THE ROOBAB— NORMAN.'

Norman?

'It'll be Norman Windsor,' said our Mother, 'well ain't that nice of him?' She looked at me as if to say: 'Is there anything between you two?'

I said: 'You can 'ave the tablecloth, Mam.'

How could I tell her how disappointed I was; how could I tell anybody?

Just to rub salt in she said: 'Norman must a-spent 'is last bit o' pay on this stuff! What does e mean: "*roobab*"?'

'I dunno.'

I didn't. I might a-done, once, but I'd forgot.

It was then I caught sight of her leaning across the chair. Her features were twisted into a face I didn't recognize.

Dad said: 'Your Mam can't *manage* any more.'

So I left work to look after her. She was in terrible pain, yes she was. The rupture was as big as that. When she sat down water came away; we had to pad her up. They said it would cost twenty pounds, the operation. We hadn't got it.

The doctor said: 'You should 'ave the operation—quick!' He said: 'If she 'as it she'll be perfect. It could be done easy.'

'Thank you, I shan't bother,' she said.

She didn't mind; she didn't want to be cut. I think she was frightened.

The doctor said: 'It's nothing!' but she wouldn't have it done.

I said: 'We'll get the money.'

Then she started falling down in the street; she was overweight, our Mother, a heavy woman, yet she never used to eat *any*thing! All she used to do was sit about, didn't go to bed, drink pop for her indigestion, and belch and belch.

Brian would run in and say: 'Can I 'ave a drink o' pop, Granny?'

'Well,' she said, 'that's all I got—but you can 'ave it.'

She didn't *bother* any more. Brian just had a bun for his dinner, or a glass o' pop. As I said, Marg did the washing, and our Ede, she was ever so good. Our Mother didn't even do the baking no more; Dad cooked the dinner. He worked damned hard. He still did the Dragon every night, collected the glasses, mopped up the beer and stuff, gave them a song when they wanted. And every morning after the fires he went back to the Dragon, to scrub. I did the rest of the school.

She couldn't do nothing. She just used to sit, dig that little bone into her apple, and eat it, like this. It was hollow, and as she scooped it filled with apple. Then she sucked.

I thought: She's old! Our Mother's old!

I wouldn't let myself think any further. It was kept locked up, in the cellar of my mind: the biggest fear of all.

*

Marg said: 'I'll take Brian off your 'ands today, Mary, take im out your way.'

They were so late coming back! I kept looking at the clock. I started to go frantic, I thought he'd been kidnapped. When they came . . .

'Ohh!'

She'd stuck his little mouth up to stop the bleeding, stuffed it with cotton wool. His teeth had gone through his lip.

She said: 'E's 'ad an accident.'

You never seen such a face in your life! I screamed!

'Why didn't you get *doctor* Marg?'

I got him to the surgery, I don't know how—I was nearly out of my mind. I thought: Oh God! 'Is looks is ruined!

What I called Marg! It seemed her Daphne had tied Brian's little trike to her two wheeler, and started to pedal away and hit a stone . . .

I said to the doctor: 'Will it 'urt 'is other teeth?'

He didn't get them for ever such a long time. The others went blue and then they dropped out. I thought when he didn't get teeth: Oh God! E ain't goin to get none! But he did. There was only the tiniest scar.

The doctor said: 'You should get your Mother to 'ave the operation. It'll kill er else.'

He was getting exasperated, you could see.

*

She said, 'There's somebody's brought flowers round.'

'*Flowers?*'

'That chap from Canning.'

I thought: Oh it's Bob.

'What's e want? Bringin you flowers? It's not *you* 'ad the accident—*this* time.' Our Mother said: 'I didn't ask im in.'

She would never let in anyone as a rule, especially chaps. She would never let me go out at night without Brian. If she so much as seen me talking to a chap . . .

'I 'spect e's got a conscience.'

I was going to say it weren't Bob's fault, my hand, then I thought: What's the point?

'Bloody should 'ave. *Flowers*! Any road,' she said, 'I've chucked em out. Lilac.'

Our Mother was that superstitious! What was the point in arguing? She was in a funny mood these days, distracted. Sometimes I thought . . .

She said: 'Cyril says its very hot.'

She'd had a letter. Our Cyril was in Yugoslavia; we didn't know that then, o' course, but 'hot' was the code. It meant hot fighting.

CHAPTER NINETEEN

I couldn't understand the war, really. You know, what it was really *for*—'cept we was winning now, and the Germans and the Italians and the Japs was on the other side. I *liked* the Germans—there, I've said it! I wouldn't a-said so, aloud, then, but I felt sorry for them. Oh and they were handsome, a lot of the German prisoners, fair hair, bright cheeks, only young chaps. They had a look reminded me . . . Early on in the war a German plane had gone over the school. I was at work, but our Mother was there, she was out feeding the hens and she said: 'I never seen a sight like it! E *waved*! To the kiddies—and me!' She said: 'The cheeky devil! The cheeky bugger! 'Ad the nerve to wave!' But she was laughing, as she remembered it.

They used to wave to *me* and all, as they went up the Alcester Road in lorries, back to their camp. They'd been working all day on the fields and farms. They waved and laughed. I think they were happy to be caught. I used to think: I wonder if *e's* a prisoner somewhere? I wonder if *e's* waving from a lorry, glad to be caught and out of the war? Somehow I never could imagine him caught. The more I wondered about it the more I thought: No, e'd a-took a risk and won a medal or bin blown to bits. That was his style.

I liked the Germans much more'n the Italians. *They* were so dark, the Italian prisoners, and all over the place, especially at the pictures. When Brian and me went to the pictures—there was nowhere else to go, see, I used to take him always, Sunday nights, well I had to, our Mother made me, unless it was an English film—it was crowded with Italians! There were hundreds of them in the queue. One queue went right from the picture house, right round, round the corner, past the Dragon and along Arden Street. That was the dear queue. We used to go in the other one, on the cheap side: up and round by Fox's back.

49. Cyril in Italy

When we got in we had a job to get a *seat*! They were near the
front, the cheap ones, and I always tried to get about four rows from
the front. I was quick: you had to be! The Italians filled them mostly.
Sometimes you could say that having to take Brian everywhere was
a handicap—but not with them! They came over and gave us
sweets, big round glassy sweets, all colours. They lasted ages. The
Italians had packs and packs of them. One showed us a lighter he'd
made from scrap: shaped like a miniature pistol, so clever, every
detail. He thought we might buy it, I 'spect. Some hopes! Oh how
Brian longed and longed for that lighter! He never said, he never
was a *grabby* lad, he just looked and I sensed how he longed for it.

The funny thing was, the Italians were so quiet. They all seemed to be on their own, even in a crowd, not mix with one another, no jabbering.

I whispered to Brian: 'Save the rest for Uncle Cyril!' and: 'Stop lookin at em!'

They used to gaze at him, sort of fierce, sad. They gave him some peculiar stares. They were so dark, rough, like tramps, or gypsies. I thought they might kidnap him. The world was mad! Upside down! Somewhere in Italy—we knowed our Cyril was in Italy now—there could a-been a woman wondering 'bout *him*: Why's e lookin at my kiddie like that? What's e thinkin, this foreign man? I didn't fancy them at all.

I had a picture in my mind's eye of Cyril sat in a cottage in Italy. We'd had a letter; it said, '*It's all olive oil, Mam!*'

'My poor babby!'

Our Cyril had gone from being a man to a boy to a babby! I thought: E'll soon be back in the bloomin womb!

He said: '*I sit at the table with the family. Its like ome hear. They pass the wine round and theirs the kiddies and the wenches. Tell Jim the wenches is v. glamorus.*'

That upset our Jim, o' course! Cyril loved to tease. He seemed to have been half way round the world: Africa, Yugoslavia, Italy. He was a bloody war hero, really.

Cyril said: '*I turned down the stripes.*'

Dad laughed. 'I did and all,' he said, 'in 'fifteen!'

'That's nothin to be proud of!'

But you could see she didn't mind *any*thing as long as Cyril was alive. We all felt the same. The relief! He asked us to send chocolate and tea and sugar. He'd got some racket going.

I thought: I wonder if e's started card parties?

And so everything we had went to Italy, 'cept milk chocolate: the Bourneville with the red label, our rations, the lot.

'*Send more chocs, and sweets,*' he said, '*and TEA.*'

We could get sugar from the brewery. Tea was the biggest challenge. Our Mother went to the Maypole, saw a woman there; she exchanged little bits of jewellry for tea. That's where those earrings went that Dad found—she'd loved them so, long ear bobs, brass but they polished up like gold. He'd found them, cleaning. I see that woman sometimes in Stratford and I think: I wonder where those ear bobs are now?

The Italians couldn't understand the film: they didn't speak the language. They watched anything, just like me. Well, *almost*! As I said, I wouldn't watch English films. I drew the line there. The actors all talked as if they'd got plums in their mouths, you couldn't tell what they were saying—the *words*!—and they was always black and white. We saw every American film that came to the picture house.

We went Sunday nights, in the shillings; the back row was one and nine. We didn't go Sat'days cos it was so rough, then. We could hear it from the school. There'd be trouble at the Dragon—a dreadful commotion—then, all of a sudden, whistles! The military police was there! Red caps jumping out of army wagons. There was different regiments, you see, at Long Marston camp; the way back was by train. They all called at the Dragon: the Pioneers, the Engineers, the RAF from Snitterfield, the Canadians. They all went to the pub on their way back to camp. There were big fights. We couldn't get to sleep for hours sometimes.

Sat'day night Dad was in the Dragon, singing. When things got nasty he got under the counter, quick. He worked all the time; how the hell he did it I do not know. Pub work was terrible hard in those days: filthy boots, spit, sick . . . Some nights he got coupons, for Brian's clothes, or he brought back chewing-gum. He cadged chewing-gum and fags off the Yanks; there was suddenly a lot of them about town. They loved his singing; they couldn't get enough of it.

Those old songs—where'd he picked them up? Once upon a time I knowed them all, inside out. He used to sing as we did the school, filled the coal buckets, shifted the desks.

> On the top of 'is tombstone
> You'll find these lines written:
> 'Now all you young men
> Take warnin from me,
> And never go courtin
> Along wi the flash girls,
> For the flash girls of the city
> Was the ruin of me.'

❧ CHAPTER TWENTY ❧

The noise of the horns woke me. Well, they didn't *wake* me, I think I was still asleep when I went to the window and looked out and saw the soldiers. There they were, waving from the biggest trucks you ever seen, and the one parked opposite the school had a great long nose with a star on top. *Yanks!* I don't know if they was beckoning *me*, they seemed to be doing: sirens going, horns, men laughing and shouting.

'Come on!' they shouted, '*come on!*'

They seemed to be shouting 'Come on, Mary!'

I took Brian in my arms, our Mother and Dad was sleeping, it was two o'clock. Blackie? He weren't about, lucky for me, he was out on the prowl somewhere.

There was a big moon that night, there must a-been. *Some*thing lit up the yard from the school house to the main road. Brian's face was a picture; he was more awake'n me.

'Shhh!' I said, 'your Granny'll 'ave a fit if she finds out!'

I was only in my nightgown and a blanket; he had pyjamas on.

'It's Victory!' the Yanks said. 'Hurry!'

And they hauled us into the back of one of the trucks. It was like a cattle truck, with rails round, full o' folks already, folks from Stratford. You sensed they was there, aside of you, but you *felt* you was alone, all alone as we thundered down Grove Road, bumped over the level crossing, past the Salmon Tail, towards the cemetery. The Yanks kept sounding the horns, sang songs I'd never heard before, songs about America.

'Look at the lights!' I said to Brian.

Lights were coming on in houses all along the Evesham Road. People could hear the din, wondered what was going on I 'spect. Nobody had to draw their curtains now. We left the town behind. Right to the top of Bordon Hill we went, right to the top. Did

359

you know that's where they found star stones, once, Bordon Hill?
Dad told us. Little stars that dropped to earth and turned to stone.
Somebody gave me a fag and I could see Brian's face all lit up with
excitement. It *was* exciting. You felt like shouting: 'I'm the King
of the Castle!'

Stratford was down there, miles and miles away. It was like a
dream; it *was* a dream! And the Yanks swung round on the top of
Bordon Hill, swung those great big trucks round, in the middle of
the road there, and down to earth we started to come, tearing
down, horns blaring. *Vroom*!

'Thank you,' I said, 'say "thank you" Brian,' but they didn't hear.

'Come to the White Swan!' they cried. That was the Red Cross
Club.

'I daren't.'

They didn't press me—they didn't have to! Past the corner by
the school we went: did I feel guilty! I wondered what our Mother
would say if she woke and found us gone, but that didn't stop me.
It was all dark at the school house, quiet as the grave. Good! I
thought.

'Mary Mary Quite Contrary!'

I smiled when they called me that. There was one G.I., he was
a joker, he'd started calling me that. He found out my name was
Mary. He came from Hollywood, he said.

'Pull the other one!'

'It's the truth! It's a real place!'

He wanted my address. I shook my head and laughed. I knew
one or two girls who'd started going with the Yanks. I liked their
films—but he was right, I *was* contrary! I have a contrary nature.
Perhaps I take after our Mother, I don't know.

'I never thought of gettin 'ome,' he said. 'I gave my lighter to a
gal in London, or I'd a-give it you! You've gotta smile'd make the
flowers come out. This your brother?'

Brian gave him a look.

'We're goin to 'ave a bonfire, sonny,' he said, 'you bet we are.'

When we got to the White Swan they ran inside and came out
with a pianna. A pianna! They pushed it into the road, by the
Fountain there, had a bit of a play and a sing-song, then two more

Yanks came running out with bits o' furniture, it was all they could find to burn, I s'ppose, and whoosh! They bust into flames and everybody was laughing and shouting '*Victory!*'

If you had asked me then, 'Did it really happen?', I would a-said 'No'. But it did, cos my nightgown was covered with oil, I never could get it off. And when I woke at six, to start work, there was Brian fast asleep aside of me, clutching a stick of gum.

*

Our Mother must a-known. When I was getting dressed, I went like a mouse always, so's not to disturb them, but she must a-heard me and she said: 'Cyril'll be comin home!'

That, I thought, is a mixed blessing. Dad was thinking the same, cos when she said, 'We'll let the fireworks off tonight, George!'— she was so excited!—he said, 'You can. *I'm* not!'

'It's Victory!'

'I'm not lettin those buggers off,' he said.

I'd never seen a fireworks show, and those fireworks was *whoppers*: like sticks o' dynamite, V-2 rockets, that long, bulging with gunpowder! One morning there they were—in the porch. Dad hadn't wanted to keep them; he was frit of fire, I don't know why. Every night he doused the fires at the school with water, tipped the ashes on the garden, still sizzling.

'I'm not 'avin em in 'ere,' he said, 'we'll give em back.'

But we didn't know *who'd* left them, we couldn't give them back, and we daren't dump them anywhere cos of the fire risk. So Dad got a pan: it was a great big crock pan, earthenware—we made wine in it. He cussed! 'Shells!' he said, 'bleedin shells!' He stacked them in the pan, in the cellar. And every night he crept out with this great big pan with the fireworks in it, and let it down over the wall by the school, 'to tek the blast,' he said. Every night he did that, when he'd put the fires out.

'We gotta let em off *some* time,' said our Mother.

'I'm not advertisin.'

'That's what they're for.'

'And 'ave all the coppers in the neighbourhood come round, sniffin about?'

'What *we* got to hide?'

Well! What we'd got in our cellar besides fireworks was *nobody's* business; our Mother knowed that as well as Dad. But she was desperate for a show, a celebration. We all was, really. Brian joined in: 'Go on Grandad!'

Dad stuck his ground. 'I'm not lettin off no shells, nor flares, fireworks, call em what you like—*ever*,' he said.

Our Mother went quiet. That afternoon after tea she sent word to the brewery, to our Jim. The message came back: 'We'll 'ave the best display they ever seen in Stratford!'

We *did*.

It was in the school yard. Jim came and set them up in the school yard, by the road. There was a lot of fumbling about with matches, and Jim trying to read the instructions: 'What does it *say*, our Mary?' Then all at once the world really did go mad! There was green and red explosions, rockets bust in the sky, and scores of parachutes came floating down. We had Catherine wheels going berserk on the gates there, the boys' and girls' gates, and a bloke with a big 'V' sign who Jim started off at the wrong end. There was burning rocket cases all over the place. They went out with little *phuts*! made me scream and jump. It was more like war'n peace!

Our Mother said: 'E'll set the school on fire!' and 'Your Dad was right!' You could see she was enjoying herself. 'E's gone balmy!' she said.

The smell! It was an exciting smell, burning black, hot, it went to your brain. It reminded me ... Then another load of rockets went up: swoosh, bang, *ohhhh*!

All the people on their way to the station had stopped dead in their tracks, you can imagine, and the soldiers, Yanks, everybody! Nurses and patients came out of the hospital, to gawp. The Dragon had no customers. Crowds of folks sat on the wall, pushing and cheering, egging us on. 'Let's 'ave another o' *those*, Jim!' They were beautiful fireworks, beautiful. Nobody had ever seen anything like them.

Our Jim started showing off. 'Now you've *all* gotta chance of seein this spectacular display!' he said, 'no charge! Not just the C.O's and the toffs!'

They'd been heading for the top brass, for a private party, bound to be. That's what our Jim reckoned. Well, he could a-been right. The people cheered and cheered. Jim fancied himself as Robin Hood.

*

We never heard from the police. That was a wonder: they must have known about it, they must have seen it! All Stratford seen that firework display and Jim spoke the truth there: it was spectacular. All except Dad. He'd gone missing; we never found him. Brian went down in the morning and there he was, hiding in the cellar; he brought him back.

'They've gone,' Brian said, 's'alright!'

He'd had a lovely time—well for a little kiddie those fireworks was magic! But even at that age he had patience with the old man, drunk or sober, more'n I had, I'll admit it. Well, I don't have to

50. Street party (Wellesbourne Grove, Stratford-upon-Avon) to celebrate Victory, 1945: Emma standing to left of table, in big hat, Brian just in front of her.

tell you, I couldn't stick him. He and Brian *got on*. When he started chunnering 'bout rats—there were rat holes all over the school, inside the classrooms, the partitions, there was one old rat with grey whiskers, a great big thing, *King Rat* by the looks on him, he was too crafty for the rat catcher—Brian said: 'I'll learn Blackie to catch em Grandad!'

Some hopes of that! Blackie had been hiding down there, and all!

The next night Jim came round again. Hullo, I thought, another blooming card party, and guess oo'll 'ave to clean up after em! But

51. Mary's young man, 1940s

he came on his own to talk to our Mother, and his voice was grim. I was under the teacher's desk, getting up the rubbish. That basket was big enough to take three footballs, but Miss Farmer couldn't aim a ball o' *hair* in straight, at twelve inches! Sometimes I reckoned she did it a-purpose.

I heard Jim say: 'Arch told me. E was there, the bastard. Arch wouldn't make a mistake. It was *im*! Watchin our bloody fireworks!'

Our Mother said something I couldn't catch.

He was always trying to impress her. It was no good; Cyril was the favourite there, always.

'This time I'll 'ave the bugger. E'll never do that to no-one, never again.'

It was *him*! It must be! He'd come back! My stomach turned over. He'd been there, at the fireworks, he could a-been near us, touching. I'd thought...maybe...I felt a real pain, here. I thought, 'E's come back to Stratford. E's alright! E got through the war.'

'There's a letter,' our Mother said, 'for Brian. It took long enough to get 'ere.'

For Brian?

'Ah,' she said, 'I opened it.'

The tears welled up in her eyes, started to stream down her face, you know, like a spring in a field—have you ever found one? The astonishment! I'd never seen her cry before, not like that. I was so astonished.

Brian said: 'I'll read it for you, Granny.'

He was crying too, practically, cos she was. But the writing was joined up; he couldn't manage. I wanted to say to her: 'Please don't cry, *please*!' I couldn't bear to see her cry.

Bert came in and he read it:

Dear Brian,

Well I'm in Germany now and it ain't much good out here their is 'nix in the winkle' and the people are none too good so I'm planning to get out as quickly as possible.

Be a good lad and remember me to your Mother, Granny, Grandad, and Bert, and I'm hoping to get my ticket next year, and then I shall stay at home for good 'I hope' so I will wish you Goodnight and God Bless you and don't forget to be a good lad, Cheerio,

Uncle Cyril
Gunner C. Hewins

'Oh,' said our Mother, 'I can die happy now.'

What had Cyril ever done to deserve so much love? How to explain it? You could see Dad thinking the same. For the first time, just for a minute, I was on his side, not hers.

*

Brian was seven years old. It was getting to be a squash in that single bed. And Blackie! I'd worked out he was over a hundred, in human years.

I thought: 'Ere's me in my bloody prime sleepin with a kiddie and a hundred year ole chap!

I was restless, counting and doing. You know, I was even counting the times a spider went across the ceiling, back'ards and for'ards, back'ards and for'ards. Blackberrying time came and went, the first Mop after the war, the first winter, the first spring, soon it would be summer. I sat looking at the ladies in the fireplace, no fire now; they didn't seem so pretty. I didn't want to go to bed; I couldn't sleep. I lay awake, tossing and turning. It was so cold, so hot! I'd got so's I was watching everywhere: watching for *him*. I thought: If I see im, just once, I'll know! I'll know e's *alive*!

You see, a dreadful idea had come into my mind. It was like being on the very edge of Bird's Pit, the pit that was flooded, nobody knew how deep or what was at the bottom yet all the time you wanted to go closer 'n' closer, have a look, find out . . .

Our Mother came to tuck Brian in. She always tucked him in, gave him a big kiss. But this night she said: 'Ow should you like to go up to London duck, to see the King 'n' Queen? You and your Mam? The day after tommorrer?'

*

We hadn't a clue what to do. We were lost—on Paddington Station! It was eleven o'clock: three hours late! We had to stand in the train, all the way. The crowds! It was a wonder we'd got so far. All the world seemed to be going to London. It was like being lost at the Mop. I was once, when I was a little kiddie. I can still feel the panic: I'd let go our Ede's hand.

There was no chance of finding Ern—he was s'pposed to be meeting us—no chance even of *seeing* him! I hung on to Brian for grim death; Gwen grabbed my coat. It was the blind leading the blind. She'd wanted to come. Else asked me: 'Will you take Gwendoline? She wants to see the Queen.' So I said 'Yes.'

'Look!' said Brian.

Flo had written: 'You catch an 88 bus.' He'd spotted a sign with '*88*' on it! We went and stood by it, and all of a sudden these Londoners, these Cockneys—well, we didn't realize they was in a queue—started shouting: 'You bleedin well get to the back!'

It was the last bus! '*Last bus!*' the conductress shouted, and there we were—stranded.

Our case was full of brown sugar; it weighed a ton. My feet hurt. I kept thinking of that doctor's words: 'Oo wears them shoes? Er'll be a cripple afore she's thirty!'

Gwen was crying, I was tearful. Well, I didn't know what to do. Some kiddies ran up: 'Carry yer bags miss? Carry yer bags?' I clung tight to it, I can tell you, and to Brian's hand. No fear, I thought. They kept running alongside of us.

'No!' I said, '*no!*'

And then Brian spotted the taxi. He never hesitated. He ran into the middle of the road—and it stopped!

'Millais Buildings!' he said, he'd got it from the films, what to do, and we piled in.

I was thinking: Oh my God what's it goin to cost? It'll take all our money!

I opened the case; I'd hid my purse in it. One of the bags of sugar had bust. There was only three pound notes.

'Oh God,' I said aloud.

That started Gwen off again. On and on went that taxi, on and on.

It's goin to cost a fortune! I thought.

Outside we could see a *river*: black and glittery and oily, half a mile wide by the looks on it, at least, you couldn't see the other bank. Horrible. And just then he stopped, outside some toilets, all brown tiles, dark brown tiles. I was frit to death.

I thought: E's goin to do us in!

'That's a pound missus,' he said.

I gave it him, quick, and we jumped out like three field mice with the cat just behind. From the darkness came *Ern*! He'd waited at Paddington, waited and waited; then he thought we weren't coming.

'Ow much did e charge?'

Gwen and me was speechless! Brian told him.

'The bugger!'

The taxi driver had overcharged us. I didn't care: we'd *got there*! So this was Millais Buildings! We couldn't believe it: brown tiles and concrete steps going up and up! Inside—oh were we glad to get inside—there was Flo and it was just like the old days. The first thing she did, before we'd got our coats off even, was count the sugar bags, weigh them. You could *hear* her brain ticking over. I thought: That's the last I'll see of them—or the results! Then she said: 'You've just come too late, our Mary! I've just 'ad to finish off the last of a bunch of *bananas*!'

Gwen's face fell, and Brian's. I'd told him about bananas. Our Flo had always *just* ate a bunch of bananas or a tin of chewing gum or a six pound walnut cake. She counted everything, weighed it up—and it had always gone, just before you arrived!

In the morning—we'd brought some bread and bacon with us, *food supplies*—I opened the window and chucked the rinds out, cos I did that at home, for the fowl.

Flo said: 'Christ, our Mary, they'll 'ave you up!'

And when I looked out, really looked out, I saw that we were high up, in the sky. I'd forgot about all those stairs, last night. There weren't no fowl. I was staring at rows and rows of wounded men, all wounded men, heads bandaged in white, legs up in the air. Two of them started waving and shouting; well, I'd only got my nightgown on. I shut the window—quick! It gave me a turn; it was a sight I wasn't expecting.

'They're officers. It's a hospital for officers,' said Flo. '*Toffs*.'

Then she had a row with Ern; she showed off. The result was, she said she wouldn't come with us to the Parade.

'I'll find my own way,' she said.

The rest of us sat on the Tate Gallery steps: Ern and me and Brian and Gwen and Flo's two boys; Teddy who'd won a scholarship to Westminster School, he was very brainy; and Jimmy. We had this good spot on the steps, *reserved*, cos our Flo worked at the Tate, cleaned it.

What's she up to? I wondered. Where's our Flo gone?

There was no sign of her.

'Where's the *Queen*?' said Gwen.

The Parade went past the steps, all the old generals and that, they were in big shiny cars, past the bottom of the steps, along the Embankment.

I remember thinking: E's only a little bloke, no bigger'n Dad!

Brian liked the army vehicles going past.

'Where's the Queen?' said Gwen.

There was somebody quite well-to-do at the Tate, must a-been, cos everybody in the Parade seemed to turn their heads and look at *us*!

The Rowes cheered and cheered, clapped like mad. We just gawped. Cockneys are different, aren't they? The war had been bad for them; they were there, all through the bombing, in the shadow of Big Ben, practically. Can you imagine? Flo told me: 'We watched em comin, up the river in the moonlight. Like shoals o' mackerel.'

And she'd been frit of *thunder*! Flo was always one step ahead of the rest of us.

There was no sign of her at the Parade. But when we got to Millais Buildings she was there before us and she said:

'You should a-come with *me*, our Mary!'

She'd found a ten-bob note!

What with the Parade, and panicking, and worrying about how long our money would last, I never had any time to think. That's what our Mother had had in mind, I 'spect. When she sent word I could come back I only thought, 'Hooray!'

Flo was crying at the station. She said: 'You remember the last time we was all together? We came to Stratford with Fred?'

How could I forget it?

'Our poor Jess,' she said.

'And Fred.'

Ern's brother young Fred was killed in the war.

Flo said: 'When me Dad seen me off he said, "Ta-ta, Flo!" ' There were tears in her eyes. 'When I got 'ome I said to Ern, "I *wished* I'd a-give im summat. I do wish I'd a-give our Dad a drink." '

I smiled to myself. Yes, it was just like the old times, only Jess wasn't there. Oh Jess, I thought, I still miss you.

52. Stall at Stratford-upon-Avon Mop, 1940s

Dad and Brian tried and tried and tried to win a Lambeth boy.* It was threepence a go. They were all afternoon trying to win him, and then they came home from the Mop so disappointed. Lambeth boys had just come out. You had tickets, see, there were flashlights; it was a proper wangle.

After tea Dad said: 'Well Emm, I got sixpence. We're goin back to 'ave another go. I'm gonna *try*!'

She grumbled. 'You'll 'ave us in the workhus yet.'

But she never could resist wasting money on Brian either. She'd spend her last pennies on a new toy for him. You could say Brian

* *Large rag doll, presumably dressed as a coster*

was the one thing they agreed on. Then she'd break into his money-box.

Blow me! Dad won the Lambeth boy! They came home with him! He had a little hat, velvety trousers and a dent in the back of his head. It was Dad's last sixpence and he got him for Brian. Praps he'd had a word with one of the moppers; most likely he did. He knowed a lot of them by name. They were a proper wangle, those stalls. The other thing they went to was the boxing booth.

Dad said: 'There's a young black chap in that booth fights like a wild cat. You seen nothin till you seen im.'

Brian brightened up—I don't know whether he *liked* the Lambeth boy really—and our Mother. She would never go to the booth at the Mop, but she always listened when Dad started to tell her about it. She listened to every word and there was a strange look in her eyes. Sometimes I thought: There's a whole half of her life I don't *know* about! That look came from there. I'd feel so jealous.

Brian said: 'I'm goin to be a boxer Gran!'

I thought: Over my dead body.

'E took me cap, after'ards, for the money! E borrowed me cap an e give Grandad a drink!' That wiped the smile off her face! 'E said: "'Ere y'are, George, get yourself a drink!"'

'Huh.'

'And there was a man. E kept followin us. Every time I turned round e was there.'

Dad said nothing. But he looked at our Mother, and she looked at me. I felt a sort of wild excitement. I hadn't felt that way for years.

I said to Brian, low: 'Us'll go back to Mop. Just the two of us, look for that man.'

*

It was the first proper Mop after the war. You never seen so many people, pushing and shoving, determined to get out, have a good time.

'There e is!' Brian shouted. To him it was a game.

A big chap had got on the cakewalk. He stumbled on, then he lost his grip. My heart turned over. He was drunk! His coat was coming off; gradually he slumped to the floor. There was something familiar . . . Everybody was screaming, but nobody heard, nobody realized. We couldn't take our eyes off him.

I thought: E'll *die*!

I started to run forwards and stopped. It was as if the cakewalk had took a *hold*—his whole body was shaking—as if something horrible had got inside of him. It was a nasty sight. We stared and stared, and in the end the Mop man realized. The shaking died down to a tremble; the whole cakewalk scrunched to a halt.

They sat him down on the steps. The grime and blood! His coat and shirt had been ripped open.

'It ain't 'im!' said Brian.

It wasn't.

'Come on,' I said. I wanted to get it out of my mind, that great big beer-filled stomach. I felt sick.

'Mam!' said Brian. He catched hold of my sleeve. I jumped! A deep voice was saying 'Ullo!'

'It ain't im, come on!' said Brian.

Another chap was leering down at me, said he'd been injured in the war. He was leering at Brian and all, summing up the situation, you could see.

'What 'bout meetin—later?' he said, 'when you've put the nipper to bed?'

'Come on Mam!'

Brian glared at him, tried to pull me away; well, I didn't need much pulling.

'It ain't im!' he said.

The game had gone sour, so had the Mop, even the sound of the organ, you know, *hellish*. The face of that tall man leered down at us.

I wanted to get home, fast. I never thought, I started back up Wood Street towards Rother Market, but hundreds of people was trying to do the same thing. I wanted to get home. Somebody panicked; kiddies screamed. They got wedged, us in the middle. Stalls started creaking, caving in.

I thought: If I faint we've 'ad it!

Brian said: 'This way Mam!'

53. Post-war Mop Fair, Stratford-upon-Avon: American Fountain towards left; behind it, White Swan Hotel.

We clambered over one of the stalls, and we got to safety.

*

I was never so pleased to see Sis in my life.

'Oh Sis!' I said; I dropped everything and threw my arms round her. How to explain? How to explain to anyone, even her?

'And ow's my little lad?'

I was washing Brian in the sink.

I said: 'E won a Lambeth boy yesterday!' I couldn't tell her the rest. She'd think I was balmy. I always washed him in the sink, his back and that. I remember Bert came by with a rabbit—the young chaps laid traps on the railway bank—cos he laughed and gave Brian a poke and said ''Ere's another Belsen victim!'

Brian's shoulder blades stuck out, he was dreadfully thin. We'd seen what the Germans had done on the news at the pictures: piles of bodies, mountains of them. Yes. You couldn't believe they could do such things, not those young lads on lorries, waving...I couldn't believe it. But it was *true*! We'd seen.

I said: 'Tek it away, it's 'orrible,' meaning the rabbit. I said: 'Ey Sis, you know that film . . . What's up?'

She said: 'Get ready for a shock. I seen im.'

'Oo?'

I knew before she said it, *who*.

'In the Horse 'n' Jockey'—she worked behind the bar there—'a while ago. I wasn't goin to tell you.'

'I don't want to know.'

''E came in bold as brass. I gave im a piece of my mind. I really let im 'ave it. Then I told him you was married.'

I should have been grateful to her for sticking up for me, that's what friends are for, as Sis said, but all I could think was: Why don't she mind er own bloody business? Why don't they *all*?

'I told you Sis, I don't want to know.'

I dried Brian fast and I sent him off. Oh my heart! It was thumping.

'Let's go outside!' I said.

It was so bright, autumn. Yellow and gold. When you looked up through the lime trees by the school house that's all you could see: yellow and gold. I told myself: You can think of im without pain, now! It was just that awful thumping.

Sis said: 'Well I 'ope it was im!' She laughed. ''E's changed.'

I had a pain then, alright. I panicked. 'What d'ye mean, "changed"?'

''Is looks.'

No! I thought, not them! Anything but them!

'I wouldn't a-known im,' she said.

Was he wounded or what? You heard stories, 'bout airmen coming back all scarred, horrible, or a soldier with a leg off, and the girl giving them up and I always thought: I wouldn't! I'd still a-loved you! I pictured myself being all noble like the heroine and taking him on, horribly wounded, knocked about, when nobody else wanted him. Like those men at Flo's . . . *They* weren't real, though, they were far enough away not to be real: in the sky, far away. The day I'd bust in and seen Dad was real. I can see him still. And I knew I could never bear it, really. 'She can't stick er Dad!' It was him all over again. Our Mother would say when I was little: 'Go on, give your Dad a kiss!' I never would. The ugliness. I couldn't.

'What's up with im?' I hardly dared ask it: 'Is e spoilt?'

Sis frowned. I had to press her.

'Well . . . it was the most mysterious thing. E'd *dyed* . . .'

I felt, you know, as if a door had blowed open somewhere, in my mind. There was a cold draught.

'E'd . . . *dyed 'is hair*! And that's not all . . . E'd got a . . . a . . .'

'*Wot?*'

'Moustache!'

'It was beautiful, 'is hair. Like . . . Oh God!'

I started to laugh. Yes, I started to laugh, and Sis did, there under the lime trees outside the school house; leaning up against one of the lime trees I nearly bust my sides. It was as if I was free of a terrible load.

'Oh my God!'

I was floating like thistledown. I can't describe it. I was free of him.

'Why?' I said, '*why*, Sis?'

She was laughing so. She said: 'What a disguise! Your Jim was lookin for im.'

'So was I!' I could say it now.

'Well, e never catched im. Good job! Might a-come off in 'is 'and! The *colour*, I mean!'

We shrieked.

'Ey praps e's joined Theatre!'

'To be or not to be—*that* is the question!'

'E always was an actor.'

'*Starring*, tonight, in the Horse 'n' Jockey . . .'

'Oh Sis, ain't it marvellous?'

It was just like old times; we was altogether.

*

Our Mother looked at me sharpish when I came back in.

'What you bin up to?'

I ran upstairs. I sang as I tucked the sheets in, shoved the beds back.

'We'll take im to the churchyard
We'll fire three volleys over im
We'll play the Dead March
As we carry im along . . .'

Even the idea of sharing with Cyril again couldn't dampen me.

'For e was a young soldier
Oo's money I squandered
E was a young soldier
Cut down in 'is prime.'

'I've 'ad a bit o' good news,' I said when I came down.
'You look as if you lost a penny an found a pound.'
'I '*ave*!'

That's done it! I thought. Soon as I said it, I could have bit my tongue off. I thought she'd ask me for it 'just till Friday'. But she never.

'Hmm,' she said, 'London did you some good by the looks on it.'
Dad said: 'She can get on with *livin*. It's 'bout time.'
'Your idea of livin ain't mine. Nor ers.'

And that was the start of another row. I was in such a good mood I didn't mind, not like I usually did. I thought: Let them get on with it! I'm home.

AFTERWORD

54. Porch, Church of England School buildings, Stratford-upon-Avon (1983). The school and the adjoining headmaster's and headmistress's houses were demolished in the early 1990s to make way for private sheltered housing.

Mary dried her eyes and took her Dad's advice. She got on with living. She never went back to 'mechanical work', though her factory days were not quite over, nor did she ever see in the porch the one figure that she had hoped might be there, one day. A few years later she married. She had no more children, and lived in Stratford for the rest of her life. As for Emma, for whom the school house had been a dream come true, she did not long survive the leaving of it when George, at seventy, retired from his caretaking job at the school. She had a massive stroke. As she lay immobile and speechless, nursed tenderly week after week, month after month, by the man whose prop she had been for over half a century, whose children she had borne and whose vicissitudes she had shared, what were her thoughts? Of all the people in Mary's story, it is Emma, 'our Mother', whom I most regret I came too late to interview, and record. To the end a contradiction, impulsive and wise, passionate and authoritarian, sometimes unfair, often generous, a product of a world all but vanished, she compels and repels me: a matriarchal figure in a fading landscape.

But before it did fade, finally and irrecoverably, a comet shot across it, changing our lives. The first signs were humdrum. In 1984 we traced a relative of Brian's biological father. The cousin and his wife, now in their late seventies, still lived in the cottage on the southern edge of the Cotswolds to which the young man had cycled after his fateful encounter with Mary's brother, all those years ago.

'There was a knock on the door and there he stood, covered in blood and bruises, a big gash here. "Oh goodness come in quick!" we said. We thought he'd been in an accident.'

Forty-five years on they were nearly as startled by the sight of Brian. The wife was visibly moved.

'It could be him stood there! He had a smile—just like yours. "Mother says 'Can I stay with you?'" He'd brought a change of clothes with him, and a fruit cake in a tin. That was all. I remember that fruit cake. The icing wasn't finished. She must have packed it in a hurry. Poor lad! And you are his *son*?'

She touched Brian wonderingly, as if she could not quite believe that he was there. Her husband was more circumspect. His face grew grim as he heard our story.

'What did I tell you, Margaret?'

Their unexpected lodger did not stay long with them. That was too long, we sensed, for his cousin's liking.

'The war started, and he left.'

Now and then over the subsequent years he had turned up, once in a taxi, they recalled, with the engine running. They had not heard from him now for many years. They supposed he had gone abroad. Perhaps he was dead. Once they had a postcard from some foreign place, saying he was working there, something to do with aircraft. That was all they knew. It was enough to help us to ascertain that he had led a peripatetic life, following the work from place to place, country to country, very much as the roadsters had done in Victorian Britain. The trail rapidly went cold. Here was a man with no roots, who did not want to be found, supposing he was still alive. And if he was, it was odds on that he would be an unpleasant surprise. We had heard from his cousin that he could drink a spectacular amount at one sitting. What other talents might he have? Common sense urged us to let sleeping dogs lie. Would Mary, who had lost her husband the year before, thank us for digging up the cadaver of her great love? Before abandoning the search, we had one last go. The young man was old enough now to draw a pension. We sent a letter c/o the DHSS on the slim chance that it might be forwarded to him. One try is all that one is allowed in such circumstances. Astonishingly, the letter reached him. More astonishingly, he replied.

And so Brian and I found ourselves flying to Los Angeles to meet his long lost father. He was still, despite the people around him, a man alone, the quality that Mary had noticed when she first saw him from her perch on the railings of Schofield's orchard. The hair was white, but the eyes, which Mary had never mentioned, were surprisingly dark and keen.

'I am,' he said ruefully, 'an asshole.'

He had the powerful attraction of a man who was both worldly-wise and vulnerable. His horror of responsibility was plain to see. It was hard not to like him, hard not to admire his guts, or sheer gall, when we telephoned Mary, and passed her on to him. What would he say? What could anyone say, in such circumstances?

'You did a good job of bringing him up, Mary,' he said. 'Better than I would have done.'

He wept when we left, and we wondered if we would see him again.

Later that year, on Guy Fawke's night, with rockets and bangers exploding behind him, he turned up on our doorstep, half a century late, too late for love from the woman he had abandoned (that had all gone to her son), but not too late to have a family, for the first time in his life. The ice was soon broken. Mary had a kind heart. She could not resist a chat and soon it was 'Whatever happened to . . . ?' 'Is he dead?' 'Did she . . . ?' It was as if they were picking up a conversation they had broken off only yesterday. In amazement we saw that they were comfortable with each other. And so it continued to be. Mary and her sister Flo cooked the Christmas dinner. Once or twice he was carried home from the pub. He lived with us in uneasy content for eight years, a septuagenarian adolescent. It was the longest time, he told us defensively, that he had ever lived in one place. We knew he would have flown if he could. We were his last bolt-hole.

In 1985, the Royal Shakespeare Company's stunning ambulatory production of 'The Dillen', first presented in 1983, was repeated, and this time it was in tandem with 'Mary, After the Queen,' in

55. Mary in 1985

an empty warehouse in Stratford. Mary and he took this raising of ghosts from the past in their stride, but it must have been an eerie experience. Most of the working girls had gone: Sis, whom he had flirted with 'to get Mary going' and who had sent him finally on his way, all but one of Mary's sisters, big Kate who had danced lightly as a bird. Unbeknown to everyone, Mary, who had entered the theatrical comings and goings with gusto ('Can I have my own *chair*, like Elizabeth Taylor?') and saw the finished production many times, was dying of cancer. Hiding the pain, she hung on until the end of the last performance. Then she told us. Three months later she died, leaving us feeling very much as she had done, thirty years before:

> *When our Mother died, Cyril said: 'Take this, our Mary, get yourself a new coat.'*
>
> *I thought, I'll buy a red costume. It ended up in a rug, in a great big centre circle of red. We was all so relieved, you see, for her. It was over.*

GLOSSARY

ash plant	an ash sapling, cut to serve as a light cane
backen	to retard, delay
bait	workman's snack
berring	burying or burial
Big House	euphemism for workhouse
blart	to cry or holloa noisily
books	euphemism for bricks
breed and seed	birth and parentage
Brummagem	Birmingham; also used to indicate something sham or worthless
builder's clerk	euphemism for builder's labourer
bull's foot	'not to know "A" from a bull's foot': to be illiterate, extremely ignorant. Originally referred to alphabet hornbooks
bury	heap of potatoes or other roots, covered with straw-lined earth for future use.
caddle	to fondle
cakey	weak minded
chit	to germinate or sprout
clerk	euphemism for labourer, in certain contexts
codge and modge	a clumsy piece of work, especially a clumsy repair
cold crowdings	bad times
crabs	crab apples
crummy	lousy
cuther	to fuss, love
dab	small quantity, sometimes used as adjective, *e.g.* dab washing
dillen	smallest of the litter, *e.g.* dillen pig; also used for the last of the family, in which sense it can have the power of fondling, darling. The Revd George Miller in *Rambles round the Edge Hills* (1900) gives the following example of usage: 'That's the dillen, missus. He be a small

	un now, but later on happen he'ull be the best o' the litter.'
donkey	shaped block for glovemaking
fashion	'in the fashion': pregnant
gentleman	'being a gentleman': being out of work, in certain contexts
giddling	giddy, thoughtless
gillies	wallflowers or gillyflowers
gollop	swallow quickly
Guffin	'The Guffin': Flowers Brewery, Stratford-upon-Avon
Guffinites	brewery workers
herden	coarse, hempen type cloth
hockle	to hack; in football to make a player hobble
jibber and jumbles	sweets
kek	cow parsley
lamming	a beating
mangels	mangel wurzels, used for winter cattle feed
miskin	midden, rubbish heap
moither	to worry, bother
Mop	annual hiring fair, held at Stratford-upon-Avon on October 12th each year (except Sundays). The 'Runaway Mop' is held a fortnight later, on a Friday
Mop rock	sweets sold at the Mop, especially striped peppermint sticks
mother	'mother of vinegar': slimy mess of bacteria used in vinegar production
mullock	dirty disorder
nammus!	be off!
offal work	coarse drudgery
packman	itinerant pedlar
pushers	girls or women of low character
quank	to settle or tame
right as the mail	on time
rock	sweets
sawney	sheepish, foolish

scrobble	scramble
slans	sloes
sliving	idle
strap	to give credit. Also used as adjective, e.g. strap shop
super	walk-on extra at theatre
tallyman	man who sells goods, usually of poor quality, on hire purchase
tater	potato
tats	tatters, rags
terrify	to destroy or vandalize
tick	'full as a tick': small blood sucking parasite
trofe	trough
wallop	to thrash; to boil violently
wapses	wasps
wench	a girl, sometimes a servant; never used derogatively
whale	to beat viciously, flog
woodnuts	hazelnuts